Counting Our Losses

THE SERIES IN DEATH, DYING, AND BEREAVEMENT
ROBERT NEIMEYER, CONSULTING EDITOR

FORMERLY THE SERIES IN DEATH EDUCATION, AGING, AND HEALTH CARE
HANNELORE WASS, CONSULTING EDITOR

Counting Our Losses

Reflecting on Change, Loss, and Transition in Everyday Life

Edited by Darcy L. Harris

Routledge
Taylor & Francis Group
New York London

Routledge
Taylor & Francis Group
270 Madison Avenue
New York, NY 10016

Routledge
Taylor & Francis Group
27 Church Road
Hove, East Sussex BN3 2FA

Printed in the United States of America on acid-free paper
10 9 8 7 6 5 4 3 2 1

International Standard Book Number: 978-0-415-87528-8 (Hardback) 978-0-415-87529-5 (Paperback)

Library of Congress Cataloging-in-Publication Data

Counting our losses : reflecting on change, loss, and transition in everyday life / [edited by] Darcy Harris.
    p. cm. -- (Series in death, dying, and bereavement)
Includes bibliographical references and index.
ISBN 978-0-415-87528-8 (hbk. : alk. paper) -- ISBN 978-0-415-87529-5 (pbk. : alk. paper)
    1. Loss (Psychology) 2. Adjustment (Psychology) 3. Change (Psychology) I. Harris, Darcy. II. Title. III. Series.

BF575.D35C68 2010
155.9'3--dc22   2010031851

Visit the Taylor & Francis Web site at
http://www.taylorandfrancis.com

and the Routledge Web site at
http://www.routledgementalhealth.com

For Brad and Lauren

Contents

SECTION I   LOSS OF THE VIEW OF THE WORLD OR OTHERS

SECTION IA   LOSS OF SAFETY AND SECURITY

SECTION IB   RELATIONAL LOSSES

SECTION II   LOSS OF MEANING OR A SENSE OF JUSTICE IN THE WORLD

SECTION III   LOSS OF THE VIEW OF SELF AS WORTHY OR VALUABLE

SECTION IIIA   LOSS OF IDENTITY

Series Editor's Foreword

As the prominent family therapist, Carlos Sluzki, once noted, "Losses are the shadow of all possessions, material and immaterial." Viewed in this sense, every person, every place, every project, and every possession we love we will someday lose—at least in a physical sense—and how we adapt to these innumerable losses shapes who we become. This book is about these inevitable transitions, particularly those precipitated by immaterial losses, as of cherished beliefs, security, self-definition, and grounding in a world we once took for granted as solid, substantial, and durable. Often, as the contributors richly illustrate, these more elusive, non-finite repercussions arise in stubbornly concrete contexts, such as relationship dissolution, progressive illness, assault, or disaster, but extend beyond the sharp outlines of the event itself, as a shadow is cast by a material object, and yet may be scarcely noticed in our habitual gaze. By shifting our vision toward the penumbra of grief, uncertainty, and anxious readjustment following in the wake of countless life events, *Counting Our Losses* brings us into full contact with this shadow, greatly extending the focus of a field often concentrated myopically on literal bereavement. Nonetheless, by situating this project in the interdisciplinary context of thanatology, the study of death and dying, Darcy Harris and her capable collaborators implicitly argue that the litany of losses to which life will expose us is better understood as occasioning grief and its integration, rather than, say, merely medicalized depression, narrowly defined trauma symptomatology, or blandly generalized "stressful life events." Common to all of these unsought transitions—whether as normative as aging and launching our children or as particular as immigrating or struggling with infertility—is the need to revise our assumptive worlds, and in doing so, to relinquish an aspect of ourselves and a life once familiar or desired. The rich description of the many contexts in which such losses occur is a cardinal contribution of this book, demonstrating amply that grieving and its complications are not reserved only for those who have lost a loved one to death.

What might surprise the reader is the way the topical coverage of many tangible losses encountered in clinical settings is complemented by thoughtful but accessible meditations on the existential realities of life, in a sense providing a "container" for the book as a whole. Indeed, the tragedy (and opportunity) of the human condition is that *we are wired for attachment in a world of impermanence*, and the book's philosophic meditation on this "noble truth" implicitly, and sometimes explicitly, informs the chapters that follow. What results is a volume that is practical in its purpose, sweeping in its scope, and occasionally poetic in its prose.

Far from leaving the reader mired in hopelessness in response to life's ineluctable losses, it offers a compassionate vision within which to engage them, moving from grief to growth, and from reassessment to resilience. I recommend it highly to all of us who are "counting our losses," as well as to those professionals who endeavor to help us live them with integrity, or perhaps even convert them to gains.

Robert A. Neimeyer, PhD
Series Editor

Acknowledgments

This book has been the culmination of many years' worth of clinical practice and personal reflection. Along the way, there have been numerous individuals to whom I owe a great deal of gratitude for how they encouraged me in my thinking and practice regarding nondeath and nondefinite loss.

First and foremost, I wish to thank the clients in my clinical practice and those who participated in my research for entrusting me with their experiences and for teaching me about the innate resilience that can manifest in the face of great pain and adversity.

I am greatly indebted to my mentor and friend, Dr. Jack Morgan, for his belief in me and his encouragement of my work and choices in the field of thanatology. It is an honor and a privilege to follow in the footsteps of this pioneer of death education.

I also wish to express my gratitude to Dr. Willson Williams, Dr. Thomas Attig, Dr. Anne Cummings, Dr. Judith Daniluk, and Dr. Kathleen Gilbert for their hard work and honest feedback. This book began under their supervision and encouragement of my research in the grief and losses associated with infertility, which then expanded into other areas of loss that did not fit neatly into specific categories.

A book such as this one involves the willingness of many individuals to come together from many different backgrounds and spheres of practice. I wish to acknowledge the work and collaboration of my colleague, Dr. Eunice Gorman, as well as Ramona Fernandez, who offered so much of this project through her patient assistance with editing and research. I am also deeply indebted to the contributing authors and their willingness to share their expertise and experiences.

I also wish to express deep appreciation to my partner, Brad Hunter, whose depth and awareness of the true nature of impermanence help to remind me that life and love are truly precious, and that every moment matters. Your unfaltering support in myriad ways means so much to me, from reading portions of the manuscript and offering suggestions for clarity to making my everyday life much lighter so that I could focus on this project—to say thank you is simply not enough.

Finally, to my daughter Lauren, as we experience both the joys and the difficulties that life offers us—for all of the changes, losses, and transitions that we have encountered and that we will journey through in the future. Your light in my life inspires me to reach out to others who find themselves struggling in dark and difficult places.

Introduction

This book began as a desire to explore how loss, change, and transition permeate our lives on a regular basis and as recognition that individuals experience grief as a result of many events that do not necessarily involve the physical death of a significant person. Rather than look at losses that are external to us (i.e., the death of a loved one), I wanted to consider the losses that are internal in nature—when something that dies is inside of us.

Throughout the course of life, we repeatedly experience events that challenge our view of ourselves, others, and the world around us. In struggling with these challenges, we often enter the grieving process, which helps us to adapt and to integrate these changes and losses into the fabric of our lives in a meaningful way. At times, this process and the losses we experience may not be consciously recognized. At other times, the losses may be overwhelming, and the grieving process may completely consume us. No matter the cause or the magnitude of the challenge, it is apparent that loss, change, and transition shape our lives and who we are as individuals. The grieving process is an important part of our human existence, as it can help us to embrace the dynamic experience of living, of which loss and change are a part.

In my clinical work, I frequently see individuals who experience profound anxiety because they can no longer live under the illusion that things can remain constant and unchanging, and this realization usually occurs as a result of the experience of a significant loss in their lives. Even though we attempt to function as if there is certainty and stability in everyday life, the world around us and even our bodies serve as metaphors for the normalcy of loss, change, and transition. The seasons change. Living things are born, grow, reproduce, and die. Many of the cells that exist in our bodies today were not present a year ago and may not be present in our bodies a month from now. This moment is gone and replaced by another moment in time. We cannot stop the changing nature of life, just as we cannot stop time in its place or change the course of events, although this topic has frequently been the subject of fantasy. Weenolsen (1988) speaks of our innate resistance to change and our belief that things can remain the same as the "fundamental illusion," functioning to allow us to feel safe and solid in the world. However, our clinging to this image causes us great difficulty when the illusion cannot be maintained, such as when a major loss event does indeed occur or when we come to the realization that we have very little control over ourselves and the people, places, and things that matter very much to us.

The purpose of this book is not to define all life experiences in the terminology of bereavement theory or to imply that we exist in an ongoing state of chronic, unresolved grief. However, there is scant writing about how the nondeath losses that we encounter on a regular basis shape who we are, how we relate to the world around us, and how we live in an environment that requires us to adapt and adjust to change on a regular basis. In response to the realization of how loss experiences of all types can have an impact on our lives, we introduced a new course in our thanatology program entitled Change, Loss, and Transition. The intention of this course is to explore different aspects of loss and the role that loss plays in human development, growth, and adjustment. When we first proposed this course, a review of the pertinent literature revealed that very little was written about this aspect of loss, as most of what was written focused on the grieving process after death-related losses. We also were hard pressed to find an appropriate text for this course because of the focus on death-related loss in the literature and other texts. Thus, the introduction of this new course led to the birth of this book and to our desire to reflect on the loss experiences in our lives in a more holistic way.

DEFINITIONS OF LOSS

Viorst (1986) stated that the losses we experience are necessary for us to grow and adapt as part of our normal functioning. In her book *Necessary Losses*, she stated that loss is natural, unavoidable, and inexorable. She further claimed that losses are necessary because we grow by losing and leaving and letting go.

> Throughout our lives, we grow by giving up. We give up some of our deepest attachments to others. We give up certain cherished parts of ourselves. We must confront, in the dreams we dream, as well as in our intimate relationships, all that we never will have and never will be. Passionate investment leaves us vulnerable to loss…. And sometimes, no matter how clever we are, we must lose. (p. 3)

The experience of loss may be subtle or overwhelming. Our losses may or may not be recognized by those around us, but it is our subjective appraisal and experience of these losses that matter. Some, like Weenolsen (1988), see the loss experience as something that needs to be conquered and worked through:

> [A loss is …] anything that destroys some aspect, whether macroscopic or microscopic, of life and self. Loss is not change, but change incorporates both loss and its overcoming. (p. 3)

Harvey (2002) discussed the role of emotional investment and attachment in the loss experience, stating that a major loss is

> … the loss of something in a person's life in which the person was emotionally invested…. By "emotional investment" I mean that we imbue these events with emotional meaning and in reaction to them we behave in ways that reflect the fact that they matter to us. They do not go away from our reflection

and memory easily. In fact, we hang on to them intentionally and memorialize their value in our lives. (p. 5)

In his discussion of the losses that are encountered in everyday life, Harvey (2002) describes the importance of experiences that demonstrate our lack of ability to control our world or exposure to experiences that confront our view of the world and shatter our assumptions about how the world should work. He also describes how losses can be "layered" on each other, magnifying their impact on our lives.

Maass (2008) discussed the role of perception and interpretation in the definition of loss. For example, an event that leads to a change in a person's normal routine may offer opportunities that did not exist before. However, the recognition of these opportunities is often overshadowed by having to let go of what was familiar, comfortable, or even safe. In her discussion of adaptation to lifestyle changes, Maass described our tendency toward dichotomous thinking (e.g., good vs. bad, positive vs. negative) rather than facing change in a way that recognizes the multifaceted and multidimensional aspects of choices and events.

THE ASSUMPTIVE WORLD

At a basic level, one's expectations about how the world works begin to be formed from birth, through the development of the attachment relationships of the infant and young child. Bowlby (1969, 1973) posited that early-life attachment experiences lead individuals to form "working models" of the self and of the world. According to Bowlby, a normal working model based on secure attachment represents the world as capable of meeting one's needs and providing a sense of safety and security. Bowlby's theory also suggested that loss can threaten these working models, leading to efforts to rebuild or restructure one's working models to fit the postloss world. Building on Bowlby's work, Parkes (1975) extended the concept of the "internal working model" to that of the "assumptive world," which he stated was a "… strongly held set of assumptions about the world and the self, which is confidently maintained and used as a means of recognizing, planning, and acting" (p. 132) and that it is "… the only world we know, and it includes everything we know or think we know. It includes our interpretation of the past and our expectations of the future, our plans and our prejudices" (Parkes, 1971, p. 103).

Parkes (1971) stated that the assumptions that individuals form about how the world works are based on their life experiences and attachments. He also emphasized that experiencing a significant loss can threaten one's assumptive world. Recent research that links attachment style to the way an individual navigates the grieving process after a significant loss would also support the role of early experiences with attachment figures as a template for how experiences are interpreted and integrated in later life (Stroebe, 2002). In her extensive work that explored the construct of the assumptive world in the context of traumatic experiences, Janoff-Bulman (1992) stated that expectations about how the world should work are established earlier than language in children and that assumptions about the world are a result of the generalization and application of childhood experiences into adulthood. Forming a belief that the world is safe is related to the sense of "basic trust" described by Erikson's (1968) model of human development.

Although attachment theory was originally founded in the psychoanalytic tradition of psychology and the discussion here draws heavily on attachment as a means of understanding how assumptions are developed, the broader context of the assumptive world goes far beyond the realm of psychological theory or cognition. If, as Parkes (1971) stated, one's assumptions are based on everything we think or know, then the assumptive world must also be informed by culture, experiences, and the social and spiritual context in which these assumptions are nurtured (Berkey, 2007). Indeed, Attig (2002) cautioned that these assumptions are much more than cognitions, as they "encompass all that we have come to take for granted as we have learned how to be and act in the world in the presence of those we love" (p. 55). In complementary research, Lazarus and Folkman's (1984) exploration of stress and coping emphasized the importance of one's individual beliefs about the world and one's self on how stressful events were perceived and assessed.

Janoff-Bulmann (1992) identified three major categories of assumptions. The first category is the belief that the world is benevolent—that there is more good than bad in the world and that people are generally trustworthy. The second category is that the world is meaningful—that good and bad events are distributed in the world in a fair and controllable manner. The category of meaningfulness emphasizes the ideas of justice and control over certain aspects of life. Most individuals tend to believe that misfortune is not haphazard and arbitrary—that there is a person–outcome contingency attached to negative life events. Research in the role of self-efficacy (Bandura, 1977) and locus of control (Rotter, 1966) also expands on this particular category of beliefs. At a basic level, negative events are generally viewed as punishment, and positive events are rewards. Janoff-Bulman stated that this assumption is "…that we can directly control what happens to us through our own behavior. If we engage in appropriate behaviors, we will be protected from negative events and if we engage in appropriate behaviors, good things will happen to us" (p. 10).

The third category is that the self is worthy and has value. Janoff-Bulman (1992) stated that these three categories of beliefs can be called world assumptions, and together they make up an individual's assumptive world. She drew on Piaget's (1954) concept of schemas to explain the nature of the assumptive world. Schemas are mental structures that represent things or events in the world. Schemas govern the interpretation of experiences (*assimilation*), or they can be revised if they are incapable of explaining or integrating a new set of experiences (*accommodation*). Rando (1993, 2002) further expanded on discussions regarding the assumptive world by differentiating between global assumptions (which are general beliefs about one's self, others, the world, and spirituality) and specific assumptions (which are more focused on what has been or is being lost).

Extrapolations of social forces that also may help shape these assumptions can be drawn from the theories of family systems (Bowen, 1985), where the valued need to belong in a social system is reinforced by the adoption of the family "rules" through socialization, which would also include the family's assumptions about the external world. Social pain theory (MacDonald & Leary, 2005) would also explain the strong need to reinforce one's adoption of the beliefs and assumptions of the social group to which an individual desired inclusion, as failure to do so would result in being ostracized from the desired group, with an accompanying negative response, which is experienced through the same neurological pathways as physiological pain.

With this foundation in place, it is apparent that the assumptive world is deeply ingrained into the fabric of how individuals live their lives and interpret life events. An individual's fundamental assumptions and themes allow for a feeling of safety and consistency in the world (Bandura, 1977; Epstein, 1991; Lazarus & Folkman, 1984; Janoff-Bulman, 1992, 2004; Poulin, 2006; Rando, 2002). Significant change or challenge to these deeply held beliefs would therefore be experienced as a threat to an individual's sense of stability and way of knowing and interpreting the world. In other words, the known is familiar and conceptually comfortable; the unknown is threatening. Significant changes challenge our feelings of safety and security (Maass, 2008). The result is a strong resistance to change in these assumptions, which Janoff-Bulman (1992) termed "cognitive conservatism" (p. 26).

Janoff-Bulman (1992) described how our basic assumptions about how the world should work can be shattered by life experiences that do not fit into our view of ourselves and the world around us. The concept of the shattering of one's assumptive world was further explored in detail by Poulin (2006), who found that there is a complex interplay between one's beliefs and assumptions about the world and other factors such as social support, age, and previous life experiences. Neimeyer, Laurie, Mehta, Hardison, and Currier (2008) discussed events that "disrupt the significance of the coherence of one's life narrative" (p. 30) and the potential for erosion of the individual's life story and sense of self that may occur after such events. What is apparent is that the experience of a significant life event that does not fit into our beliefs can throw us into a state of disequilibrium. Coping, healing, and accommodation after such experiences are part of a greater process that individuals undertake in an effort to "relearn" their world in light of confrontation with a reality that does not match one's expectations or assumptions (Attig, 1996).

Obviously, these life-altering events and losses cause a major shift and upheaval in our lives, and the process of adjusting to a world that is different from what we thought or believed will involve a great expenditure of energy. In putting together this book, experiences that may lead to the loss or challenge of specific assumptions about the world, such as the loss of the self as worthy or valuable, loss of the belief in the benevolence or basic goodness of others, loss of the belief that there is justice or meaning to events that occur, or the loss of the belief that the world is a safe place.

OVERVIEW OF THE BOOK

We begin with an exploration of the recent literature on losses that are not a result of the death of someone and the grief experience after such losses. In this first section, we will discuss in more detail specific aspects of nondeath loss, explore the concepts of nonfinite loss, ambiguous loss, and chronic sorrow, and then look at how these constructs may be applied to the various losses that are described in subsequent chapters. As a backdrop to the discussion of the topics in this book, a chapter that explores the social context of grief, including the concept of disenfranchised grief as defined by Doka (1989, 2002) will be provided.

The specific losses described in this book are presented in three distinct sections, founded on the basic assumptions as described earlier by Janoff-Bulman (1992). At the start of each of these sections, a brief introduction will be offered, tying together the specific topics to the overall theme of that section. Special contributions have been submitted by authors with specific expertise or experience in the listed topic areas to help provide clarity and description to these experiences.

The first descriptive section includes losses of assumptions related to the view of the world and others: for example, topics such as the loss of safety and security on a macro level, such as in mass disasters and large-scale events, and personal violations, such as rape and harassment. There is also a chapter on vicarious trauma and compassion fatigue in professionals, as it is recognized that professionals who work with traumatized individuals often find their view of the world to be altered as they are repeatedly exposed to stories of human pain, suffering, and helplessness (Pearlman & Saakvitne, 1995). The next chapter in this section explores relational losses that may occur, such as through separation and dissolution, adoption, and specific developmental milestones, such as the postparental transition (i.e., "the empty nest").

The second descriptive section examines the loss of meaning or a sense of justice in the world. Topics in this heading include existential losses pertaining to one's belief system, the realization of the human condition and existential suffering, the recognition that life has very little certainty, and the loss of one's faith community as a result of changes in one's beliefs.

The third descriptive section includes the loss of the view of one's self as worthy or valuable. In losses such as these, the loss of one's identity may lead to a redefinition of the self in ways that cause an individual to struggle for a sense of worth, value, identity, or of belonging. Topics in this section include the loss of the self through abuse or neglect, the loss of one's homeland and identity through immigration or moving, the loss of employment, the loss of reproductive ability, losses experienced by gay men when they "come out" publicly, and the loss of functionality that occurs with aspects of the aging process, degenerative conditions, and head injuries.

After the chapters that describe specific losses, there is a section that explores how individuals cope with losses in life, which will discuss the concepts of resilience, posttraumatic growth, and the role of meaning making with nondeath losses. We conclude with a summary of how loss, change, and transition can be integrated in life in a way that is healthy and adaptive and the potential for transformation that may occur after these experiences.

Doka (1989, 2002) discussed the importance of losses being acknowledged and validated. This book is designed to help individuals articulate their losses, both in the identification of what has actually been lost and the depth of the loss experience. Clinicians recognize the importance of bearing witness to an individual's subjective appraisal of an experience and of validating that experience because they are aware that only that person really knows what is important to himself or herself. Thus, loss, change, and transition are universal experiences, but the personal responses and appraisals of these experiences are highly individual and unique. The ability to name and describe an experience fully allows us the opportunity to reflect and consider its implications for our lives and our future choices. The need to grapple with our experiences and to try to understand them (even if they initially seem beyond our comprehension) is a key part of our human need to understand ourselves and to make sense of our world. I hope that this book provides a greater understanding of specific aspects of nondeath loss and that it also opens the door for further discussion of the losses that occur when something inside of us dies.

REFERENCES

Attig, T. A. (1996). *How we grieve: Relearning the world*. New York: Oxford University Press.

Attig, T. A. (2002). Questionable assumptions about assumptive worlds. In J. Kauffman (Ed.), *Loss of the assumptive world: A theory of traumatic loss* (pp. 55–68). New York: Brunner-Routledge.

Bandura, A. (1977). Self-efficacy: Toward a unifying theory of behavioral change. *Psychological Review, 84*, 191–215.

Berkey, K. (2007). The spiritual assumptive world of suddenly bereaved parents: A qualitative study. *Dissertation Abstracts International, 68*(10)B (UMI no 3286061).

Bowen, M. (1985). *Family therapy in clinical practice*. Northvale, NJ: Aronson.

Bowlby, J. (1969). *Attachment and loss: Attachment* (Vol. 1). New York: Basic Books.

Bowlby, J. (1973). *Attachment and loss: Separation* (Vol. 2). New York: Basic Books.

Doka, K. J. (1989). *Disenfranchised grief: Recognizing hidden sorrow*. Lexington, MA: Lexington Books.

Doka, K. J. (2002). *Disenfranchised grief: New directions, challenges, and strategies for practice*. Champaign, IL: Research Press.

Epstein, S. (1991). The self-concept, the traumatic neurosis, and the structure of personality. In D. Ozer, J. Healy Jr., & A. Stewart (Eds.), Perspectives in personality (Vol. 3, Part A, pp. 63–98). London: Kingsley.

Erikson, E. (1968). *Identity: Youth and crisis*. New York: Norton.

Harvey, J. H. (2002). *Perspectives on loss and trauma: Assaults on the self*. Thousand Oaks, CA: Sage.

Janoff-Bulman, R. (1992). *Shattered assumptions: Towards a new psychology of trauma*. New York: Free Press.

Janoff-Bulman, R. (2004). Post-traumatic growth: Three explanatory models. *Psychological Inquiry, 15*, 24–30.

Lazarus, R., & Folkman, S. (1984). *Stress, appraisal, and coping*. New York: Springer.

Maass, V. S. (2008). *Lifestyle changes: A clinician's guide to common events, challenges, and options*. New York: Routledge.

MacDonald, G., & Leary, M. R. (2005). Why does social exclusion hurt? The relationship between social and physical pain. *Psychological Bulletin, 131*, 202–223.

Neimeyer, R. A., Laurie, A., Mehta, T., Hardison, H., & Currier, J. M. (2008). Lessons of loss: Meaning-making in bereaved college students. In H. Servaty-Seib and D. Taub (Eds.), *Assisting bereaved college students* (pp. 27–39). San Francisco: Jossey-Bass.

Parkes, C. M. (1971). Psycho-social transitions: A field for study. *Social Science & Medicine, 5*, 101–115.

Parkes, C. M. (1975). What becomes of redundant world models? A contribution to the study of adaptation to change. *British Journal of Medical Psychology, 48*, 131–137.

Pearlman, L. A., & Saakvitne, K. W. (1995). *Trauma and the therapist.* New York: Norton.

Piaget, J. (1954). *The construction of reality in the child.* New York: Basic Books.

Poulin, M. J. (2006). *When do assumptions shatter? A prospective investigation of negative events and world assumptions.* Retrieved October 5, 2007 from ProQuest Digital Dissertations (AAT 3236684).

Rando, T. A. (1993). *Treatment of complicated mourning.* Champaign, IL: Research Press.

Rando, T. A. (2002). The "curse" of too good a childhood. In J. Kauffman (Ed.), *Loss of the assumptive world* (pp. 171–192). New York: Brunner-Routlege.

Rotter, J. (1966). Generalized expectancies for internal versus external control of reinforcement. *Psychological Monographs, 80*, 1–28.

Stroebe, M. (2002). Paving the way: From early attachment theory to contemporary bereavement research. *Mortality 7*(2), 127–138.

Viorst, J. (1986). *Necessary losses.* New York: Simon & Schuster.

Weenolsen, P. (1988). *Transcendence of loss over the life span.* New York: Hemisphere.

About the Editor

Darcy L. Harris, PhD, RSW, FT, is a professor in the Department of Interdisciplinary Programs at King's University College at the University of Western Ontario, in London, Ontario, Canada, where she is the coordinator of the thanatology program. She also maintains a private clinical practice with a focus on issues related to change, loss, and transition. She serves as a consultant for the Southern Ontario Fertility Treatment Program in London, Ontario, as well as a community consultant for victims of traumatic loss.

Prior to her teaching responsibilities at King's University College, Dr. Harris worked as an expanded role nurse in the areas of oncology and hospice care in the United States for 15 years. She then completed graduate training in counseling psychology and maintained a full-time therapy practice for another 10 years prior to completing her doctoral studies in psychology and thanatology at the Union Institute and University, Cincinnati, Ohio.

Dr. Harris planned and developed the undergraduate degree program in thanatology at King's University College, which provides students from around the world with the opportunity to study death, dying, and bereavement. She has implemented coursework in thanatology in the specific interest areas of critical theory, social justice, and the exploration of grief after nondeath losses. She is also adjunct faculty in the College of Graduate Studies at the University of Western Ontario, and she is on the board of directors for the Association for Death Education and Counseling. She is currently engaged in research on the topic of grief after various nondeath losses.

Dr. Harris has written extensively and frequently provides presentations on topics related to death, grief, and loss in contemporary society. Topical areas include the social context of grief in Western society, women's experiences of reproductive losses, and shame and social stigma in death and grief.

About the Contributors

Susan Abercromby, MEd (counseling psychology), is the coordinator of the Community Group Program for Children and Mothers Exposed to Woman Abuse in London, Ontario. She has worked in the field of violence against women and children for 10 years. She offers training and workshops on violence against women and children to audiences including teachers, child protection workers, students, and various community groups both locally and internationally.

Tom Attig, PhD, applied philosopher, is professor emeritus in philosophy at Bowling Green State University in Ohio. He is the author of *The Heart of Grief: Death and the Search for Lasting Love* (Oxford, 2000) and *How We Grieve: Relearning the World* (Oxford, 1996). A past president of the Association for Death Education and Counseling and vice chair of IWG, he currently lives in Victoria, British Columbia, Canada, and devotes his time to writing, speaking, and online teaching.

Pamela Cushing, PhD, is an associate professor of social justice and peace studies and disability studies at King's University at the University of Western Ontario in London. Her cultural anthropology PhD and postdoctorate involved a year of ethnographic fieldwork with L'Arche communities across Canada and then Camphill Schools in Scotland.

Eunice Gorman, PhD, RSW, is an assistant professor at King's University College in the thanatology program. She has worked in the areas of oncology, palliative care, bereavement, perinatal bereavement, professional caregiver support, and chronic illness as a clinician, teacher, researcher, administrator, and speaker. She is a member of numerous Canadian and international professional associations related to illness, grief, and loss.

Doug Harvey, MDiv, BCC, CT, is ordained with the Christian Church (Disciples of Christ) and has served for many years in the area of health-care ministry. His previous experiences include ministry to the residents and staff of the Christian Health Center in Louisville, Kentucky, Hospice of Louisville, and Hospice of the Bluegrass in Lexington, Kentucky. Doug has also served as an on-call chaplain with the University of Kentucky Hospital. Doug is currently serving as the interim pastor of Third Central United Christian Church (DOC) in Louisville, Kentucky, and is an active member of the Association of Death Education and Counseling and the Association of Professional Chaplains. He retired from the Army Reserve in 2006 with a total of 25 years of military service.

Brad Hunter, BA, CHT, began a career working in the area of death and bereavement in the early 1970s. At the same time, he started training in various meditative disciplines. These parallel paths converged about 10 years ago as he began introducing others to meditative practices and adapting some of these practices to therapeutic interventions for anxiety, trauma, grief, and depression.

Jessica Isenor, BSc, earned her degree in biology and psychology from Dalhousie University. She has worked in the private sector as a corporate trainer and volunteered at Dalhousie's Frank G. Lawson Career Information Centre and the Metro Immigrant Settlement Association. She is currently completing her MEd degree in counseling psychology at the University of Western Ontario.

Jeffrey Kauffman, MA, LCSW, FT, is a psychotherapist in private practice in suburban Philaldelphia. He is author of *Guidebook on Helping Persons With Mental Retardation Mourn* (Baywood Publishing, 2008) and editor of *Loss of the Assumptive World* (Routledge, 2002) and *The Shame of Death, Grief and Trauma* (Routledge, 2010).

Phyllis Kosminsky, PhD, LCSW, FT, is a clinical social worker at the Center for Hope in Darien, Connecticut, and in private practice. For the past 13 years, she has worked with bereaved adults and children individually and in groups. She is the author of *Getting Back to Life When Grief Won't Heal* (McGraw-Hill, 2007), which deals with the complications of grieving dependent and conflictual relationships and traumatic losses. Along with her experience as a clinician, Dr. Kosminsky has a background in public policy and program development and has taught courses in these subjects as a member of the faculty of Northeastern University in Boston.

Nieli Langer, PhD, received her master's in gerontology from the College of New Rochelle in New York (1985) and her PhD in social welfare (gerontology concentration) from Fordham University, New York (1989). From 1989 until 1994 she taught social work and gerontology at Our Lady of the Lake University in Texas and then chaired the Division of Gerontology at the University of the Incarnate Word (1995–1999) in San Antonio, Texas. Since her return to New York, Dr. Langer has mentored in the doctoral program of Walden University, has been adjunct professor at Fordham University, and has taught in the graduate division of the College of New Rochelle since 2001. Dr. Langer has authored three books in adult education and gerontology and over 40 peer-reviewed and invited articles and chapters. She is a tenured full professor at the College of New Rochelle.

Laura Lewis, PhD, RSW, is an associate professor at the School of Social Work, King's University College at the University of Western Ontario. She is also cross-appointed to the Department of Family Medicine in the Schulich School of

Medicine, also at the University of Western Ontario. Prior to her full-time academic appointment, she provided many years of community-based counseling services to people contending with many diverse dimensions of loss. Her research interests are in the area of grief and bereavement and primary health care.

Carl MacMillan, MA, is director of L'Arche Daybreak in Richmond Hill, Ontario. Before joining L'Arche in 1988, he worked as an advocate for people with intellectual disabilities in Boston, Massachusetts. Carl received his master's in the management of human services from the Heller School for Social Policy & Management at Brandeis University in the United States.

M. Thérèse (Terrie) Modesto, PhD, is founding director of the T.E.A.R. Center in Washington, D.C. She is a member of the Association of Death Education and Counseling as well as the Hospice Association of America Professionals. Additionally, she is a member of the International Critical Incident Stress Foundation, International Cemetery and Funeral Association, and the Association of Gravestone Studies.

Wanda Sawicki, BA, OATR, MAPPC, is an art therapist registered with the Ontario Art Therapy Association (OATR), having received a diploma in art therapy from the University of Western Ontario in London, Ontario, Canada. She has a master of arts in pastoral psychology and a counseling (MAPPC) degree from St. Stephen's College, Edmonton, Alberta, Canada. She has a private practice specializing in issues related to loss and grief in London, Ontario, Canada.

Jennifer Schachter is an adult adoptee who lives in Boston, Massachusetts, and is product manager with SensAble Technologies in Woburn, Massachusetts.

Sherry Schachter, PhD, FT, is the director of bereavement services for Calvary Hospital and Hospice in New York where she develops, coordinates, and facilitates educational services for staff and facilitates bereavement groups for families. In addition, Dr. Schachter has a private practice and also publishes and lectures on issues related to dying, death, and loss. She is past president of the Association for Death Education and Counseling (ADEC) and an active member of the International Work Group on Death, Dying and Bereavement (IWG). She is the biological mother of three, the adoptive mother of two children, and the grandmother of eight.

Derek Scott, BA, RSW, is a certified gestalt therapist and group leader (Gestalt Institute of Toronto—five-year training program) and a registered social worker with a BA (honors) in psychology from Keele University in England and has worked in the field of counseling and therapy since 1981. He has experience with a variety of insight-based holistic modalities including action-method psychodramatic work, gestalt two-chair and contact boundary work, body-focused awareness, cognitive therapy and reframing, chakra system and guided imagery, and the Internal Family Systems (IFS) model.

1

Grief From a Broader Perspective
Nonfinite Loss, Ambiguous Loss, and Chronic Sorrow

DARCY L. HARRIS and EUNICE GORMAN

Sorrows are our best education. A person can see farther through a tear than a telescope.

Lord Byron

BACKGROUND

*I*n the bereavement theory classes that we teach, we ask students to complete an assignment where they take an inventory of the losses that they have experienced in their lives and then relate these losses to the course content. It is not uncommon to have our younger students approach us on receipt of this assignment and tell us that they have not experienced any losses and that they are concerned about their ability to complete this project as a result. The "light bulb" usually goes on when we ask them about things like moving, losing friends as a result of a move to a new school or home, having to discontinue participation in a sport they love due to a career-ending injury, the ending of their first romantic relationship, or if their parents separated. Many of the students reply that they had never considered these events as losses in their lives because they did not involve a death but that on reflection they can see how their view of themselves and their world had to be adjusted or changed as a result of these or similar experiences. These adjustments occurred with the initiation of a process that helped them to integrate what had happened into the course of their lives—the grieving process.

In the process of living our lives, we do encounter losses on a regular basis, but we often do not recognize their significance because we tend to think of loss in finite terms, mainly associated with death and dying, and not in terms of adaptation to life-altering change. In the exercise described in the previous paragraph, our students create a "loss line," where they draw a line on a piece of paper, with their birth at the left side of the paper and the present time on the right side. All along this line on the paper, we suggest they place tick marks at specific ages to indicate when they experienced significant loss events in their lives. Once students are able to grasp the broader sense of loss as something that caused their lives to change in a significant way or that required them to make a significant adaptation in some way, the line is filled quickly with tick marks. Frequent examples include those already given, and often there are losses involving hopes and dreams, such as when they had planned that their lives would go in one direction and they realized that what they had hoped for was not going to be as they had anticipated. Some students realize at this time that, while the losses they have experienced are very real, they may also be intangible and difficult to describe concretely. Further examples of these losses may be lost beliefs that they once held about how the world should work or their ability to trust others. Or they may have somehow lost themselves. In our clinical practice, we hear many stories of individuals who have either been diagnosed with or must take care of family members who have degenerative physical or mental conditions, of intimate relationships that end with an aftermath that continues long after the relationship does, and of individuals who are attempting to rebuild their lives after losing their employment. Many of these descriptions can be identified as *nonfinite losses* or *ambiguous losses,* which we will explore in greater detail in this chapter.

NONFINITE LOSS AND CHRONIC SORROW

Nonfinite loss is defined as an enduring loss that is usually precipitated by a negative life event or episode that retains a physical or psychological presence with an individual in an ongoing manner (Bruce & Schultz, 2002). Some forms of nonfinite loss may be less clearly defined in onset, but they tend to be identified by a sense of ongoing uncertainty and repeated adjustment or accommodation. Three main factors separate this experience from the experience of a loss due to a death event:

- The loss (and grief) is continuous, although it may follow a specific event such as an accident or diagnosis.
- The loss prevents normal developmental expectations from being met in some aspect of life, and the inability to meet these expectations may be due to physical, cognitive, social, emotional, or spiritual losses.
- The inclusion of intangible losses, such as the loss of one's hopes or ideals related to what a person believes should have been, could have been, or might have been (Bruce & Schultz, 2001).

In their writings, Bruce and Schultz (2001) go on to describe several cardinal features of the experience of nonfinite losses:

- There is ongoing uncertainty regarding what will happen next.

- There is often a sense of disconnection from the mainstream and what is generally viewed as "normal" in human experience.
- The magnitude of the loss is frequently unrecognized or not acknowledged by others.
- There is an ongoing sense of helplessness and powerlessness associated with the loss.

Jones and Beck (2007) further add to this list a sense of chronic despair and a sense of ongoing dread, as individuals try to reconcile themselves between the world that is now known through this experience and the world in the future that is now anticipated.

In short, the person who experiences a nonfinite loss is repeatedly asked to adjust and accommodate to the loss. At the same time, because nonfinite loss is often not well understood, the experience may go unrecognized or unacknowledged by others. Support systems may tire of attempting to provide a shoulder to lean on when they also see potential joy, as well as sorrow, in a situation. For instance, partners who have had ongoing problems with infertility finally are able to have a baby. However, the baby is born prematurely and with some health concerns. The couple is at once ecstatic but worried about the future and sad because of the potential roadblocks and concerns that may arise over the course of the new baby's life. Well-wishers will stress the joy at having a new baby in the couple's life and may not recognize, or perhaps even tolerate, any discussion of the mixed emotions of sadness and disappointment that the baby was not "perfect" and that the delivery did not occur after a full-term pregnancy.

A related concept to nonfinite loss is that of *chronic sorrow,* a term first proposed by Olshansky (1962) after his observations of parents whose children were born with disabilities. He noticed that these parents experienced a unique form of grieving that never ended as their children continued to live and that the hopes they had for these children were repeatedly dashed as time went on. Shortly after the introduction of the concept by Olshansky, a few articles were written about the adjustment and coping in parents of children with various developmental disabilities. Since then, most of the research associated with the concept of chronic sorrow has been reported in the nursing literature. In 1989, the Nursing Consortium for Research on Chronic Sorrow was formed to further investigate the phenomenon in individuals with chronic or life-threatening conditions as well as the caregivers of these individuals (Burke, Eakes, & Hainsworth, 1999). The concept has been empirically proven in multiple sclerosis (Ahlstrom, Gunnarsson, & Isaksson, 2007; Liedstrom, Isaksson, & Ahlstrom, 2008), parenting a child with a mental health problem (Angold, Messer, & Stangl, 1998; Corrigan & Miller, 2004; Godress, Ozgul, Owen, & Foley-Evans, 2005; Hinshaws, 2005), Alzheimer's disease (Mayer, 2001), autism (O'Brien, 2007), mental illness (Jones, 2004), and caring for a child with disabilities (Berube, 1996; Green, 2007; Langridge, 2002). Chronic sorrow has also been linked to Parkinson's disease, mental retardation, neural tube defects, spinal cord injury, schizophrenia, and chronic major depression (Roos, 2002). Chronic sorrow is found in situations involving long-term care giving. It has also been recently associated with loss of homeland, language, culture, and customs in immigrants (Melvin, 2005). Samuels (2009) shed light on chronic sorrow in young adults who have moved through the foster home system and now live in homes outside the social service network. These young people mourn the loss of a sense of home that would have grounded them as children.

Chronic sorrow is defined by Roos (2002) as:

> a set of pervasive, profound, continuing, and recurring grief responses resulting from a significant loss or absence of crucial aspects of oneself (self-loss) or another living person (other-loss) to whom there is a deep attachment. The way in which the loss is perceived determines the existence of chronic sorrow. The essence of chronic sorrow is a painful discrepancy between what is perceived as reality and what continues to be dreamed of. The loss is ongoing since the source of the loss continues to be present. The loss is experienced as a *living loss*. (p. 26)

Chronic sorrow remains largely disenfranchised and often escalates in intensity or is progressive in nature (Roos & Neimeyer, 2007). While chronic sorrow is often linked to a defining moment, a critical event, or a seismic occurrence, it can just as easily be the hallmark of the slow insidious realization of what a diagnosis means over time and how it has caused change for the lives in its wake. In this book, the term nonfinite loss will refer to the loss or event itself, and chronic sorrow will refer to the response to ongoing, nonfinite losses.

Burke et al. (1999) define chronic sorrow as "grief-related feelings that emerge in response to an *ongoing disparity* resulting from the loss of the anticipated 'normal' lifestyle of these persons" (p. 374). Teel (1991) states that, in addition to the disparity that exists between what is expected or hoped for and what actually is in reality, the chronicity of the feelings and the ongoing nature of the loss separate chronic sorrow apart from other forms of grief. According to this author, chronic sorrow can be precipitated by the permanent loss of a significant relationship, functionality, or self-identity. Delp (1992) links living loss experiences to mental suffering, lamentation, sadness, regret, and the sense of emotional heaviness.

Lindgren (1992) defines the characteristics of chronic sorrow to include the following: (1) a perception of sadness or sorrow over time in a situation with no predictable end; (2) sadness or sorrow that is cyclic or recurrent; (3) sadness or sorrow that is triggered internally or externally; and (4) sadness or sorrow that is progressive and can intensify. Chronic sorrow is differentiated from the grief response after a death in that the loss itself is ongoing, and thus the grief does not end. Lindgren goes on to stress the peaks and valleys, resurgence of feelings, or periods of high and low intensity that distinguish chronic sorrow from other types of grief responses. An individual's emotions might swing between flooding of emotion and numbness at the two extremes of an emotional pendulum. Most people who experience chronic sorrow reside somewhere between these two end points.

Roos (2002) also states that the loss involved in chronic sorrow is a lifetime loss and remains largely unrecognized for its significance. She also notes that the first realization of the loss is the *trauma* that launches chronic sorrow. One's assumptive world is shattered, and there is no foreseeable end, with constant reminders of the loss. She states that an undercurrent of anxiety and trauma also separates this construct from grief after a death and that the person usually continues to function, separating it from primary clinical depression. Chronic sorrow differs from posttraumatic stress disorder (PTSD) because of the ongoing nature of the loss and because it is not a reaction to an event that has occurred, even though there may be an event that defines when the loss began. The traumatic material in nonfinite loss is related to the degree of helplessness and powerlessness that is felt in light of a situation that has profound, ongoing, and life-altering implications for the individual.

Roos (2002) makes the point that chronic sorrow may apply more to those who are caregivers, as the affected individual may not be able to internalize the world to be able to have dreams or life goals, and the intensity of the experience of chronic sorrow is related to the potency and magnitude of the disparity between the reality of the situation and the dream to which a person may cling. The outcome is really unknown, or the progression of what will unfold is unknown, so unpredictability complicates the process. The ongoing presence of the person or the loss inhibits reinvestment into other aspects of life, and there are "surges" of loss that are often triggered by various events, as might occur in individuals whose loss was related to the death of another individual (Teel, 1991).

It is important to stress the cyclical nature of chronic sorrow. Peterson and Bredow (2004) remind us that tipping points, triggers, or milestones can cause an upsurge of sorrow. These can be either externally or internally driven. Something as simple as a touch, smell, or sound might bring feelings of sadness rushing to the forefront of a person's day-to-day experience. Triggers might be anniversary dates or reminders sparked by a happy or sad event in another person's life, such as a wedding or baby shower. Fears, disappointments, and sorrow can be brought to mind easily. However, it is important to note that it is a disservice to the individuals struggling with chronic sorrow if we view the experience as permanent despair. It is not. Instead, there is mounting evidence that sorrow occurs periodically through-out day-to-day life, and there are also moments of joy. Johnsonius (1996) describes this as cycles of withdrawal, or loss of connectedness with an outward appearance of happiness, or real happiness, despite continued pain in an environment that is never free of the reminders of what has been lost.

AMBIGUOUS LOSS

Many of the nondeath losses experienced by individuals are very difficult to name, describe, or validate. As stated previously, many losses are not clearly defined because there is no identifiable "death." For many individuals, it may be unclear exactly what has been lost. The loss may or may not involve a person, and there may not be a defining experience to denote where the loss actually originates. In her development and exploration of loss experiences where there was significant ambiguity, Boss (1999) first used the term *ambiguous loss*. She described two situations where ambiguous loss occurs. In the first scenario, the *person is perceived as physically absent but psychologically present.* Examples may be when a person is missing, such as in divorced families when the noncustodial parent is absent but very much present in the minds of the children. Prisoners, kidnapping victims, relatives serving their country overseas, adoptive families, and situations when a person is absent or missing but very much present in the minds or awareness of their loved ones also may also fit this description. Another frequent example would be grandparents who lose contact with their grandchildren after the parents of these children divorce. In the second scenario described by Boss, ambiguous loss may be identified when *the person is physically present but perceived as psychologically absent.* Examples of this type of loss may be when a family member has Alzheimer's disease, acquired brain injury, autism, or a chronic mental illness or is psychologically unavailable due to addictions or some type of ongoing distraction or obsession. Each of these scenarios leaves individuals feeling as if they are "in limbo" (Boss & Couden, 2002) as they struggle to learn to live with ambiguity (Boss, 1999, 2006, 2007; Tubbs & Boss, 2000).

Boss's first observations of this phenomenon occurred when she engaged with families in a therapeutic setting, where the family system was outwardly intact, but one of the members was absent psychologically from the family through obsessive workaholism or addiction.

Key aspects of ambiguous loss include (Boss, 2007) the following:

- The loss is confusing, and it is very difficult to make sense of the loss experience (as when a person is physically present but emotionally unavailable).
- Because the situation is indeterminate, the experience may feel like a loss but not be readily identified as one. Hope can be raised and destroyed so many times that individuals may become psychically numb and unable to react.
- Because of ongoing confusion about the loss, there are frequent conflicting thoughts and emotions, such as dread and then relief, hope and hopelessness, wanting to take action and then profound paralysis. People are often "frozen" in place in their reactions and unable to move forward in their lives.
- Difficulty problem solving because the loss may be temporary (as in a missing person) or permanent (as in an acquired head injury).
- There are no associated rituals and very little validation of the loss (as opposed to a death where there is official certification of the death and prescribed rituals for funeral and disposition of a body).
- There is still hope that things may return to the way they used to be, but there is no indication of how long that may take or if it will ever happen (e.g., if a family member enters treatment for an addiction or if a couple enters marital therapy).
- Because of the ambiguity, people tend to withdraw instead of offer support because they do not know how to respond, or there is some social stigma attached to the experience.
- Because the loss is ongoing in nature, the relentless uncertainty causes exhaustion in the family members and burnout of supports.

Boss (1999) and Weiner (1999) describe the experience of ambiguous loss like a "never-ending roller coaster" that affects family members physically, cognitively, behaviorally, and emotionally. Physical symptoms may include fatigue, sleep disturbances, and somatic complaints that may affect various body systems. Cognitive symptoms may include preoccupation, rumination, forgetfulness, and difficulties concentrating. Behavioral manifestations may be expressed through agitation, withdrawal, avoidance, dependence, or a pressing need to talk at times. Emotionally, individuals may feel anxious, depressed, irritable, numb, or angry. It is not uncommon to be misdiagnosed with an anxiety disorder or a major depressive disorder (Weiner).

There is a great deal of overlap between nonfinite loss and ambiguous loss. Perhaps much of the distinctions have to do with their origin in different lenses of study. In the literature, nonfinite loss is described more from an intrapersonal perspective, with the loss experience focusing on the individual's perspective and coping (i.e., what did I have that I have now lost). In contrast, ambiguous loss is a concept that was formulated within a family stress model, and the loss is described in terms of how the family members perceive and define the loss according to the boundaries of the family system (i.e., who is absent from the family system that should be present). In the descriptions of nonfinite loss and ambiguous loss, the common features include dealing with ongoing uncertainty that causes emotional exhaustion, shattering of one's assumptions about how the world should be, and the lack of rituals and validation of the significance of these losses. Nonfinite loss, ambiguous loss, and chronic sorrow may be linked not only to real losses but also to perceived, symbolic, or secondary losses. Nonfinite loss, ambiguous loss, and chronic sorrow may all be accompanied by shame and self-loathing that further complicates individual authenticity and truthfulness in other relationships, thereby adding to the struggle with coping.

THERAPEUTIC IMPLICATIONS

In losses where there is a high degree of ambiguity regarding what is actually lost or when the loss experience may (if ever) end, such as in nonfinite losses, some important general guidelines may be of benefit in helping individuals with these types of loss experiences.

Identify and Label the Loss Experience

Validation of the experience and the perceptions of the affected individuals are very important, so the loss is recognized for the significance it has to the persons involved. There may also be "layers" of loss present as the experience takes its toll on family members physically, cognitively, behaviorally, and emotionally (Boss, 1999; Betz & Thorngren, 2006).

Place the Problem With the Situation and Not the Person

Understand that the issue is with the ambiguity of the situation and its occurrence outside of what is considered "normal" human experience rather than there being something wrong or dysfunctional with the person or family that is experiencing it. The inability to resolve the grief is due not to personality defects or deficiencies but to the situation that has been created by the loss itself. Naming the ambiguity as an external entity helps to diminish crippling self-blame and family shame (Boss, 2004).

Gather Information and Resources

Knowledge is power, and information can be very empowering to individuals. Information from the Internet, books, articles, and popular culture may help to normalize what has been perceived as an abnormal response to an ongoing, ambiguous loss experience. Popular movies can also be powerful sources of information and inspiration for placing these types of losses into context. For example, the movie *Regarding Henry* (Nichols & Rudin, 1991) accurately demonstrated the impact of an absent, workaholic father who rebuilds his family life after suffering a head injury. *A Beautiful Mind* (Howard & Grazer, 2001) portrayed the losses associated with mental illness. *Away From Her* (Polley & Egoyan, 2006) and *Iris* (Eyre, Pollock, Minghella, & East, 2001) are provocative examples of the effects of Alzheimer's disease on individuals and their families. Many clients find "movie therapy" to be very helpful, especially if they are unable to concentrate for long periods to read more detailed written information.

Insularity, disassociating from family and friends, secret keeping, and isolation add to the struggles experienced by individuals and families coping with a living loss. Furthermore, role entrapment and protectiveness can make matters worse. Linking individuals to supports and assisting them to follow through with help seeking is of the utmost importance.

Identify and Validate Emotions That Are Present

It may be helpful to explore what the "rules" around emotions have been to that point for an individual or within a family system. For example, in many families, it is not appropriate to express strong emotions or there may be gender-specific rules about who can express which emotions. Often, the presence of conflicting emotions is very confusing—and it is important to normalize the multifaceted aspects of human responses. Parents can feel strong love and concern for their son who has stolen things from them to support his drug habit, and they can also feel anger and regret that he is their son at the same time. In addition, the roller coaster experience of the cycles of hope and disappointment leaves family members exhausted and numb (Betz & Thorngren, 2006). It is important to allow negative feelings to be part of the dialogue (Collings, 2008), but, at the same time, ways to move forward need to be considered.

Recognize the Loss and Identify What Is Not Lost

It is easy to focus on the loss and how it has negatively affected the world of that individual. However, some aspects of life and the person have not been lost. This aspect of intervention focuses on the innate strengths of an individual that are not lost as a result of the experience. Focusing on what is still present and what has not been lost is not meant as a form of distraction or negation of the heavy toll that the loss has taken on the individual or family. Rather, the focus is on identifying innate strengths and abilities that are apparent and on which healing can occur. You may be able to identify how the loss has taken away control and choice from a person, but then you may be able to focus on the choices that are possible within the limitations created by the loss (Boss, 1999).

Recognize That There Is No Perfect Solution

There must be permission to acknowledge the pain of what has happened, that life may never be the same again, and that the ambiguity may continue indefinitely. Within the context of what is no longer possible or probable, what are the realistic possibilities? Mastery in a situation of nonfinite or ambiguous loss will focus on changing what is internal, such as perceptions, feelings, or memories, and not on external things like other people, the situation, or the environment (Boss, 1999). Promoting realistic aims, supporting hope, and assisting to find optimism can benefit people in problem solving and decision making. Recognition for people's efforts, empathy, compassion, and respect can go a long way toward helping people feel that they have been heard and understood (Bowman, 2005; Gordon, 2007; Melvin, 2005).

Allow for the Possibility of Meaning Making and Growth

Times of great pain and despair are also times when we identify what is most important in our lives and when we also recognize positive aspects of ourselves that we may have never known before. Although it would be highly insensitive for a therapist to ask clients in the midst of an excruciatingly painful experience about the meaning they have attached to that experience, they will often reflect on their experiences and identify positive aspects of themselves or things they have learned from going through such an arduous event. Many clients will speak of being more sensitive to others facing similar losses or of increased awareness that, even when they may not be able to make sense of what has happened, they will somehow use this experience to help others or to have a view of the world that is more accommodating to a diverse range of human experiences. The concept of the *wounded healer* is often birthed from having to tend to one's own wounds during a very painful time.

Initiate Rituals Where None Exist

Rituals give symbolic meaning to significant events in life. Clients may be able to identify rituals that symbolize the loss they have experienced or give validation to the importance of the experience. For example, a client in my (D.H.) clinical practice who went through several years of infertility treatment made a clay model of her uterus and then formed several small balls of clay that represented the embryos transferred into her body during the various infertility procedures.

She initially placed each "embryo" into the clay uterus and then took each one out, one by one, and said goodbye to the children she would never bring into the physical world with her. She then buried each of these clay balls to symbolize a funeral for them.

Honoring the Human Spirit

Individuals and their supports systems find ways of coping with the curveballs that life throws at them. It is important to look for ways to honor people's strengths and to recognize ambiguous gains (Boss, 2007) as well as to identify, find, and support sources of resilience. This may be undertaken in a number of ways including linking people with others who have encountered similar losses and have flourished.

Letting Go of Time-Bound Assumptions

Given the ongoing nature of nonfinite loss, ambiguous loss, and chronic sorrow, it is important to remember that there is not a linear movement through stages, phases, or tasks related to grieving. Instead, individuals and their support systems are called on to integrate grief over a lifetime. In our society, we are often quick to want end points and time frames. The notion that there is a natural progression toward closure, resolution, acceptance, or reconciliation does not lend itself well to living loss, as the cyclical and recurrent upswings of grief can last a lifetime. Furthermore, the continuity of the loss is often complicated by contradictory feelings where joy and grief are felt simultaneously, as mentioned earlier. Clients who feel pressure to fit their grief into an arbitrary time frame may feel that they have somehow failed or are not grieving properly. It is important to remember that each person is different, each situation unique, and each loss experience distinctive. While recognizing the ongoing nature of living loss, clinicians must also be aware of depression, prolonged grief, and acute or long-term complicated grief; to be able to distinguish these experiences from nonfinite loss, ambiguous loss, and chronic sorrow; and to offer in response more intensive interventions as indicated.

CONCLUSION

The constructs of nonfinite loss, chronic sorrow, and ambiguous loss are interesting as theories and descriptions of unique aspects of loss. However, we see these theories as highly relevant to working with individuals who are in the throes of ongoing losses in their lives that are often not recognized for their significance because they are either intangible or not caused by a physical death. If one of the most important aspects of therapeutic work with these individuals is the validation of their loss experience, then these theories provide the words from which validation will initially take place. Consider the spouse who feels abandoned in her marriage by a husband who is a good provider, is able to engage socially with friends at functions, but who spends almost all of his waking time at home in front of a computer screen while his wife tries to occupy herself because he is emotionally unavailable to her on a regular basis. To describe her experience as a form of loss with words that validate her experience gives her the opportunity to realistically see the situation and make conscious choices regarding how she will both address the issue with her husband and choose to care for herself in the process. Giving words that are accurate in their description and useful in their ability to acknowledge a loss experience provides a basis on which therapeutic movement can occur.

Things to Consider

1. Think of situations in your own life when you simultaneously felt joy and sadness related to the losses with which you are living, for instance, loss of dreams, hopes, and health.
2. Are there losses not related to death with which you are living that sometimes cause distress or intrusive feelings or preoccupy your mind to cause disruptions in your day-to-day life?
3. What activities or interventions might help someone cope with, manage, or adjust to these feelings?
4. What might hinder a person's efforts to make sense of or make meaning of living losses?

REFERENCES

Ahlstrom, G., Gunnarsson, L.G., & Isaksson, A.K. (2007). The presence and meaning of chronic sorrow in patients with multiple sclerosis. *Journal of Nursing and Healthcare in Chronic Illness, 16*, 315–324.

Angold, A., Messer, S.C., Stangl, D., Farmer, E.M.Z., Costello, E.J., & Burns, B.J. (1998). Perceived parental burden and service use for child and adolescent psychiatric disorders. *American Journal of Public Health, 88*(1), 75–80.

Berube, M. (1996). *Life as we know it: A father and an exceptional child.* New York: Pantheon.

Betz, G., & Thorngren, J. M. (2006). Ambiguous loss and the family grieving process. *The Family Journal: Counseling and Therapy for Couples and Families, 14*(4), 359–365.

Boss, P. (1999). *Ambiguous loss: Learning to live with unresolved grief.* Cambridge, MA: Harvard University Press.

Boss, P. (2004). Ambiguous loss research, theory, and practice: Reflections after 9/11. *Journal of Marriage and Family, 66*, 551–566.

Boss, P. (2006). *Loss, Trauma and Resilience: Therapeutic work with ambiguous loss.* New York: Norton.

Boss, P. (2007). Ambiguous loss theory: Challenges for scholars and practitioners. *Family Relations, 56*(2), 105–111.

Boss, P., & Couden, B.A. (2002). Ambiguous loss from chronic physical illness: Clinical interventions with individuals, couples and families. *JCLP in Session: Psychotherapy in Practice, 58*(11), 1351–1360.

Bowman, K. (2005). Commentary on "Loving-kindness meditation for chronic lower back pain." *Journal of Holistic Nursing, 23*(3), 305–309.

Bruce, E.J., & Schultz, C. L. (2001). *Nonfinite loss and grief: A psychoeducational approach.* Baltimore: Paul H. Brookes.

Bruce, E.J., & Schultz, C. (2002). Non-finite loss and challenges to communication between parents and professionals. *British Journal of Special Education, 29*(1), 9–13.

Burke, M.L., Eakes, G.G., & Hainsworth, M.A. (1999). Milestones of chronic sorrow: Perspectives of chronically ill and bereaved persons and family caregivers. *Journal of Family Nursing, 5*(4), 374–387.

Collings, C. (2008). That's not my child anymore! Parental grief after acquired brain injury (ABI): Incidence, nature and longevity. *British Journal of Social Work, 38,* 1499–1517.

Corrigan, P.W., & Miller, F.E. (2004). Shame, blame and contamination: A review of the impact of mental illness stigma on family members. *Journal of Mental Health, 13*(6), 537–548.

Delp, K.J. (1992). Beyond chronic sorrow: Psychosocial intervention strategies for professionals. *Psychosocial Aspects of Genetic Counseling. Birth defects, 28*(1), 75–77.

Eakes, G.G. (1993). Chronic sorrow: A response to living with cancer. *Oncology Nursing Forum, 20*(9), 1327–1334.

Eakes, G.G., Burke, M.L., & Hainsworth, M.A. (1998). Middle-range theory of chronic sorrow. *Journal of Nursing Scholarship, 30*(2), 179–184.

Eyre, R. (Director), Pollock, S. (Producer), Minghella, A., & East, G. (Producer). (2001). *Iris* [Motion picture]. United States: Miramax.

Godress, J., Ozgul, S., Owen, C., & Foley-Evans, L. (2005). Grief experiences of parents whose children suffer from mental illness. *Australian and New Zealand Journal of Psychiatry, 39,* 88–94.

Gordon, M. (2005). *Roots of empathy: Changing the world child by child.* Toronto: Thomas Allen.

Green, S.E. (2007). "We're tired, not sad": Benefits and burdens of mothering a child with a disability. *Social Science and Medicine, 64*(1), 150–163.

Hainsworth, M.A. (1994). Living with multiple sclerosis: The experience of chronic sorrow. *Journal of Neuroscience Nursing, 26*(4), 237–240.

Hainsworth, M.A. (1996). Helping spouses with chronic sorrow related to multiple sclerosis. *Journal of Psychosocial Nursing and Mental Health Services, 34*(6), 36–40.

Hainsworth, M.A., Burke, M.L., Lindgren, C.L., & Eakes, G.G. (1993). Chronic sorrow in multiple sclerosis: A case study. *Home Healthcare Nurse. 11*(2), 9–13.

Hainsworth, M.A., Busch, P.V., Eakes, G.G., & Burke, M.L. (1995). Chronic sorrow in women with chronically mentally disabled husbands. *Journal of the American Psychiatric Nurses Association, 1*(4), 120–124.

Hainsworth, M.A., Eakes, G.G., & Burke, M.L. (1994). Coping with chronic sorrow. *Issues in Mental Health Nursing, 15,* 59–66.

Hinshaws, S. P. (2005). The stigmatization of mental illness in children and parents: Developmental issues, family concerns, and research needs. *Journal of Child Psychology and Psychiatry, 46*(7), 714–734.

Howard, R. (Director, Producer), & Grazer, B. (Producer). (2001). *A beautiful mind* [Motion picture]. United States: Universal Studios.

Johnsonius, J.R. (1996). Lived experiences that reflect embodied themes of chronic sorrow: A phenomenological pilot study. *Journal of Nursing Science, 1*(5–6), 165–173.

Jones, D.W. (2004). Families and serious mental illness: Working with loss and ambivalence. *British Journal of Social Work, 34,* 961–979.

Jones, S.J., & Beck, E. (2007). Disenfranchised grief and non-finite loss as experienced by the families of death row inmates. *Omega, 54*(4), 281–299.

Krafft, S.K., & Krafft, L.J. (1998). Chronic sorrow: Parents' lived experience. *Holistic Nursing Practice, 13*(1), 59–67.

Langridge, P. (2002). Reduction of chronic sorrow: A health promotion role for children's community nurses? *Journal of Child Health Care, 6*(3), 157–170.

Liedstrom, E., Isaksson, A.K., & Ahlstrom, G. (2008). Chronic sorrow in next of kin of patients with multiple sclerosis. *Journal of Neuroscience Nursing, 40*(5), 304–311.

Lindgren, C., Burke, M., Hainsworth, M., & Eakes, G. (1992). Chronic sorrow: A lifespan concept. *Scholarly Inquiry for Nursing Practice, 6*, 27–40.

Mayer, M. (2001). Chronic sorrow in caregiving spouses of patients with Alzheimer's disease. *Journal of Aging & Identity*, 6(1), 49–60.

Melvin, L. (2005). Health needs of immigrants: Rights to treatment and confidentiality. *Journal of Family Planning and Reproductive Health Care, 31*(4), 331–332.

Nichols, M. (Director), & Rudin, S. (Producer). (1991). *Regarding Henry* [Motion picture]. United States: Paramount Pictures.

O'Brien, M. (2007). Ambiguous loss in families of children with autism spectrum disorders. *Family Relations*, 56(2), 135–146.

Olshansky, S. (1962). Chronic sorrow: A response to having a mentally defective child. *Social Casework, 43*(4), 190–192.

Peterson, S.J., & Bredow, T.S. (2004). *Middle range theories: Application to nursing research*. Philadelphia: Lippincott Williams & Wilkins.

Phillips, M. (1991). Chronic sorrow in mothers of chronically ill and disabled children. *Issues in Comprehensive Pediatric Nursing, 14*(2), 111–20.

Polley, S. (Director), & Egoyan, A. (Producer). (2006). *Away from her* [Motion picture]. Vancouver, Canada: Lionsgate Films.

Roos, S. (2001). Theory development: Chronic sorrow and the Gestalt construct of closure. *Gestalt Review, 5*(4), 289–310.

Roos, S. (2002). *Chronic sorrow: A living loss.* New York: Brunner-Routledge.

Roos, S., & Neimeyer, R. (2007). Reauthoring the self: Chronic sorrow and posttraumatic stress following the onset of CID. In E. Martz & H. Livneh (Eds), *Coping with chronic illness and disability* (pp. 89–106). New York: Springer.

Samuels, G.M. (2009). Ambiguous loss of home: The experience of familial (im)permanence among young adults with foster care backgrounds. *Child and Youth Services Review, 31*(12), 1229–1239.

Teel, C.S. (1991). Chronic sorrow: Analysis of the concept. *Journal of Advanced Nursing, 16*(11), 1311–1319.

Tubbs, C.Y., & Boss, P. (2000) Dealing with ambiguous loss. *Family Relations, 49*(3), 285–286.

Weiner, I. (1999). *Coping with loss*. Mahwah, NJ: Lawrence Erlbaum.

2

The Social Context of Loss and Grief

DARCY L. HARRIS

You know, there's a lot of talk in this country about the federal deficit. But I think we should talk more about our empathy deficit—the ability to put ourselves in someone else's shoes; to see the world through the eyes of those who are different from us—the child who's hungry, the steelworker who's been laid-off, the family who lost the entire life they built together when the storm came to town. When you think like this—when you choose to broaden your ambit of concern and empathize with the plight of others, whether they are close friends or distant strangers—it becomes harder not to act; harder not to help.

Barack Obama

INTRODUCTION

A book that explores various aspects of loss would be remiss if it did not discuss the context in which these losses occur and the socially mediated factors that affect the response to these losses. It can be said that we do indeed walk alone at times on our life's path; however, which path we choose, how we walk that path, and what possible alternative paths we may have are all highly influenced by the social context in which we live. There is often a tendency on the part of clinicians to focus on grief in terms of an individual's personal reactions to a loss. After all, the focus of most clinical work is on the individual, either in private counseling or in small group work focused on the issue at hand. Yet, when we work with individuals, we recognize that they exist within family systems, organizational systems, and even social and political structures that have an influence on these individuals' experience of loss and the manifestation of their grief. It is with this thought in mind that this chapter is devoted to the "bigger picture" of loss, hoping that by so doing the individual experience is situated as part of the larger social context of loss.

MICRO, MEZZO, AND MACRO PRACTICE

The mainstay of clinical practice is typically the office of the therapist, where clients come for help in dealing with life difficulties they encounter. This form of help is often referred to as *micro practice* in the social work literature (Dietz, 2000; Wronka, 2008). In micro practice, the focus is on the intrapsychic aspects of clients' experience and their perceptions and beliefs about what is happening in their life, with interventions focused on their beliefs, perceptions, and feelings. In this practice setting, the professional helper also has the opportunity to "bear witness" to clients' stories, which can be a very powerful healing experience for the clients. *Mezzo practice* focuses on work with small groups at a local level, such as employees of a specific workplace, members of an extended family system, or a support group that has formed around a specific issue or experience. In mezzo practice, the skills of active listening and reflection used in micro practice are enhanced by understanding and working with group dynamics as they occur in the interactions and communication between individuals who are present in the group setting. The focus in mezzo practice is on facilitation by the helper. *Macro practice* focuses on larger systems, such as organizations, communities, and even political structures and governments. In macro practice, the focus is on advocacy, with the goal of changing organizational, social, and political policies that have a negative effect on the individuals who are part of these larger groups (Kirst-Ashman & Hull, 2008).

Looking at these levels of intervention is very important, as the strict focus on micro practice alone will not address the profound social influences under which individuals must live and function. The intrapsychic focus of clinical work can have the potential to individualize social problems rather than to identify that some problems may actually be the result of social norms in conflict with individuals' experiences. Thus, working with clients' "self-talk" in a micro practice setting can become an exercise in identifying the social messages that have been internalized by clients about themselves. In this setting, it is possible to look at these internalized messages with a "macro lens," exposing the underlying social messages that have been adopted into their values and self-judgments.

It has often been said that grief is related to our innate tendency to form attachments. This innate tendency to attach identifies human beings as primarily social in nature and needing the acceptance of and affiliation with others to feel safe and secure within the world. Thus, the social messages and beliefs held by the dominant group into which individuals belong will have a powerful influence on how they perceive themselves and also on how their experiences will be interpreted and validated or invalidated. If we need to feel socially connected to others to feel safe in the world, then experiences that cause us to feel disconnected from our affiliated "group" will be highly disruptive to our sense of safety and security at a very basic level.

A good portion of this chapter is spent looking at how the macro level of social and political influences has a direct impact on the micro level of the internal world of individuals in their experiences of loss. This interaction of individuals' experiences with the social and political spheres is the foundation of both feminist and critical theorists, who state that individual change and social change are interdependent entities (Morell, 1987). Political and social structures have a direct impact on the individuals that are part of these systems, and the subjective experience of individuals can be an impetus to advocate for social and political change as well.

SOCIAL AND POLITICAL UNDERPINNINGS

When we begin to explore social and political influences on individuals, we are essentially talking about how power is distributed within a society. Power in this context can be defined as the ability to have influence, control, superiority, or an advantage over others (Brown, 1994). It is important to see that systemic power relations exist between social groups identified in a society. We are all born into social groups, which preexist us as social structures. The social and political significance of social groups is established and maintained socially (i.e., not by nature or by divine intervention). Group identities are socially elevated or diminished in relation to one another, establishing structural power relationships between these groups. Individuals are oppressed or privileged by virtue of their membership in social groups, which may be defined by race, class, gender, religion, culture, or type of work performed (i.e., blue-collar vs. white-collar workers). Membership in groups because of certain experiences may also lead to oppression or privilege, depending on the group and the experience. For instance, individuals who win a large amount of money through a lottery may find a great deal of social power and influence usually associated with the dominant group that was not theirs prior to the experience of winning the lottery.

Social power is "built into" society in three ways:

1. *Institutionally*, through corporations and businesses, family systems, churches, schools, the military, and government bodies
2. *Cultural and symbolic practices*, which include the use of language, cultural rituals, religious rituals, advertising, television shows, movies, literature, folk and fairy tales, and iconic figures in popular culture
3. *Individually*, through the influence of one's habits, consciousness, perceptions of self and others, attitudes, and beliefs. In addition, power in social structures is maintained through the use of social norms and social rules, which may widely perpetuate stereotypes and a sense of an "us versus them" mentality.

Some sanctions also reinforce these norms, such as rewards and praise for hard work and punishment and marginalization for individuals perceived as slacking off or draining the resources of the group. Specific laws reinforce the imbalance of power between groups or limit the ability of some to have meaningful autonomy over their lives (e.g., voting laws or marriage laws). Finally, one group may use violence against another to maintain existing power structures. This violence may range from subtle forms of psychological and emotional violence or manipulation to brutal physical violence exacted by one group against another. Some of this violence may be presumed as "legitimate" in the use of military, police, or familial rights, and some of it may be illegitimate, or not sanctioned by the broader social context.

The purpose of discussing power and social groups in this context is to help to contextualize some very important questions about what is deemed socially appropriate or socially inappropriate within a given group. There are three basic questions to ask when exploring issues within their social context:

1. Whose interests or well-being are being served by these social rules and norms?
2. Whose life is eased, enriched, made more comfortable, or protected by the status quo in this situation?
3. How do the generally accepted social rules and norms serve the members of a given society?

SOCIAL NORMS AND SOCIAL RULES IN GRIEF AND LOSS

Grandin and Barron (2005) define social rules as "those guidelines, norms, requirements, expectations, customs, and laws, written and unwritten, spoken and unspoken, that reflect a society's attitudes, values, prejudices, and fears, and determine the roles we play and the actions we take, as we interact with other people in society as individuals and as groups" (p. ix). It is in this context that we examine the social rules in Western society that surround loss and grief. Several social rules for validation of loss experiences and for grieving in most Western societies are not stated explicitly but are widely known and recognized. These social rules identify who, in a given society, is granted the privilege of any exemption from roles and responsibilities because of a socially recognized condition that is legitimized through a political structure or authority figure, such as a physician. Exclusions from work and social responsibilities are legitimized through social rules as well as through the granting of special social support by identification with the prescribed role of mourning in losses that meet the criteria of acceptability. These rules are not posted on the doors of funeral homes and religious centers; they are implicit and imbued with a great amount of power in their ability to ascribe legitimacy to the grief response in a mourner. In general, social rules surrounding loss experiences suggest that individuals should keep their loss experiences to themselves or share these experiences and their feelings with a select few individuals, to "get over it" as soon as possible, to return back to a normal routine within short order, and to remain strong and stoic.

Western industrialized societies are built on capitalism, which encourages a market-based productivity orientation. Capitalism also favors patriarchy, which usually embraces hierarchical structures and emotional stoicism to promote greater productivity and profit. Nonproductive members of capitalistic societies may be pitied at first, but eventually they are resented and stigmatized for their lack of contribution toward the materialistic goals set by the market-based, consumer-oriented system (Sherman, 2006). Because loss of productivity can be seen as a challenge to our way of being and our "way of life," there is a great deal of social pressure to minimize any experience that may interfere with our functionality or to at least suppress it into a very narrow place of acceptance, typically in private places only.

What does this mean for individuals who experience profound losses? We are urged to silence our grief or ignore our feelings about our loss experiences. We also feel the pressure to carry on with our lives and our routines as before, being praised for "being strong" in the face of adversity. And because this type of society also emphasizes "doing" with tangible products at the end to prove our worth, there is not much allowance for a reflective process that is often required when we are called to renegotiate our assumptive world after it has been assaulted. As a result, individuals who experience profound losses may turn inward, perhaps being able to share their thoughts and feelings with a select few but still expected to maintain their functionality in the public sphere. It is no wonder that compulsive behaviors such as obsessive eating, drinking, shopping, and gambling arise as outlets in response to the need to maintain such a high degree of emotional control and stoic focus on prescribed roles—and if these do not work, we are urged to take medication to "fix" ourselves quickly (interesting to note that all of these "fixes" are focused on consumerism in various ways).

In my private practice, I often hear clients say, "I need to stop wallowing in all of this." On exploration, I am often dumbfounded by the degree of expectation that people have regarding their functionality in light of major life-changing and traumatizing events. I have often wondered why these individuals would beat themselves up emotionally when they are obviously (and understandably) affected by the experience of significant losses in their lives. After much thought, I realized that these attitudes represent internalization of the social messages surrounding the value and worth of individuals in our society; the message is clear: Their productivity and ability to maintain functionality must remain intact, no matter what life experience they endure. There is praise for the father who remains "strong" after his child dies from a traumatic accident. In this context, any person in the same social system would understand that "strong" means stoic, rational, functional, probably articulate, and even gracious. This is the bar to which all members of this society are measured, and it is an oppressive burden to many.

Internalized social messages keep us within the boundary of acceptance by our social group. In industrialized societies, social pressures to maintain functionality and to suppress feelings that may be seen as a sign of weakness are a form of oppression on its members. Oppression can be defined as the act of using power to empower or grant privilege to a group at the expense of disempowering, marginalizing, silencing, and subordinating another group (Brown, 1994). The root of the word oppression is the key element, press. Individuals within a social group adopt the norms and values of the dominant group, which becomes the measure by which they hold themselves for evaluation (Freire, 1993). The experience of oppressed people is that the living of one's life is confined by barriers that are not accidental and, thus, are unavoidable. These barriers are also systematically related to each other in such a way as to catch one between and among them and restrict or penalize motion in any direction (Frye, 1998).

In the context of bereavement, separating out social expectations of how bereaved individuals are expected to respond to loss (i.e., how they should respond) from the actual reality of their loss experience (i.e., how they actually do respond or need to respond) normalizes the human response to loss without the oppressive factor of shame and the inhibition caused by external social constraints that may have the potential to suppress adaptive but socially uncomfortable or stigmatized responses. Gender socialization and stereotyping are also strong social forces that shape the expectations of how individuals should grieve. For example, men who are sensitive or who express vulnerable emotions publically are often characterized as "weak" or effeminate. Women who do not cry or express vulnerable emotions outwardly often are labeled as "frigid" or insensitive (Martin & Doka, 2000). Strong emotions of any type are usually stigmatized, and bereaved individuals may express embarrassment for "losing control" of their emotions in front of others.

When these messages are experienced as internal expectations of oneself, it is apparent that the social messages have now become internalized oppression and that what is actually a systemic or structural issue in a society becomes labeled as an individual's psychological problem or shortcoming (Tappan, 2006). Oppression in this context is often represented individually through self-deprecation, shame, humiliation, self-loathing, and low self-esteem. Because the social messages are internalized, the individual takes ownership of the problem instead of recognizing the actual source of the problem in social norms and forces that are unrealistic. To address structural issues such as this in a purely individualistic manner perpetuates the oppressive social factors that are at play in these situations (Dietz, 2000). It is as if these social messages represent a distorted mirror that is being held up for viewing with an insistence that the distortion is reality, and, if this distortion is not accepted as reality by individuals, there will be a price to pay socially through marginalization or internally as shame or self-loathing. For this reason, it is important to recognize that individuals who experience ongoing emotional pain after significant loss events may live in a society that can perpetuate this pain through rigid social rules that do not allow for the validation of these losses or the opportunity to engage meaningfully in a grieving process that would permit adaptation and healing.

CLINICAL IMPLICATIONS—MICRO PRACTICE WITH MACRO AWARENESS

Since most clients come for therapeutic help and support through one-on-one therapy or small group sessions, the broader issue becomes how to support clients in these micro practice settings while maintaining awareness of how social rules and political policies profoundly affect their well-being. Lee and Hipolito-Delgado (2007) emphasize the need for clinicians to cultivate personal awareness of how they have been and are influenced by social and political forces to be able to identify and disentangle the potential detrimental impact of these forces on their engagement with their clients.

Clinical work rooted in social awareness explores how issues of power are manifest in the life of the client (Aldarondo, 2007). Innate in this exploration is the concept of client empowerment, which is described as a process of dialogue through which clients are continuously supported to explore the range of possibilities they see as appropriate to their needs. In an empowerment model, clients are identified as the "experts," and their subjective experiences and perceptions form the center for all decisions that are made in the therapeutic setting (Rose, 1990). It is important to note that an empowerment model seeks to identify sources of oppression in clients, validates clients' subjective experiences that have been objectified or marginalized through oppressive forces, focuses on the client's innate strengths and resilience, and supports advocating for social change to address oppression at the structural level (Gerber, 2007; Lee, 2007). Specific areas for exploration and awareness for clinicians may include the following:

- **Monitor the use of language and terminology.** Clinical language and "jargon" are often drawn from the medical model of assessment and diagnosis of disorders, which may lead to the objectification of individuals through diagnostic labels rather than the empowerment of individuals to identify choices and the range of possible responses to loss. Words such as *dysfunctional, disordered, impaired,* or *pathological* or identifying a person with a *diagnosis* may reinforce the social vulnerability individuals experience after a life-altering loss event (Dietz, 2000). Given the hegemonic propensity for diagnoses to be used as a dividing line between those who are "healthy" and those who are mentally ill, great care must be taken when associating a client's distress and pain with a reified set of criteria in a diagnosis code. There is often a conflict created for clinicians in this issue, as insurance companies often require a diagnostic code to be assigned for reimbursement of services.
- **Validate the subjective experience and expertise of the individual.** Clinicians need to recognize individuals' expertise in their own experiences, which occur within a social context. It is important to be able to enter the reality experienced by clients, as they feel it, understand it, and participate in it, to fully appreciate their world (Rose, 1990). The process of validation occurs through an ongoing dialogue, where the clinician actively listens to clients' descriptions and feelings, checking assumptions or intuitive thoughts with them for verification, and acknowledges with clients the impact of these experiences on their world. This aspect of the therapeutic relationship is of primary importance, as discussed in the previous section. One of the most important interventions with clients who have experienced nonfinite losses is to name and validate these losses for the significance in which clients actually experience them—not as they are expected to do so by the social rules surrounding the loss experiences. In this process, it is important to identify where clients' experiences have been invalidated, pathologized, or marginalized by social rules and where oppressive factors have robbed persons of their subjective expertise and agency.

- **Recognize the common human experience that we share with clients.** Within the boundary of a professional relationship, clinicians must be able to work from a framework that emphasizes bearing witness to the experience of another human being rather than adopting a role of authority over clients' experiences. Empowerment begins when individuals feel seen, heard, respected, and validated. This process has a greater potential to counter experiences that have been suppressed or stigmatized by social rules and dogma than a clinical focus on interpretation and diagnosis (Dietz, 2000). In this model, it is understood that to be fully engaged with clients it may not be possible to remain purely objective—and most certainly, the most appropriate response to oppression is not *affective neutrality*, which is encouraged by the medical model (Dietz, 2000).
- **Focus on clients' strengths and innate resilience rather than on pathology.** Using language that opens possibilities helps to encourage people to identify their ability to adapt and create meaning within change. Individuals feel empowered when the focus is on their strengths and resilience rather than on their perceived dysfunction. Focusing on the clients' innate strengths can provide a powerful catalyst for growth in contrast to the paralyzing effects of oppressive social expectations. Some clients may initially resist identifying their strengths and attempts to cope with adversity due to the presence of internalized negative beliefs and attributions toward themselves. In my clinical practice, I call this "reality testing" with my clients, because we will gently explore how their negative beliefs of themselves began and how these negative self-beliefs are reinforced in their daily lives. We often talk about the social rules and expectations that augment these negative self-perceptions, which gives clients the opportunity to differentiate their actual experiences and responses from social expectations that are intended to serve the purposes of a materialistic culture. By naming these rules and acknowledging their influence on daily life, clients have the opportunity to see their strengths more clearly and to identify where they have actively engaged in coping and surviving in the context of situations that have made them feel powerless and helpless.
- **Take social action or advocate for change when possible.** There are times when we, as clinicians, may be moved deeply by our clients' suffering in their social context, and our reasonable response may need to include social action of some form. Involvement in groups that raise social awareness of issues that have remained in the background of social formation directly connects micro practice with macro practice. For example, the group Mothers Against Drunk Driving (MADD) was begun by a group of women who lost family members as a result of drunk drivers. This group has had a powerful impact on how society views drinking and driving—an issue in the past that was ignored for its significance, as drunk drivers were seen only as a comical nuisance and not taken seriously in courts of law.
- **Involvement in social action may offer a way to transcend oppression and as such can provide a very meaningful outlet for individuals**

who were at one time stigmatized through a loss experience. It is difficult to work with individuals and groups whose loss experiences cause them to be socially stigmatized and marginalized and to not be moved to engage in some form of consciousness raising, social action, or advocacy. Social activism and advocacy may take many different forms, such as writing, incorporating social awareness into presentations and publications, financial support, involvement in political debate and policy formation, and direct involvement in socially aware organizations.

CONCLUSION

It is my hope that clinicians will become more aware of the social context of loss issues and be able to identify how social forces influence the process of adaptation to loss. We are social beings, and as such, we are all interconnected by our shared human experiences, with loss being one of these. We cannot define ourselves in isolation, and we all experience the dynamic interplay between our individual selves and the social and political structures in which we live. All of us experience many different types of losses in life, and we need the ability to recognize these losses and have the freedom to respond to them in ways that are congruent with our needs, free from the dictates of social rules that may deny or invalidate our deeply human experiences.

Compassion is the radicalism of our time. –H.H. The Dalai Lama

REFERENCES

Aldarondo, E. (2007). Rekindling the reformist spirit in the mental health professions. In E. Aldarondo (Ed.), *Advancing social justice through clinical practice* (pp. 3–17). Mahwah, NJ: Lawrence Erlbaum.

Brown, L. S. (1994). *Subversive dialogues: Theory in feminist therapy.* New York: BasicBooks.

Dietz, C. A. (2000). Responding to oppression and abuse: A feminist challenge to clinical social work. *Affilia, 15*(3), 369–389.

Freire, P. (1993). *The pedagogy of the oppressed.* New York: Continuum.

Frye, M. (1998). Oppression. In P. S. Rothenberg (Ed.), *Race, class, and gender in the United States* (pp. 146–149). New York: St. Martin's.

Gerber, L. A. (2007). Social justice concerns and clinical practice. In E. Aldarondo (Ed.), *Advancing social justice through clinical practice* (pp. 43–71). Mahwah, NJ: Lawrence Erlbaum.

Grandin, T., & Barron, S. (2005). *The unwritten rules of social relationships.* Arlington, TX: Future Horizons.

Kirst-Ashman, K. K., & Hull, G. H. (2008). *Understanding generalist practice* (5th ed.). Belmont, CA: Brooks/Cole.

Lee, C. C. (2007). A counselor's call to action. In C. C. Lee (Ed.), *Counseling for social justice* (2nd ed., pp. 259–264). Alexandria, VA: American Counseling Association.

Lee, C. C., & Hipolito-Delgado, C. P. (2007). Introduction: Counselors as agents of social justice. In C. C. Lee (Ed.), *Counseling for social justice* (2nd ed., pp. xiii–xxviii). Alexandria, VA: American Counseling Association.

Martin, T. L., & Doka, K. J. (2000). *Men don't cry … women do: Transcending gender stereotypes of grief*. Philadelphia: Brunner Mazel.

Morell, C. (1987). Cause is function: Toward a feminist model of integration for social work. *Social Service Review, 61*, 144–155.

Rose, S. M. (1990). Advocacy/empowerment: An approach to clinical practice for social work. *Journal of Sociology and Social Welfare, 17*, 41–51.

Sherman, H. J. (2006). *How society makes itself*. Armonk, NY: M. E. Sharpe.

Tappan, M. B. (2006). Reframing internalized oppression and internalized domination: From the psychological to the sociocultural. *Teachers College Record, 108*(10), 2115–2144.

Wronka, J. (2008). *Human rights and social justice*. Thousand Oaks, CA: Sage.

Section *I*

Loss of the View of the World or Others

*I*n this section, several authors explore experiences that are related to one's sense of safety in the world and in relationships with others. These losses affect how we view the world and the people who share that world with us. Most individuals grow up with the sense that the world is basically a safe place and that people are generally well-meaning and trustworthy. The experience of the loss of one's sense of safety in the world or of others in our world with whom we have associated feeling safe can result in a significant assault on previously held assumptions about the world and others.

In the first part of this section, three authors explore ways an individual may experience the loss of a sense of safety and security in the world. In her chapter on personal violation, Susan Abercomby explores the depth to which one's ability to move freely and relate to others is affected when an individual has been subjected to abuse and trauma. She raises an important point for individuals who may have never truly experienced feeling safe in their lives: Can they grieve the loss of something they never really had or experienced in the first place?

Therese Modesto explores loss of safety and security from a macro perspective—when the loss of safety is experienced on a large scale, almost unfathomable prior to the event. Here, the idea of the lost or shattered assumptive world as a shared experience provides a unique backdrop to the experience of the individuals who are affected by such events.

Eunice Gorman looks at the effects of cumulative exposure of professional caregivers to hearing and seeing the effects of trauma, abuse, suffering, and injustice in their clients. Caregivers may not have a direct experience of feeling unsafe or traumatized, but the fact that they can lose a sense of the world as a safe place by hearing the stories of their clients can have profound implications for the caregiver as a person. The simple acts of bearing witness and being fully present to individuals with these types of experiences can be demoralizing and foster disillusionment, eventually crippling the caregiver's effectiveness.

The next part of this section explores losses that have a direct relational context. Certainly, the dissolution of intimate relationships is an experience of great commonality; however, the familiarity of this loss does not equate with ease of adjustment after the loss and the depth to which this loss affects those who experience it. This chapter explores both the social context and the unique personal aspects of the loss of a relationship where the individuals continue to live but the relationship itself is what dies.

Sherry Schachter and Jennifer Schachter offer a chapter to explore the unique losses associated with adoption, from the perspective of both the adoptive mother and the adopted child. This chapter brings to light the complexities associated with adoption for both the adoptive parent and the child who is adopted. There is often an assumption that adoption is an ideal solution for both the parent and the child, but these authors caution that, although the outcome can be very positive, some aspects of grief and loss for both participants in the adoptive process need to be honored as well.

Laura Lewis and Eunice Gorman discuss the postparental transition (frequently referred to as the "empty nest") as an experience that is rich with contradictions and adjustment. During this time, a parent often struggles with competing simultaneous urges to "let go" and "hold on." It is also a time of great redefinition of roles, relationships, and priorities that have been established for almost 20 years. These authors explore the possibilities for grief that is intermingled with many other feelings when a grown child leaves home.

Pamela Cushing and Carl MacMillan raise the issue of grief in nonkinship groups when there is staff turnover and transitioning. These authors describe the commonplace occurrence of the coming and going of caregivers in a residential environment for developmentally disabled individuals, the impact of the loss of these caregivers on residents and other staff members, and how this particular community adjusts and adapts to these inevitable changes and experiences of loss that result.

Section *IA*

Loss of Safety and Security

3

Are You Safe? Understanding the Loss of Safety for Women and Children Who Experience Abuse

SUSAN ABERCROMBY

INTRODUCTION

*I*t is serendipitous that I was asked to write a chapter on the loss of safety for women and children who have experienced abuse. It has evolved into an area of interest, of query and conjectures of a clinical practice that has developed over the last decade. This chapter is an attempt to pull together thoughts on the topic, combining the experiential and a journey through the literature and research.

I am writing of experiences of women and children who have had their lives altered by male violence in intimate partner violence and sexual abuse by men. I include also experiences of children and youth who have had exposure to violence against their mothers, and in some cases, against themselves. This chapter queries the meaning and concept of *safety*, the loss of safety, safety plans, and the clinical significance of *being safe*.

It is my hope that the clinical implications section at the end of the chapter will complement and strengthen the work of many professionals in the arena of treatment of the impact of violence toward women and children. It is a limitation of this chapter, however, that my work is only with adult women and male and female children and youth. I cannot speak for the adult male experience or offer clinical intervention suggestions.

In 2006, I wrote a chapter in a group manual I use on a daily basis (Loosley, Drouillard, Ritchie, & Abercromby) about the implications of children and women exposed to woman abuse: "When women abuse has been identified the safety of the women (Mothers) and children must be a priority for assessment because women are not able to support their children when they are not safe. They cannot be emotionally nor psychologically available for treatment if they fear retaliation from the abuser. A safety plan for the women and children must be considered. It is essential to assess what is the most salient factor in supporting the family after safety has been addressed" (p. 241).

In the personal revisiting of the concept of safety, I am reminded of the dynamic process of our work. Then, I suggested not only that safety was the most salient factor during initial assessments but also that there was a need for specific safety plans. I have since queried the helpfulness of the notion of safety plans when there is an absence of a complex assessment or analysis of an individual woman's situation. As clinicians, we see our clients through a lens that has its own interpretation and way of knowing of what it means to be safe, and the clinician's personal level of compassionate fatigue or vicarious trauma can alter and shift that lens over time.

It is not that assessment is no longer crucial or imperative; the questions and emerging research have moved me to consider connections between thanatology and traumatology literature as a challenge to current approaches to treatment of women and children who have experienced trauma. The clients I have the honor of knowing continue to teach me and to challenge my current practice to better meet their diverse and unique needs.

Therefore, what does it mean to be safe or to be in a state of being safe? According to the *Collins Essential English Dictionary* (2006), to be safe is defined as "freedom from danger, risk or injury." Safety is a quality or a state of being free from danger, an impregnability or invulnerability. It is "having the strength to withstand attack." The *Oxford English Dictionary* (2009) states that "to be safe is to not have exposure to danger, based on good reasons or evidence and not likely to be proved wrong." Many know what it is to feel safe, many have experienced a loss of the sense of safety in their lives, and others may never have known what it means to be safe.

When asked at the conclusion of group what safety looks like after leaving her abusive partner, one client stated, "It looks like there are no worries, that you're not walking on eggshells and that you can be yourself, that you're free to say what you want, what you feel, and that there's no hurt." This woman appears to have experienced the *Collins Dictionary* definition of safety. She speaks of a sense of freedom, a sense of control, and power. She exhibits a sense of safety. She has known what it means to feel safe and the converse, because she experienced danger and the loss of safety. However, she can also speak to the hope and empowerment of being in a state of being free from danger, risk, or injury. She has perhaps regained a sense that the world is benevolent and meaningful (Janoff-Bulman, 1992).

Conversely, how does one experience the loss of safety when one may not know safety as it is defined and, moreover, may not know what constitutes danger? Trust and sense of safety becomes stunted or nonexistent after trauma. Many researchers and clinical specialists in the area of grief and loss write of the "loss of safety" (Janoff-Bulman, 1992; Kauffman, 2002). For some, there is indeed the loss of safety, the loss of the *assumptive world* when they have experienced trauma. For some, there may be a precursor to the loss of a safety. Some of the women and children I have known have never experienced the state of being safe. In her argument for a new psychology of trauma, Janoff-Bulman writes, "Our penchant (as human beings) for preserving rather than changing knowledge structure suggests the deeply embedded, deeply accepted nature of our beliefs…" (p. 51). For those who have not experienced safety, as in the cases of early childhood trauma (i.e., exposure to domestic violence or sexual abuse), there is the penchant to what is familiar. Familiarity is powerful and danger is familiar. Basic woundedness is the loss of the power to assume a safe world (Kauffman). A safe world, at the most basic level, is unknown. It cannot be defined, and therefore the clinical implications are vast and complicated. Safety becomes the salient clinical issue, as Kauffman purports.

During assessments, we have asked our clients questions such as: Are you safe? On a scale of 1 to 10, how safe are you? Do you have a place of safety? Is this a safe number? Do you have a safety plan? Yet often we do not query in depth what each woman's concept of safety and danger is. I invite all of us to look underneath and outside the margins of our work. Can we stretch our understanding and expand our clinical practice to shift our thinking, our approach, and our beliefs to better assist our clients who have had their lives altered by traumatic experiences?

SOCIAL CONTEXT

The reactions, emotions, and current intervention tools that clinicians assume in response to traumatic events affect their interpretation, assessment, and practice. We use a plethora of tools that may not be effective regarding the diverse nature in the loss of a sense of safety of many of our clients.

Many of us have used the safety plans as well as risk and lethality assessment tools created to keep our clients safe and away from harm. It would be irresponsible of me to suggest the discontinuation of these widely known and used interventions; however, I invite all of us to ask different questions and to use the tools in a more individualized and cautious approach. Sometimes it is not clear that an individual's present perspective or life choices have been influenced by past traumatic experiences. Early childhood trauma is often an invisible wound. Consequently, it is imperative to take into account the pretrauma personality characteristics of adult survivors, such as their attachment patterns or coping styles (Neimeyer, 2001). As clinicians, we often give importance and place emphasis on the traumatic event, and justifiably so. However, clients' life narratives may be crucial to understanding their sense of safety.

It is of clinical importance to also recognize and acknowledge the coping mechanisms of children, especially preschool and latency-aged children. We cannot dismantle the coping systems that have been a mode of survival for them. These coping mechanisms, such as the belief that consuming alcohol is the cause of the violence of their caregivers, give them meaning to the chaotic nature of their world.

I acknowledge that we often use safety plans in response to crises of immediate danger. Safety plans must not be seen as absolute or static or linear but as a dynamic tool. Each situation must be seen as unique with careful and thorough assessment. We cannot assume our clients know the most fundamental, radical, or basic awareness and knowledge of what it means to be safe. We must look underneath our internalized assumptions and theories and outside our usual systems to really understand our clients who may not fit into our current notions of treatment and understanding.

EXPERIENTIAL CONTEXT

Those of us who have the honorable yet often difficult task of assisting clients in their journey of healing and of bearing witness to incredible atrocities and unparalleled testimony of human strength and perseverance understand that it is complicated work. Some women may not know safety, yet they know survival. We must continue to empower and honor our clients' experiences. To offer a safety plan without the consideration of their survival strategies can be disempowering and may not be helpful. There are no easy solutions; however, it has been my observation that safety planning has become the default intervention given to women in all circumstances. Sometimes we end up giving women the service we have to give rather than the service they want or need (A. Cunningham, personal communication, October 15, 2009).

Safety is not linear, nor must our intervention be without modification or clinical query. During the writing of this chapter, I heard the term safety used on a daily basis. It is a household word: safety pin, fire safety, safety belt, and safety boots. It is apparent that safety is a word that is crucial and important to our daily lives, our possible assumptions of our world. A woman experiencing domestic violence is "safer" living in a shelter. She may be physically safe for a time, but what of her and her children's psychological and emotional safety? Additionally, it is not enough to offer the woman a safety plan without considering that multiple adversities such as poverty, homelessness, or no social network may co-occur (Everett & Gallop, 2001). Moreover, she may respond to questions of her safety without the knowledge of what it means to be safe.

CLINICAL IMPLICATIONS

In my practice of group treatment with women and children who have experienced violence, I inform them that I will do my best to provide a sense of safety; however, absolute safety cannot be promised. Providing routine in treatment, such as the use of ritual and a predictable environment, is crucial to building trust and providing a sense of safety. Structure, nurture, and routine are tools I use in all aspects of my practice. For example, I use bookends (i.e., a consistent beginning and ending for each group session), such as a consistent song or story at the beginning and end of the scheduled group time for children, to provide a sense of the expected (Munn, 2000). The outcome of the procedure is that children arrive, sit down beside me, and state, "I know what we are going to do now." In the bewildering, chaotic, and unpredictable environment of domestic violence or childhood sexual abuse, this fostering and commitment to relational, emotional, and physical safety is essential.

For adult women, a predictable environment is also a building block for a sense of safety: a consistent room setup, the same chair for each session, the same reading or breathing exercise at the onset and conclusion of group. Coffee, tea, or water offered at group is part of providing structure and basic human needs. It is my experience that the offering of food in every group for adults and children provides a predictable cadence to meetings and soothes anxiety. It is also recognition of Maslow's (1943) hierarchy of needs: Food is a basic human requirement. Children who have experienced neglect and maltreatment especially respond positively to food offered in a group setting.

Rituals such as these can be both subtle and powerful. They use the same mechanics that are present in the development of attachment in early childhood when all information is received through the senses. The same smells or tastes or sounds communicate predictability. One 10-year-old boy responded gleefully to the offer of Arrowroot cookies: "These are baby cookies, aren't they?"

The consistent use of props such as puppets, stuffed animals, mandalas, and Play-Doh also supplies the elements of nurture, structure, and predictability for both women and children. The presence of mandalas for coloring and Play-Doh for molding can assist in reducing anxiety or providing an opportunity to "tune out" from a group discussion that may be particularly difficult.

I use soft and pliable stuffed animal puppets and present them to children at the first group session. They can choose one for their entire group participation. The puppet awaits children's arrival on their chair each group session, again, offering a sense of what can be predictable and a building block for safety. Interestingly, even 12-year-old boys use the stuffed animals for comfort and a sense of security. Women in treatment groups also respond positively to the opportunity to hold a stuffed animal for reassurance. Helping our clients to learn to self-soothe is crucial to their healing. Children who have not experienced a safe world may not have the innate ability to self-soothe. I teach the butterfly hug, which is a dual-attention stimulation exercise that consists of crossing your arms over your chest, so that with the tip of your fingers from each hand you can touch the area located under the connection between the clavicle and the shoulder, simulating the flapping wings of a butterfly (USF, 1997). This is a grounding technique for all group participants. In another example, blowing bubbles helps younger children learn the concept of deep breathing, which assists in reducing anxiety and provides a sense of calm.

While the suggestion of props is fundamental for the building of the sense of trust and safety, it is the client–professional relationship that provides the foundation for healing and, therefore, fosters a sense of safety. It is the therapeutic relationship that heals (Herman, 1992). The client–professional relationship provides the opportunity for clients to begin to experience healthy, human relationships through the consistent relational components of respect, clear communication, caring, empathy, authenticity, accountability, consistency, and, most importantly, connection. Connection is at the core of human growth and development (Jordan, Walker, & Hartling, 2004). Consequently, the consistency of a group facilitator's presence is also necessary.

According to Kauffman (2002), "traumatization is an exposure of the self in which the self fragments, loses it protective illusions and value, and hides in the unnamable shame" (p. 206). The self hides within shame and becomes isolated from the self and from others in the world. Isolation, according to the Stone Center model (Jordan et al., 2004), is seen as the primary source of suffering. When women and children recover and reconcile the notion of safety after experiencing trauma, it allows them an opportunity for reconnection and integration of the self and, ultimately, connection to others and a meaningful community. For those who have never known safety, or those who have experienced the loss of safety after exposure to trauma, integration and connection can begin to grow amid the concepts of nurture, routine, structure, and predictability. Predictable environments for treatment are essential, but it must also be recognized that any modality of treatment requires careful and thorough assessment, as "one size does not fit all."

I feel deep gratitude for the group therapy models I use in my practice and to my colleagues who created them. However, modification is always an important consideration to meet the diverse clinical needs of our clients. Group manuals need to be used as guidelines only. The use of safety plans is recommended in the group manual for children; however, safety plans were never developed for children. They were created for adults. Currently, there is no research to support the global use of safety plans for children. An intervention approach is most helpfully matched to reach a child's unique situation, preceded by an assessment of needs and directed at areas in which the child is experiencing difficulties (A. Cunningham, personal communication, October 17, 2005).

Because of conjecture and queries over a decade, I no longer use safety plans for children in a group format. I ask them what safety might smell like, taste like, feel like. I encourage children to draw pictures of safety. I use the Narrative format (White & Epston, 1990) of asking questions to externalize concepts, such as safety, danger, or anger. I might ask, "Can you draw a picture of the anger?" or, "What does the 'danger' say to you?"

For women, I ask them to tell me about a time when they might have felt safe. I ask them to qualify safety in sensory terms. When women tell me that they have never experienced a safe world, I ask their permission to give them an example of what may be a dangerous decision or action. I look for ways within the therapeutic relationship to help clients reduce their danger. It is an attempt to make clearer the illusions and assumptions of safety so that I might assess clients' needs more thoroughly and accurately.

> It is to live the questions…. And the point is to live everything. Live the questions now. Perhaps then, someday far in the future, you will gradually … live your way into the answer. (Rilke, 1984)

REFERENCES

Collins essential English dictionary. (2006). Retrieved October 30, 2009 from http://www.google.ca/search?hl=en&source=hp&q=collins+dictionary&meta=&aq=1&oq=Collins

Everett, B., & Gallop, R. (2001). *The link between childhood trauma and mental illness: Effective interventions for mental health professionals.* Thousand Oaks, CA: Sage Publications.

Herman, J. (1992). *Trauma and recovery.* New York: Basic Books.

Janoff-Bulman, R. (1992). *Shattered assumptions: Towards a new psychology of trauma.* New York: The Free Press.

Jordan, J., Walker, M., & Hartling, L. (2004). *The complexity of connection: Writings from the Stone Center's Jean Baker Miller Training Institute.* New York: Guilford.

Kauffman, J. (2002). Safety and the assumptive world: A theory of traumatic loss. In J. Kauffman (Ed.), *Loss of the assumptive world: A theory of traumatic loss* (pp. 205–212). New York: Brunner-Routledge.

Loosley, S., Drouillard, D., Ritchie, D., & Abercromby, S. (2006). *Groupwork with children exposed to woman abuse: A concurrent group program for children and their mothers.* London, Canada: Children's Aid Society of London and Middlesex.

Maslow, A. (1943). A theory of motivation. *Psychological Review,* 50(4), 370–396.

Munns, E. (Ed.) (2000). *Theraplay: Innovations in attachment-enhancing play therapy.* Northvale, NJ: Jason Aronson.

Neimeyer, R. (Ed.) (2001). *Meaning reconstruction and the experience of loss.* Washington DC: American Psychological Association.

Oxford English dictionary. (2009). Retrieved October 30, 2009 from http://www.google.ca/search?hl=en&source=hp&q=oxford+english+dictionary&meta=&aq=1&oq=oxford+

Rilke, R. (1984). *Letters to a young poet.* New York: Random House.

University of South Florida (USF). (1997). *International Traumatology Institute.* Retrieved October 30, 2009 from http://www.emotionalrelief.org/articles/article-butterflyhug-jarero.ht

White, M., & Epston, D. (1990). *Narrative means to therapeutic ends.* Adelaide, South Australia: Dulwich Centre.

4

Traumatic Events and Mass Disasters in the Public Sphere

M. THÉRÈSE MODESTO

For we live under continual threat of two equally fearful, but seemingly opposed, destinies, unremitting banality and inconceivable terror.

Susan Sontag (as cited in Brown, 1988)

INTRODUCTION AND OVERVIEW

*I*n the first decade of the 21st century, individuals, communities, and nations across the world have had to face some of the most terrifying disasters and critical incidents in recent history, in which people have experienced multiple losses of life, belongings, community, and peace of mind. In many ways, the assumptive world that individuals and society have known and believed concerning safety and security will never again be thought of in the same way. In a 10-year period from 1900 through 1909, there were a total of 73 national-level natural disasters worldwide. Within the first 5 years of the 21st century, disasters on the national level have escalated to 2,788, and this figure continues to rise, according to the International Strategy for Disaster Reduction (2006, p. 1).

WHAT IS A DISASTER, CRITICAL INCIDENT, OR CRISIS?

To begin our discussion, it is important to work from a mutually understood definition of what is a disaster or critical incident. A disaster is a sudden natural occurrence, limited in time and location, that is a severe disrupter to individuals' or a society's living experience. A critical incident is an event of human design. It can be either intentional, such as a terrorist-initiated event, or an accidental event such as a gas pipeline rupture causing an explosion with significant loss of life, property damage, and overall hardship physically and emotionally to individuals, communities, and the environment.

> A crisis is a sequence of actions and events that are unstable and possibly dangerous physically, emotionally, socially or economically leading to individual life or community altering change. These events generally produce upheaval and destabilization in a person, family/household or community's ordinary experience of life. (Modesto, 2009, p. 6)

Historically, it was believed that disasters were events that happened to people and that they were considered "victims" of such painful experiences with little to no control over the situation. Many professionals in thanostic (death-related) disaster management and critical incident studies currently view this concept differently. It is now understood that disasters are a combination of naturally occurring events and individual and community actions. For example, due to the intentional geographical selection by individuals, corporations, and recreational services in areas of frequent hurricanes, the risks of natural disasters are elevated. Given the combination of factors just described, the disaster understanding of the term *victim* is considered incorrect. Additionally, the term victim has the connotation that disaster- or critical-incident-affected survivors are powerless or helpless in affecting their current and future situation. This perception is also inaccurate since individuals, communities, and societies have the active ability to work toward their survival and future well-being. This understanding has special importance when considering the traumatic loss resiliency and recovery issues. Throughout this chapter the terms *disaster-* or *critical-incident-affected survivor* or *disaster-* or *critical-incident-affected* surviving community will be used instead of the term victim. By using the words *affected* and *survivor* there is a more accurate understanding of circumstances and responsibilities in the event discussed and the avoidance of the erroneous worldview of victimization and powerlessness.

LIMITATIONS OF RESEARCH AWARENESS

Numerous research studies, articles, and books have been written since the terrorist attacks on September 11, 2001, in the United States, Hurricane Katrina, and the Indian Ocean tsunami. Blunenfield (2008); Melloan (2005); Bloomfield (2006); Norris, Stevens, Pfefferbaum, Wyche, and Pfefferbaum (2008); and Pfefferbaum (2005) addressed topics such as emergency management, continuity, and resiliency with respect to disaster-affected survivors of tragic events. Even with all that has been written and researched recently, little attention has been offered directly on the issues of how individuals and societies currently view the assumptive world of security and safety after a disaster. Because of these direct and indirect disasters and critical incidents, affected survivors' have undergone profound experiences that have transformed how they see issues related to safety and security. Often in studying disasters and mass tragedies, the focus is on the tasks of mitigating the physical impact of a disaster event. In the initial response, the physical needs of individuals and communities, from food and shelter to emergency medical needs, are the priority (Rodriguez & Aguirre, 2006). These are obviously important topics to discuss but are not the only topics to be considered. After the initial tasks are attended, the focus changes to assessment and redressing the infrastructural needs of a disaster-affected location. As quickly as possible, there is a desire for many to make the images of the disaster disappear (Thomas, 2007).

It is assumed by many professionals in the disaster management field that showing the destruction and devastation is a sign of weakness, vulnerability, and pain (Blumenfield & Ursano, 2008). However, Shalev & Errera (2008) discuss "virtual safety maps" that critical-incident and disaster-affected survivors use as a way to restructure components of the traumatic event. These eight ways that either weaken or even totally miss resilience in various coping mechanisms are (1) dramatize; (2) pathologize; (3) catastrophize; (4) create negative expectations; (5) blur boundaries; (6) misinform, mislead, manipulate, or even lie about certain information; (7) intervene with the top-down process of experts at the expense of individual and group critical-incident or disaster-affected survivor resourceful-ness; and (8) ignore or demonstrate reluctance to share.

In summary, a major critical thanostic task from either natural disasters or from intentionally designed critical incidents is the action of addressing and redressing the image and living out the daily life understanding of safety and security. It is a major postdisaster component of reaffirmation of life that individuals and communities must face, wrestle with, and ultimately come to honor and move from.

THE SEVEN TYPES OF DISASTER SECURITY AND SAFETY ASSUMPTIVE WORLDVIEWS

From our earliest life, we are constantly experiencing, observing, and learning about the world around us. These opportunities help us to develop and construct assumptions and beliefs. However, when there is a trauma, such as a critical incident or disaster that affects the survivor and the community, the assumptive world-view is often shattered or heavily impacted, resulting in chaos. The former ways of handling the trauma and loss from a former assumptive perspective are not compatible. This causes a great disruption in the foundation and framework of how critical-incident or disaster-affected survivors operate and see their world. In addressing the chaos of loss for the critical-incident or disaster-affected survivors and community, individuals are called on to revise their assumptions and beliefs about themselves and their world. These challenges are in addressing not only the realities of death but also of losses in numerous ways. Individuals and communities may respond in one or more of the following seven ways of making sense of security and safety within the context of their assumptive worldviews.

Transform

This occurs when individuals or communities change their form, appearance, or structure in how they conduct their daily living after a critical incident or disaster.

When such a radical disruptor in their lives has occurred, they grieve the loss of what were comfortable routines and expectations of life.

For example, the U.S. Department of Homeland Security Transportation Security Administration (TSA) required massive changes in airport security screening since the attempted bombing of the American Airlines Flight 63 by Richard Calvin Reid ("the shoe bomber") on December 22, 2001. Now we have long lines for inspection of personal belongings and body scans. Bomb-sniffing dogs are employed, and shoes are checked for bomb-making materials. And limited amounts of liquid items are now allowed on any airplanes (TSA, 2009). This intense control has caused a loss of privacy for passengers that has transformed the collective understanding of airline travel from an assumptive worldview that travel was safe, enjoyable, and easy to navigate to one of insecurity and a potentially unsafe environment and experience

Transcend

Transcendence occurs when individuals or communities rise above or go beyond the initial limits of thought because of the breach of initial safety and security assumption.

An example of this is Coventry Cathedral in England, which was bombed in the Nazi Blitz on November 14, 1940. A total of 515 enemy planes bombed over 4,000 homes, and 75% of all factories were destroyed in one night. The attack killed 568 known civilians, and there were possibly 1,000 deaths in total (Taylor, 2005). It had been understood during military actions that churches and hospitals were off limits as enemy targets. This was not the case that night. The largest church in Coventry was St. Michael's Cathedral, which was totally destroyed by the Nazi Blitz (http://en.wikipedia.org/wiki/Coventry_Cathedral; Baker, 1994). The bombings emotionally shattered the people not only of Coventry but of England as a country.

To transcend the altered assumption of safety and security, the Church of England helped to rebuild the bombed cathedral. Instead of reconstructing the original design of the destroyed cathedral, Sir Basil Spence, the principal architect, insisted that the remaining 14th-century Gothic structure of the cathedral be incorporated into a highly modern design. Physically, emotionally, and spiritually, there was a uniting of the two buildings with the use of Hollington sandstone as the structural element in both buildings, thus uniting the past with the new (Mansell, 1979). A German emigree inscription artist named Ralph Beyer, whose Jewish mother died in Auschwitz during World War II, was commissioned to engrave the highly honored baptismal font. His homeland and its government had been the enemy of England and the direct destroyer of the cathedral. This construction of the new cathedral reinforces the transition from life is good through the safety and security assumption to a transcendent world assumption of life and the world having meaning. The cathedral community lives out the transcendence worldview by actively working in its established International Center for Reconciliation and the International Network of Communities of the Cross of Nails (http://en.wikipedia.org/wiki/Coventry_Cathedral).

Transfer

This occurs when individuals or communities cause the feelings of grief or loss to pass from one person to another as thoughts, power, or qualities. When individuals or communities have had a major disruption of their assumptive worldview, often there is the passing of fear, uncertainty of the future, confusion, or disaster amnesia silence. In a disaster or critical-incident era, many feel powerless and thus construct the assumption that life is bad and that it is unlucky to speak of such devastation or discuss such matters for fear that it could happen again.

A prime example of disaster amnesia silence and the assumptive worldview of loss of safety and security is the influenza pandemic of 1918 (i.e., the Spanish flu), which killed 50 to 100 million. The sense of loss of safety and security from an invisible disease was tremendous at a time when there was no pharmacological intervention or vaccination. The terror was so profound that public officials required newspapers to refrain from printing all the obituaries as a way to stem the terror in the local community (Barry, 2005; Greene & Moline, 2006). The lack of historical reporting and reference for over 80 years indicated the depth of the terror and power this illness had on the collective and individual physical and emotional mindset of a generation internationally (Barry).

Conversely, patriotism resurged throughout the United States after the terrorist attacks on September 11. Many individuals passed on the emotional pride of their country by exhibiting U.S. flags on cars, homes, and business signs. This transfer of patriotism is still evident in many settings even years later (Ross, 2005).

Translate

This occurs when individuals or communities change the conditions or form of security requirements or translate security terminology that can be more easily understood by the general public.

The intention of the U.S. Department of Homeland Security was to provide an effective means of communicating the potential for a terrorist attack (Department of Homeland Security, 2003; Plotnick, Gomez, White, & Turoff, 2007). A common term used by the media was "terror alert" (Lehrer, 2001). Since there was no independent way for citizens to verify the current level of threat as accurate, the terror alert generated great anxiety. Such is the case with a woman and her teenage sons, who suffocated from using the plastic and duct tape precautions advised by the government against possible terrorist chemical and biological threats (Dan, 2003). For family members who grieved the loss of three family members, they grieved not only their loss but also the loss of security that a directive intentionally constructed to save lives was the instrument that took lives. The terror alert system provided ongoing confusion as to what was a reliable threat level and feelings of strong possibility of political manipulation by government authorities (Ridge, 2009).

Transpose

Transposition occurs when individuals or communities attempt to change the order, sequence, or relative position of a critical-incident or disaster-affected physical setting to give the appearance of turning back the hands of time-experience to a predisaster or pre-critical-incident era. This is done to attempt to emotionally correct, change, and alleviate the pain, fear, and insecurity that results from a devastating event and to return a stable assumption of safety and security.

A prime example of this is the rebuilding of the Pentagon after September 11, 2001, such that it visibly appears to show no difference in pre- and postattack. The military determined that the Pentagon should and would be repaired to its original appearance by the first anniversary of the terrorist attack (Inglesby, 2002). This repair requirement was intentional to reestablish the image of security and safety in the power and resilience of the U.S. military in general, and the Pentagon in particular, both nationally and internationally (Modesto, 2009). It should be noted that this is in direct contrast to the transcend assumption worldview model of safety and security described earlier. The attempts to transpose the assumptive worldview order by removing all indications of the trauma and loss is in contrast to the transcendent assumptive world order, which elevates the assumptive worldview to a higher level of well-being and meaning of life.

Transvalue

This is when individuals or communities reestimate the value of a person, event, or position due to a readjustment of the assumptive worldview of safety and security.

An example of this is the general public's view of firefighters, emergency medical technicians, and police in New York City. Since the terrorist attacks on September 11, these civil servant positions have been elevated even higher than before in esteem and emotional value. Currently it is popular to wear items such as T-shirts that bear the New York City Fire Department logo as a way to show appreciation and support for these heroes. People love heroes. It gives security and reassurance. When people's assumptive worldview has been shattered, the desire to have a superhero available to rescue them is very strong. Society and individuals have transvalued superhero protection ability from the fantasy level of comic books and fictional stories onto the dedicated service personnel of the fire, rescue, and police departments (Modesto, 2009).

The assumptive worldview regarding New York emergency service personnel is much different during and after the second terrorist attack on the World Trade Center in 2001 from the first terrorist attack of the World Trade Center in 1993. The key lies in the level of change to the assumptive worldview: (1) the first critical incident was not as significant in the number of fatalities and injuries; (2) there was no damage to the collective pride in having lost not one but two of the world's largest buildings in their personal city as in the second attack; (3) in the first attack on the World Trade Center there was a sense of justice achieved since terrorist perpetrators and organizers were identified, arrested, and convicted; therefore, in the idea that "the good won over the bad," there was still the sense of power and control in operation. It is interesting to note that for over 40 years there has also been the assumptive viewpoint that the United States was so strong and powerful that it would never allow a foreign attack on homeland soil after experiencing the attack on Pearl Harbor.

Transport

Transport occurs when individuals or communities either must move away from one place or another or are sent into banishment or a long-term penal restricted situation.

When such a critical incident or natural disaster occurs, there is a great deal of grief and loss of homeland or community experience. There is also compounded loss of community identification, familiarity, heredity, and community pride, to name a few. When individuals or communities are forced from their home, their sense of security and safety is drastically diminished, such as in the case of the forced emigration of Cherokee Native Americans from eastern Tennessee to Oklahoma, known as *Nunna dual Isunyi* ("The Trail Where We Cried," or the Trail of Tears). Approximately 20,000 Cherokee, Choctaw, and Creek Indians were forced to complete an 800-mile migration in the winter of 1838–1839. More than 8,000 Native Americans died of disease, exhaustion, exposure, and starvation under federal military constriction authorized by the authority of President Andrew Jackson (Satz, 1979).

SUMMARY

While conducting research for this chapter, it became obvious that little attention has been focused on addressing the issues of loss of safety and security in critical-incident and disaster events. While safety of life and property is the first order of business in a disaster, the long-term ramifications regarding refuge and well-being can stay with individuals a very long time and, in some incidences, the rest of their lives. While this chapter does not afford the opportunity to explore the topic extensively, it demonstrates the need to continue to explore the ramifications of the assumptive worldviews of security and safety in the plethora of disaster and critical-incident experiences.

Personal safety, home, and belongings must be safeguarded and grief and loss mourned once a disaster or critical incident has occurred. The issues of critical incident and disaster loss are multifaceted, and the methods of assistance to address these complex concerns are in their infancy in research and design. Disaster management research is a very new field of academic and professional field of study. Over its short lifetime, it has gone from studying the most obvious aspects of destruction to now expanding its understanding into the psychosocial aspects of disasters and their impact. It is important to note that disasters can have an impact on cultural collections, causing disruption of the assumptive worldview of personal and cultural worth (Personal communications, 2009). Diane Myers

(2001) summed it up well in her excellent paper "Weapons of Mass Destruction and Terrorism: Mental Health Consequences and Implications for Planning and Training": "Viktor Frankl, a psychiatrist who survived the holocaust and wrote *Man's Search for Meaning* (1963), said 'What is to give light must endure burning.' As disaster planners and responders, we attempt to 'bring light' (or recovery and healing) to the darkness of events such as terrorism. Mental health and spiritual support services can add greatly to this team effort, providing succor to both victims and responders."

In our current life experience in the early years of the 21st century, many consider life to be much different from what it was in the past. Often, we are tempted to look longingly for the "good old days" and consider it a safer, more secure, and a better place to have lived. In some ways, perhaps so; in other ways, it is far from the idealistic truth we paint with a wide-sweeping brush of nostalgia. Now we live with fears of airplanes intentionally crashing into buildings by enemies of the state, children being slaughtered in their classrooms by other students full of hatred and pain as a result of bullied abuse, and uncontrollable climate disasters that sweep over large segments of the country in a few terrifying hours. Our current worldview is shaken by the new ways that dangers are expressed in all corners of our world. Yet when we look throughout history, we also see that disasters and critical incidents of various forms have had traumatic results and have shaken the foundations of individual and community assumptive worldviews. However, the courage of the human heart, the tenacity of the community spirit, and the efforts of many hands hasten resiliency and recovery. These qualities have helped to address the fears and insecurities of our assumptive worldview in times of snares and dangers of life. These qualities are what have helped and will continue to help us address our assumptive worldviews in ways that are encouraging, sustaining, and fortifying to the human race throughout time.

> The only real security in life lies in relishing life's insecurity. (Peck, 1996, p. 136)

REFERENCES

Baker, S., & Terris, O. (1994). *A to Z: A for Andromeda to zoo time: The TV holdings of the National Film and Television Archive, 1936–1979*. London, British Film Institute.

Barry, J. M. (2005). *The great influenza: The story of the deadliest pandemic in history*. New York: Penguin Group.

Bloomfield, P. (2006). The challenging business of long-term public–private partnerships: Reflections on local experience. *Public Administration Review, 66*(3), 400–411.

Brown, J. (1988). A is for atom, B is for bomb. *Journal of American History, 75*(1), p. 68.

City of Oklahoma City Document Management. (1996). *Final report: Alfred P. Murrah Federal Building bombing April 19, 1995*. Stillwater, OK: Department of Central Services Central Printing Division.

Dan, U. (2003, March 18). Israelis dead in survival "bunker." *New York Post*, p. 7.

Department of Homeland Security. (2003, February 28). *Homeland Security Presidential Directive 5: Management of domestic incidents*. Retrieved December 13, 2009 from http://www.dhs.gov/xabout/laws/gc_1214592333605.shtm

Greene, J., & Moline, K. (2006). *The bird flu pandemic: Can it happen? Will it happen?* New York: Thomas Dunne Books.

Inglesby, T. (2002). The Phoenix Project: Rising from the Pentagon's ashes. *Masonry Magazine*. Mason Contractors Association of America. Retrieved December 11, 2009 from http://www.masonrymagazine.com/8-02/rising.html

International Strategy for Disaster Reduction. (2006). *Disaster statistics occurrence: Trends-century.* Retrieved November 13, 2009 from http://www.unisdr.org/disaster-statistics/pdf/isdr-disaster-statistics-occurrence.pdf

Lehrer, J. (News Anchor & Producer). (2001, November 2). Terror alert. *News Hour with Jim Lehrer.* [Television broadcast]. Washington, DC: Public Broadcasting Service. Retrieved December 13, 2009 from www.pbs.org/newshour/bb/terrorism/july-dec01/alert_11-02html

Mansell, G. (1979). *Anatomy of architecture*. Cedar Falls, IA: A & W Publishers.

Melloan, G. (2005). What are the lessons of Katrina? *Wall Street Journal*, 13, p. A17.

Modesto, M. T. (2009). *What is critical incident thanatology?* Presented at Argosy University 5th Annual Truamatology Symposium, Sarasota, FL, TEAR Center.

Myers, D. (2001). *Weapons of mass destruction and terrorism: Mental health consequences and implications for planning and training*. Presented at Weapons of Mass Destruction/Terrorism Orientation Pilot Program, Clara Barton Center for Domestic Preparedness, Pine Bluff, Arkansas. Retrieved December 11, 2009 from www.icisf.org/articles/Acrobat%20Documents/TerrorismIncident/WMD_Myers.html

Norris, F., Stevens, S., Pfefferbaum, B., Wyche, K., & Pfefferbaum, R. (2008). Community resilience as a metaphor, theory, set of capacities, and strategy for disaster readiness. *American Journal of Community Psychology, 41*(1–2), 127–150

Peck, M. S. (1996). *In search of stones: A pilgrimage of faith, reason and discovery*. London: Simon & Schuster.

Pfefferbaum, B., Reissman, D., Pfefferbaum, P., Klomp, R., & Gurwitch, R. (2007). Building resilience to mass trauma events. In Doll, L., Bonzo, S., Mercy, J., & Sleet, D. (Eds.), *Handbook of injury and violence prevention* (pp. 347–358). New York: Springer Science.

Plotnick, L., Gomez, E., White, C., & Turoff, M. (2007). *Furthering development of a Unified Emergency Scale using Thurstone's law of comparative judgment: A progress report.* Information Systems Department, New Jersey Institute of Technology.

Ridge, T. (2009). *The test of our times: America under siege … and how we can be safe again*. New York: St. Martin's Press.

Rodriguez, H., & Aguirre, B. (2006). Hurricane Katrina and the healthcare infrastructure: A focus on disaster preparedness, response, and resiliency. *Frontiers of Health Services Management, 23*(1), 13–23.

Ross, M. E. (2005, July 4). *Poll: U.S. patriotism continues to soar: Years after 9/11, fervor stays high across racial, religious, political lines*. Retrieved December 13, 2009 from http://www.msnbc.msn.com/id/8410977/

Satz, R. (1979). *Tennessee's Indian peoples: From white contact to removal, 1540–1840.* Knoxville: Tennessee Three Star Books, University of Tennessee Press.

Shalev, A., & Errera, Y. (2008). Resilience is the default: How not to miss it. In Blumenfield, M. & Ursano, R. (Eds.), *Intervention and resilience after mass trauma* (pp. 149–172). New York: Cambridge University Press.

Taubenberger, J. K., & Morens, D. M. (2006). *1918 influenza: The mother of all pandemics*. Last retrieved on December 10, 2009 from http://www.cdc.gov/ncidod/EID/vol12no01/05-0979.htm

Taylor, F. (2005). *Dresden: Tuesday, February 13, 1945.* New York: HarperCollins.

Thomas, W. M. (2007). Community resilience—Exploring the conceptual framework. *Bulletin of the American Meteorological Society, 88*(3), 406.

TSA. (2009). *TSA travel assistant—The screening experience.* Transportation Security Administration, U.S. Department of Homeland Security. Retrieved December 13, 2009 from http://www.tsa.gov/travelers/airtravel/screening/index.shtm

5

Vicarious Trauma and Professional Caregiver Stress
Occupational Hazards or Powerful Teachers?

EUNICE GORMAN

*F*acing crisis, multiple loss, and sadness is not an abstract experience for professional caregivers. Every time professional caregivers enter into a therapeutic relationship, they put themselves at risk for exposure to death, emergencies, and trauma. Being intimately involved in situations where patients or clients are facing crises takes a toll over the short and long term in the careers and personal lives of those who seek to support others. Care giving and guiding individuals and their families and friends through change, transition, and loss does not occur without having an impact on the professional. This experience of responding to ongoing and repetitive strains related to professional care giving has been given a number of names including *burnout, compassion fatigue, vicarious trauma,* and *professional caregiver stress.*

BURNOUT

Burnout can be defined as the reaction over time to moral distress, ethical dilemmas, exposure to sadness, and the crisis nature of the work. Often, people experience unhappiness, stress, alienation, or work dissatisfaction or feel overly responsible and drained by not only the external demands of their work but also the internal demands they place on themselves. Ultimately, burnout has an impact on job performance as well as the physical and mental health of the caregivers and their family and friends. Some common signs and symptoms of burnout include long-term exhaustion, cynicism, and diminished interest in both personal and work pursuits and activities (Jevne & Reilly Williams, 1998; Maslach, 1982; Maslach, Schaufeli, & Leiter, 2001; Maslach & Leiter, 1997; Maslach & Leiter, 2008; McKenna, 1998; Wolin & Wolin, 1993).

Freudenberger and North (1985) outlined 12 stages or phases related to burnout:

1. The compulsion to prove oneself
2. Increased input or working harder (e.g., feeling indispensible)
3. Neglecting one's own needs (e.g., not taking time for breaks)
4. Repression or displacement of needs and conflicts (e.g., forgetting things, lack of energy)
5. Reinterpretation or revision of values (e.g., avoiding social situations, relationship problems)
6. Increasing occurring problems (e.g., denial of cynicism, aggression, other negative feelings)
7. Definitive withdrawal (e.g., empty feeling, psychosomatic reactions)
8. Clearly visible behavioral changes (e.g., others notice the changes in you)
9. Loss of feelings for one's own personality (e.g., sense of alienation)
10. Feelings of inner emptiness (e.g., panic attacks, numbness)
11. Depression and exhaustion (e.g., feelings of hopelessness and self-doubt)
12. Complete burnout and exhaustion (e.g., physical, spiritual, and emotional impact is severe)

Although this theory is over 25 years old, it still stands as an elegant way to shed light on the downward spiral from high enthusiasm to complete exhaustion. These 12 stages, or phases, are not sequential and can happen in rapid succession or over a very long time. Professionals coping with death, loss, and sadness on a day-to-day basis may skip several steps in the progression, especially if concurrent stressors are present in their personal life. So we can see by tracking these 12 phases that people start out with high expectations for themselves and for their work life and disregard some of their needs to perform well on the job. As time goes on, work life takes precedence, and self-care seems like something for which there is no time. They then begins to chronically put themselves to one side. Over time, not only does their personal and emotional life suffer, but their work also begins to be fraught with reduced productivity and feelings of alienation and negativity. Over time these people may seek to soothe or comfort themselves and try to fill the inner emptiness with food, recreational drugs, shopping, or other diversions as a means to ward off growing feelings of dissatisfaction and fatigue. It is not uncommon for people, after pushing so hard, to come to a point where they are physically unwell and unable to work. The antithesis of burnout, according to Maslach and Lester (1997) is engagement, which is characterized by energy, involvement, and efficacy.

COMPASSION FATIGUE

Compassion fatigue can be defined as the response to suffering that is continuous and unresolved. There is a gradual lessening of compassion over time because of the constant exposure to stress and anxiety. Often people with compassion fatigue report feeling hopeless, a decreased experience of pleasure, negative attitude, feelings of self-doubt, and incompetence. Figley (1982) also called compassion fatigue secondary victimization. It is referred to as secondary traumatic stress (Figley, 1995, 1999) or simply as secondary trauma (Pearlman & Saakvitne, 1995). In essence, the care providers give and give until they feel that they can no longer meet the demands, real or imagined, external or internal, placed on them by their work. Even more telling is when professional caregivers begin to resent perceived and real requests and lose their wish and desire to respond at all.

VICARIOUS DRAMA

Vicarious trauma is the ongoing process of change over time because of exposure to, witnessing, and listening to people's suffering and traumatic experiences. Constantly bringing other people's pain into our own awareness over time can have a cumulative impact. Some people maintain that vicarious trauma is the cost of caring and the cost of being empathetic. As a result, professionals may experience psychological, physical, or spiritual repercussions, or existential angst. Vicarious trauma is not uncommon in relief workers and first responders to trauma or civic and national emergencies. The overwhelming nature of the devastation of famine, flood, searching for survivors, or body removal can cause individuals to have recurrent problems managing the images and memories that intrude in their daily lives after the crisis has passed.

Professional caregiver stress is related to all of the aforementioned but is often more closely aligned with the family caregiver stress literature (Balevre, 2001; Bride, 2007; Katz & Johnson, 2006).

The difficulty in professional care giving is that we are called to simultaneously care and be engaged and to be detached. We hear talk of professional distance, boundaries, limit setting, professional detachment, and other such terms to refer to ways to be connected and at the same time distant enough to provide some protection for our emotional and psychological lives. It can be challenging to find a path where emotional involvement is manageable, where you feel that you are making a difference and fulfilled, while at the same time protected from emotional pain and preserving your ability to recuperate and have a life outside of work.

EMOTIONAL LABOR

Emotional labor is often performed at a high personal cost (Martinez-Inigo, Totterdell, Alcover, & Hollman, 2007). The cumulative impact of responding to chronic interpersonal stressors on the job cannot be ignored. Entering into other people's suffering, witnessing their pain, and connecting with our wounded humanity can slowly chip away at the enthusiasm and idealism brought to professional roles by young men and women. Professionals who begin in a care-giving career in their 20s, relatively unencumbered with personal responsibilities, may be shielded to some degree because they can focus on their work with little interference from, or concern about, balancing their personal life with work. One could also argue the opposite and say that newly minted professionals are at higher risk for work dissatisfaction and stress given that they have not had time to develop coping mechanisms or personal and professional support systems. Furthermore, they may be quickly disillusioned about their ability to withstand daily onslaughts of witnessing the pain and suffering of others. As professionals gain experience, they may be better able to weather work storms and upheavals, but they must also work harder to dovetail personal and professional responsibilities. Healthcare professionals in their 40s, for instance, find that they not only must balance their work life but may also be care giving at home, struggling with life transitions, managing work stress, parenting, supporting elderly parents, and even dealing with their own changing health. To admit that earlier altruism is now slipping away or even that resentment at being called to care at work and at home can lead to feelings of shame, embarrassment, and anger. Feelings of helplessness, hostility, sorrow, and restlessness can build and leave professionals exploring their options outside of health care or social work for what they perceive as less stressful pastures. One young woman joked that she might like to work as a cashier at the local supermarket; however, when she asked the woman working at the counter if she found her job stressful she was given a full and clear description of ways dealing with the public in a large grocery store was enough to make one dream of winning the lottery and never working again. Judging from this encounter, it is clear that everyone has work stress, but somehow the crisis nature of much of the work in health care and social work makes it seem like professional caregiver stress is more challenging. Perhaps the accompanying human connectedness and often intense and long-term relationships leave professional caregivers feeling open to burnout, vicarious trauma, and compassion fatigue.

PERSONAL SAFETY

Perhaps the more insidious changes do not occur in response to the day-to-day stressors or even the organizational shortcomings in attempts to support workers but rather because of exposure to the evil and wretchedness of the world. Organizations often have little awareness of the human toll of the work. Managing widgets on a conveyor belt and supporting human beings in crises are not the same thing. When professionals come face to face on a regular basis with anger, hatred, crime, violence, threats, and the very worst that the world can offer up it has an impact. Workers can feel a lack of safety, a sense that the world is fundamentally flawed, and that trust in our fellow human beings is misplaced. Their sense of the assumptive world is shifted. Workers who have seen it all, or have seen too much, can develop a jaundiced view of people and relationships that spills over into their own life. Having constant exposure to rage, waiting for train wrecks to happen, and worrying about clients we view as high risk but still competent to make their own decisions can leave a worker feeling a loss of control, diminished self-efficacy, lack of power, and ultimately a sense that their own world is not safe nor just. Dealing with this sense of unease and mistrust can lead to professionals not feeling that they are capable or willing to continue in their work roles. At this point, they may leave their workplace for another less stressful job, transfer to an area that is not in direct client contact, or leave the profession completely.

Whatever the case, all individuals have their own thresholds of coping with work stress just as they have their own personal list of ways their body, mind, or spirit let them know they need a break. Table 5.1 provides a list of signs and symptoms that might occur as people manage the daily stressors in their work. The list is by no means exhaustive, nor does it account for the very individualized signs and symptoms people feel when they are overloaded or overwhelmed. Having one or two symptoms or problems on the list does not mean that someone is at risk for burnout, vicarious trauma, or compassion fatigue; however, those with a number of symptoms in rapid succession or all at once might want to reevaluate their current self-care practices.

THE BODY KNOWS

Just in case we believe that the continual exposure to stress is something that is felt only psychologically, we need to remind ourselves of our body's physiological response to stress. When we are stressed, our bodies respond by releasing adrenaline; our heart rate increases, as does our blood pressure. We experience an increased respiratory rate, increased muscle tension, increased sensitivity in our sensory organs, neuro-hormonal dysregulation, and difficulty adjusting to arousal levels, resulting in an overly responsive startle reflex. Moreover, the overproduction of catecholamines causes anxiety and sleep problems, while the underproduction of serotonin results in reactivity, irritability, and impulsivity. The underproduction of cortisol, or the antistress hormone, compromises the immune system. The center in the brain known as the hippocampus shrinks with prolonged exposure to stress hormones, thus leading to memory problems. Clearly, asking people to deal with their stress on the job as if their bodies were not reacting on many levels is inadequate, especially in long-term and ongoing exposure to stress (Clark, 2002).

By its very definition, a care-giving relationship is based on receptivity, relatedness, and responsiveness and does not allow for reciprocity. Professionals often view the therapeutic relationship is a sacred contract. The components of the caring relationship include humility, courage, advocacy, patience, honesty, trust, presence, and constancy (Mayeroff, 1971). The nursing, social work, psychology, and medical literature have paid much attention to these characteristics. They are all dedicated to the process of providing care for others. There is no expectation that you will be cared for in return. In fact, many young people seek care-giving professions for just this reason: They want to help people. Your clients or patients will never be called on to support you, although to overlook the immense benefit gained by offering care and the self-actualization that often is a by-product of entering into the caring process would be a mistake.

Professionals absorb the pain of others, expose themselves to emotional contagion, and experience shared trauma (Morrissette, 2004) with little preparation and the certain knowledge that it is their responsibility to manage work-related stress. If we add personal issues of never feeling good enough (Mate, 2003), being too nice (Sommers, 2005), being afraid of making mistakes, or struggling with workaholism (Killinger, 1991), we can see that professional self-care and setting limits or boundaries becomes challenging. Add to these personality traits specific areas of

TABLE 5.1   Signs and Symptoms of Professional Caregiver Stress

Fatigue	Blaming	Decreased functioning
Moodiness	Guilt	Decreased self-worth
Oversensitivity	Remorse	Guarded conversations
Aches and pains	Emptiness	Resistance/stonewalling
Dry mouth	Sadness	Acting out
Weight gain	Sense of betrayal	Hatred
Weight loss	Constriction of interests	Evasion
Decreased joy	Preoccupation	Judgmentalism
Decreased libido	Suffering	Uncertainty
Health concerns	Egocentricity	Avoidance
Sleep problems	Insecurity	Confrontation
Pain	Mood changes	Bitterness
Loneliness	Suicidal thoughts	Despair
Disengagement	Crying	Blaming
GI problems	Apathy	Intellectualizing
Hyper alertness	Feeling hopeless	Memory loss
Immune system weakness	Decreased productivity	Overworking
Decreased empathy	Dreams or nightmares	Lack of concentration
Lack of motivation	Ambivalence	Guilt
Decrease creativity	Flare-up of health/mental health conditions	Work as burden
Envy	Self-reproach	Arrogance
Feeling helpless	Feeling inadequate	Omnipotence
Gallows humor	Skin problems	Narcissism
Hampered problem solving	Resentment	Boredom
Difficulty making decisions	Boredom	Lack of feeling
Cynicism	Rage	Increased conflict
Gossip	Defensiveness	Powerlessness
Alienation	Minimizing	Feeling stuck
Risk taking	Shortness of breath	Irritability
Sweating	Decreased energy	Alcohol use
Hot flashes	Tightness in throat or chest	Recreational drug use
Chills	Increased sensitivity to light or noise	Coping problems
Shaking	Hair loss	Decreased self-efficacy
Trembling	Self-absorption	Isolation
Absentmindedness	Calling in sick	Grief
Sighing	Being late	Restlessness
Denial	Heart palpitations	Racing thoughts
Anger	Lack of sleep or increased sleep	Panic attacks

(continued)

TABLE 5.1   Signs and Symptoms of Professional Caregiver Stress (Continued)

Numbness	Headache	Doing "for" rather than "with"
Disorganization	Tension	Boundary violations
Anxiety	Aimlessness	Fears of failure, the unknown, embarrassment, change, new people, new situations

Sources: Anderson, 2000; Anewalt, 2009; Berglas, 2001; Berry, 1988, 1991; Bruhn, 1990; Dane & Chachkes, 2001; Grosch & Olsen, 1994; Heyward, 1993; Peterson, 1992; Rabin, Saffer, Weisberg, Kornitzer-Enav, Peled, & Ribak, 2000; Weiss, 2004; Young, 2007.

vulnerability, prejudice, past history of feeling overwhelmed in a caretaking role, not liking certain clients, or feeling that your efforts go largely unrecognized, and you have the potential for people struggling to fit themselves into the care-giving equation. If we also consider the felt lack of voice that some professionals experience, the fear of contagion, or those who find that the needs and demands of work leave them feeling swamped by emotions, it is a small wonder that many individuals find themselves tired, worn out, and wishing for that elusive lottery win.

WORKPLACE FACTORS

Organizational hierarchies, bureaucracies, power relations, work tensions and multiple accountabilities (lateral, upward, downward, and corporate), turf issues, role stress, and role overlap add to the already difficult work of supporting people in pain and distress. Compounding the relationship aspects of the work are ethical dilemmas, value dilemmas, moral distress (Zlotnick Shaul, 2006), the push to be relentlessly cheerful (McGillicuddy, 2006), and the crisis orientation of the work. In fact, many professionals point to the politics, the organization, or leadership stressors as more difficult to cope with than patients who are gravely ill, dying, or in crisis. The constantly changing nature of the work world and the psychosocial risks at work, including transference and countertransference, add to the stress of high caseloads, dealing with cutbacks, resource allocation questions, job content, job demands, workload pace, scheduling, and control issues (Dollard, Skinner, Tuckey, & Bailey, 2007; Foster, 2004). Furthermore, stifled grief and bereavement are very much a part of the workplace for professional caregivers (Eyetsemitan, 1998). Fear of job loss in the ever-changing economy and previously mentioned stresses all combine to produce "wounded healers" (Conti-O'Hare, 2002) or "walking wounded." Often, the term wounded healer connotes a person very much in touch with past hurts and exquisitely compassionate to fellow human beings as a result. Add to this picture rapidly advancing technology, constant pressure to learn more, do more, and get more credentials, and you have individuals who started out loving their work and their career suffering from burnout, compassion fatigue, vicarious trauma, and professional caregiver stress.

GIFTS IN THE WORK

Caregivers speak of self-transcendence, dedication to a cause, being part of something that is bigger than they, and feeling fully human and present in their work life. Kottler (1999) writes about the benefits inherent within helping roles including reflection, creativity, altruism, growth, intimacy, legacy, drama, power, curiosity, and voyeurism. So to answer the oft-asked question, "How do you do the work that you do? It must be so depressing!" many professional caregivers will answer honestly and quickly that they get so much more back from the people they work with—that the lessons they learn, the experience of the power of the human spirit, and the love they see in the self-sacrifice of family members all combine to provide a rich and fulfilling work life.

Radley and Figley (2007) highlight the positive impact of care giving when they talk about compassion satisfaction. Others have written about benefit finding (Tennen & Affleck, 2002), or the positive emotions found in the stress experience. Clearly, positive and negative emotions go hand in hand with stress (Folkman, 2008). This benefit finding and then calling up these benefits, or what some call benefit reminding, or focusing on the benefits within the experience aids in coping and making meaning.

Of late there has been increased emphasis on the positive aspects of working with trauma (Arnold, Calhoun, Tedeschi, & Cann, 2005), meaning making, hardiness (Harrisson, Loiselle, Duquette, & Semenic, 2002), and inner strength (Dingley, Roux, & Bush, 2000). The positive aspects of providing support include feeling needed and wanted, fulfilling a duty, feeling that your occupation is worthwhile and useful, as well as being of service. For some the challenge, sense of mastery, competence, and continually learning new skills are the draws within the work. For others a sense of solidarity, living faith, giving back, responsibility for our fellow humans, and moral experience are central to their regard for their careers in the helping professions. For still others, the wisdom gained from being at the bedside or across a room from someone who is in emotional pain lends them a greater appreciation for life. Folkman (2008) reminds us that there is often a co-occurrence of positive and negative emotions in stress. There is a restorative function in positive emotions with respect to physiological, psychological, and social coping resources. Kinds of coping processes that generate positive emotions include benefit finding and reminding, adaptive goal processes, reordering of priorities, and infusing ordinary events with positive meaning (Folkman). Positive emotions help to restore resources and sustain coping. Meaning-focused coping including appraisal and drawing on values, beliefs, existential goals, purpose, and guiding principles all add to the positive aspects of care giving. In these ways the negative impact of stress is buffered by the positive emotions not often talked about as resources for managing work life stress.

VICARIOUS RESILIENCE

Still others have begun to talk about vicarious resilience (Engstrom, Hernandez, & Gangsei, 2008; Hernandez, Gangsei, & Engstrom, 2007; Hurley, 2008; Hurley & Martin, 2009). Vicarious resilience refers to the benefits clinicians or practitioners gain from seeing clients or patients do well. When clinicians see them surmount obstacles, meet problems head on, survive, and even thrive, they benefit from their resilience. Hernandez and colleagues take this concept one step further when they argue not only that front-line workers can experience vicarious resilience but also that agencies and organizations can and should find ways to promote vicarious resilience within clients, the agency, and the employees of the organization.

Reflective practitioners (Schon, 1983; Skovholt, 2001) continually seek ways to look at themselves and the work that they do, not only for the benefit of the clients that they serve but also for self-care and a desire to perform at the highest level possible. Resilient clinicians often further develop these critical self-reflection skills, find outside support, and develop particular self-care strategies (Anderson, 2000; Kearney, Weininger, Vachon, Harrison, & Mount, 2009; Norcross & Guy, 2007; Smith, 1997; Wicks, 2008).

However, we do all professional caregivers a great disservice if we place responsibility for stress control and management squarely on their shoulders without taking into consideration organizational roles in vicarious trauma and professional caregiver strain and stress (Maslach & Leiter, 2008). Destructive environments (Cyrulnik, 2005), role socialization, toxic work environments, less-than-ideal team functioning, and other workplace issues add to the personal cost associated with providing care.

Coombs (2001, p. 134) describes the "living workplace" as a place with the following:

Integrity
Love
Appreciation
Truth
Respect
Dignity
Honesty
Acceptance
Honor

For many working on busy medical units, managing work life becomes secondary to getting the work done. Team building, managing conflict, and paying attention to work life feel like luxuries no one has the time or energy to undertake. However, more and more teams and organizations are realizing that to attract, retain, and maintain excellent staff or to be considered magnet organizations they need to spend the necessary time, effort, and occasionally funds on team building, worker support, training, and organizational change. More and more, they are looking to the guidance and wisdom of people like Coombs (2001) to assist them in their efforts to improve patient and client care by assuring that the people working in the organization are well supported. They see it as an investment and not a frill or something that might be nice but not necessary in today's work climate.

CLINICAL RECOMMENDATIONS

According to Papadatou (2006), professionals are called on to simultaneously grieve and contain grief to keep their humanity and to retain their professionalism. It is important that stressed caregivers be given the opportunity to talk about their experiences. The power of narrative to make sense, elicit memories, integrate, normalize, add coherence, and express a full range of feelings and responses cannot be underestimated. Edward (2005) talks about the importance of insight, good counsel, support, flexibility, humor, creativity, experience, perspective, faith, and ongoing professional development.

Second, limit setting and practicing what has been termed *compassion wellness* (Anewalt, 2009), awareness, acknowledgment, and action (Katz & Johnson, 2006; Wogrin, 2007) in a safe and nonjudgmental manner with a supervisor, employee assistance program, therapist, or staff support group is essential. Even discussing struggles to manage workplace stress with a trusted colleague or friend who is able to keep confidentiality and listen with an open heart and mind can be of enormous benefit.

The importance of hope in coping with difficult patient and family situations cannot be underestimated. Even in the face of crisis, death, and deep sadness in the workplace, professionals who possess hope about making a difference, providing exemplary care, or shoring up their clients' hopes can reduce the wearing impact of constant care giving.

Self-Awareness

People who have a history of difficulties, abuse, or trauma may be at more risk for compassion fatigue, vicarious trauma, professional caregiver stress, or burnout. While it is important for all caregivers to pay close attention to the impact that their work has on them, it is particularly critical for those at risk to do so. Ongoing journaling, talking with a mentor, reflecting, or confiding in a trusted friend or colleague when issues arise will help to protect caregivers from the adverse effects of working in service professions.

Prevention

Knowing that burnout is a possible side effect of a career in a care-giving profession, it is imperative that people not wait until they are feeling the first indicators that their work may be exhausting them. Instead, self-care needs to be a regular and integral part of day-to-day life. The efforts made on your behalf need not be grand gestures but may be small incremental steps toward counting yourself into any and all care-giving equations.

Social Support

Support is fundamental to our daily lives. Researchers have stated time and again that social support is a huge part of predicting who will do better in terms of difficult times or bereavement (Bonanno, 2004). The buffering hypothesis states that support is beneficial only for those who are stressed or ill. The main effect hypothesis, on the other hand, states that support is health enhancing for everyone. Certainly, social support is critical in defraying the emotional costs associated with care giving. A mentor, friend, clergy person, or colleague who can offer a sympathetic ear and helpful suggestions can mean the difference between individuals feeling that they can remain in their current role or feeling like they need to leave their profession.

Care-giving organizations (Kahn, 2005) are ones committed to supporting and, one might argue, retaining their staff. Organizations might consider offering programs or activities in their efforts to encourage staff to seek help or to have mechanisms like peer support, buddy systems, critical-incident stress debriefing, and supervision in place. The organizational structure needs to be committed to building workplace morale (Bruce, 2003), spirited leadership, and trust on the job (Castro, 1998). Moral and ethical workplaces (Kidder, 2005) tend to offer some of the following:

Health promotion
Support groups—personal and organizational culture
Team-building exercises
Offsite retreats
Support for ongoing training and development and expertise building
Conflict management training
Journal clubs
Regular rehashing and debriefing
Prevention
Employee assistance plans
Critical-incident stress debriefing
Wellness programming
Career development

Programming needs to be two-pronged, targeting (1) the individual (problem-based coping and focusing on causes in the environment and appraisal-based coping that looks more closely at what is causing the stress for the individual) and (2) the organizational origins of pressure and strain. Workplaces must aim to support employees coming forward with their concerns without fear of reprisal or being seen as weak or somehow not fit for care-giving work. In fact, the person who does feel the pain and suffering of others and who cares deeply is who you want at your bedside when you are gravely ill. Organizations should work toward keeping empathetic, compassionate, and committed professionals around for a long time.

Maslach and Leiter (2008) refer to six areas of work life that are important in burnout: workload, control, reward, community, fairness, and values. If there is a discrepancy or lack of fit between the person and the organization in any of these six areas, there can be an increased risk for burnout. Therefore, prevention needs to happen on not only an individual level but also on an organizational level.

TRAINING AND PREPARATION FOR PRACTICE

To better prepare and support young people as they enter into professional care-giver roles, we need to educate reflective practitioners (Clark, 2006: Milner & Criss, 2006; Papadatou, 2006) who understand the importance of self-awareness, professional issues, and self-care. Kearney (2009) stresses that professionals need to be capable of *dual awareness*, or the ability to simultaneously focus on the patient and on themselves in any interaction. Moreover, information and training for practice needs to include the potential impact of the work personally and professionally while offering self-care strategies and practices. Symptoms of work overload need to be reviewed. Being forewarned is to be forearmed. Stress related to the work should not come as a surprise but instead should be something that new professionals know about and can therefore work toward guarding against.

Although many professionals share that they enjoy working in areas where they give of themselves, this sharing is not always welcome. It is not acceptable in some circles to rave about how much you love your work. As a society, we seem much more comfortable with focusing on the negatives or on complaints. Part of what caregivers need to do is reject this type of shop talk as the main way that work is discussed and instead remind themselves and their colleagues that along with the stress there can be enormous benefits. Professional care giving is a gift, a privilege, and an honor and something that can bring a sense of fulfilment and pride to those who make a career of supporting those in need.

THINGS TO CONSIDER

1. What brought you to this work? Are there sensitivities or risk factors of which you need to be aware?
2. What sustains you? How do you get physical and emotional rest and nourishment?
3. Do you have an inner voice that occasionally prods you with the word "enough"? What do you do when you hear it?
4. In what ways is caregiving a gift?
5. Do you have a mentor (a trusted responsive committed professional that can support you, guide you)? Are you a mentor?
6. Do you have a personal inventory of self-care practices (physical, social, emotional, psychological, interpersonal, and spiritual) in which you are committed to engaging on a regular basis? If not, do any of the aforementioned ones appeal to you?
7. Do you think organizations' roles and responsibilities related to decreasing workplace stress, promoting wellness, managing conflict, and confronting bullying and bad behavior go beyond financial compensation?
8. Do you work in a rural or remote setting (or even in an urban setting where you have a unique role) where it is difficult to separate work from life when you consistently run into clients or patients at the hockey arena, grocery store, church, or dance recitals (dual relationships)? How do you set limits and keep boundaries clear for you and for your clients?

REFERENCES

Anderson, D.G. (2000). Coping strategies and burnout among veteran child protection workers. *Child Abuse and Neglect, 24*(6), 839–848.

Anewalt, P. (2009). Fired up or burned out? Understanding the importance of professional boundaries in home health care and hospice. *Home Healthcare Nurse, 27*(10), 590–597.

Arnold, D., Calhoun, L.G., Tedeschi, R., & Cann, A. (2005). Vacarious posttraumatic growth in psychotherapy. *Journal of Humanistic Psychology, 45*(2), 239–263.

Balevre, P. (2001). Professional nursing burnout and irrational thinking. *Journal for Nurses in Staff Development, 17*(5), 264–71.

Berglas, S. (2001). *Reclaiming the fire: How successful people overcome burnout*. New York: Random House.

Berry, C.R. (1988). *When helping you is hurting me.* San Francisco: Harper and Row.

Berry, C.R. (1991). *How to escape the Messiah trap: A workbook for when helping you is hurting me*. New York: Harper Collins Publishers.

Bonanno, G.A. (2004). Loss, trauma, and human resilience: have we underestimated the human capacity to thrive after extremely aversive events? *American Psychologist, 59*(1), 20–8.

Bride, B.E. (2007). Prevalence of secondary traumatic stress among social workers. *Social Work, 52*(1), 63–70.

Bruce, A. (2003). *Building a high morale workplace*. New York: McGraw-Hill.

Bruhn, J.G., Levine, H.G., & Levine, P.L. (1994). *Managing boundaries in the health professions.* Springfield, IL: Charles C. Thomas Publishers.

Castro, E. (1998) *Spirited leadership: 52 ways to build trust on the job.* Allen, Texas: Thomas More.

Clark, C.C. (2002). Stress: Physiological and immune system effects. In C.C. Clark (Ed.), *Health promotion in communities: Holistic and wellness approaches* (p. 213). New York: Springer.

Clark, J.L. (2006). Educating spiritually reflective practitioners. Presentation at the First Annual North American Conference on Spirituality and Social Work. May 25–27, Renison College, Ontario, Canada.

Clark, P.C. (2002). Effects of individual and family hardiness on caregiver depression and fatigue. *Research in Nursing and Health, 25*(1), 37–48.

Clarke, D.M. & Kissane, D.W. (2002). Demoralization: Its phenomenology and importance. *Australian and New Zealand Journal of Psychiatry, 36*(6), 733–742.

Conti-O'Hare, M. (2002). *The nurse as wounded healer: From trauma to transcendence*. Sudbury, MA: Jones and Bartlett Publishers.

Coombs, A. (2001). *The living workplace: Soul, spirit and success in the 21st century.* Toronto: Harper Business.

Crawford, R. (1998). *How high can you bounce? Turn your setbacks into comebacks*. New York: Bantam Books.

Cyrulnik, B. (2005). *The whispering of ghosts: Trauma and resilience* (trans. Susan Fairfield). New York: Other Press.

Dane, B., & Chachkes, E. (2001). The cost of caring for patients with an illness: contagion to the social worker. *Social Work in Health Care, 33*(2), 31–51.

Dingley, C.E., Roux, G., & Bush, H.A. (2000). Inner strength: A concept analysis. *Journal of Theory Construction and Testing, 4*(2), 30–35.

Dolan, Y. (1998). *One small step: Moving beyond trauma and therapy to a life of joy.* Watsonville, CA: Papier-Mache Press.

Dollard, M., Skinner, N., Tuckey, M.R., & Bailey, T. (2007). National surveillance of psychological risk in the workplace: An international overview. *Work and Stress, 21*(1), 1–29.

Edward, K.L. (2005). The phenomenon of resilience in crisis care mental health clinicians. *International Journal of Mental Health Nursing, 14*(2), 142–148.

Endicott, L. (2006). *Self-care of the professional: Managing compassion fatigue and burnout in one's practice.* Paper presented at the NACSW Convention, October, Philadelphia.

Engstrom, D., Hernandez, P., & Gangsei, D. (2008). Vicarious resilience: A qualitative investigation into its description. *Traumatology, 14*(3), 13–21.

Eyetsemitan, F. (1998). Stifled grief in the workplace. *Death Studies, 22,* 469–479.

Figley, C.R. (Ed.) (1989). *Treating stress in families.* New York: Brunner/Mazel.

Figley, C. (Ed.) (1995). *Compassion fatigue: Coping with secondary traumatic stress disorder in those who treat the traumatized.* New York: Brunner/Mazel.

Figley, C. (Ed.) (1999). *The traumatology of grieving: Conceptual, theoretical and treatment foundations.* London: Taylor & Francis.

Flach, F. (1988). *Resilience: Discovering a new strength at times of stress.* New York: Fawcett Columbine.

Flach, F. (1997). *Resilience: The power to bounce back when the going gets tough.* New York: Hatherleigh Press.

Folkman, S. (1997). Positive psychological states and coping with severe stress. *Social Science and Medicine, 45*(8), 1207–1221.

Folkman, S. (2008). The case for positive emotions in the stress process. *Anxiety Stress and Coping, 21*(1), 3–14.

Foster, R. (2004). Self-care. Why is it so hard? *JSPN, 9*(4), 111–112.

Freudenberger, H.J. (1980). *Burn-out: The high cost of high achievement.* New York: Doubleday.

Freudenberger, H.J., & North, G. (1985). *Women's burnout: How to spot it, how to reverse it and how to prevent it.* New York: Doubleday.

Glouberman, D. (2003). *The joy of burnout: How the end of the world can be a new beginning.* Makawao, Maui, HI: Inner Ocean Publishing.

Godwin, L. (2004). *From burned out to fired up: A women's guide to rekindling the passion and meaning in work and life.* Deerfield Beach, FL: Health Communications.

Grosch, W., & Olsen, D.C. (1994). *When helping starts to hurt: A new look at burnout among psychotherapists.* New York: W.W. Norton.

Harrisson, M., Loiselle, C.G., Duquette, A., & Semenic, S.E. (2002). Hardiness, work support and psychological distress among nursing assistants and registered nurses in Quebec. *Journal of Advanced Nursing, 38*(6), 584–591.

Helgesen, S. (2001). *Thriving in 24/7: Six strategies for taming the new world of work.* New York: Free Press.

Helliwell, T. (1999). *Take your soul to work: Transform your life and your work.* Toronto: Random House.

Hernandez, P., Gangsei, D., & Engstrom, D. (2007). Vicarious resilience: a new concept in work with those who survive trauma. *Family Process, 46*(2), 229–241.

Heyward, C. (1993). *When boundaries betray us: Beyond illusions of what is ethical in therapy and life.* San Francisco: Harper.

Hurley, D. (2008). *Resilience.* Paper presented at King's University College, UWO, London, Ontario, Canada, March 7.

Hurley, D., & Martin, L. (2009). *From the zone of risk to the zone of resilience.* Social Work Research day, November 6, King's University College at the University of Western Ontario, London, Ontario, Canada.

Jevne, R.F., & Reilly Williams, D. (1998). *When dreams don't work: Professional caregivers and burnout.* Amityville, NY: Baywood Publishing Co.

Johns, C. (2000). *Becoming a reflective practitioner: A reflective and holistic approach to clinical nursing, practice development and clinical supervision.* Oxford, UK: Blackwell Science.

Joinson, C. (1992). Coping with compassion fatigue. *Nursing, 22,* 116–120.

Jones, S. (1995). *Coping with change at work.* London: Thorsons.

Kahn, W.A. (2005). *Holding fast: The struggle to create resilient care giving organizations.* New York: Brunner-Routledge.

Katz, R.S., & Johnson, T.A. (Eds.). (2006). *When professionals weep: Emotional and countertransference responses in end-of-life care.* New York: Routledge.

Kearney, M. (2000). *A place of healing: Working with suffering in living and dying.* Oxford, UK: Oxford University Press.

Kearney, M., Weininger, R., Vachon, M., Harrison, R., & Mount, B. (2009). Self-care of physicians caring for patients at the end of life. *Journal of the American Medical Association, 301*(11), 1155–1165.

Kidder, R.M. (2005). *Moral courage.* New York: Williams Morrow.

Killinger, B. (1991). *Workaholics: The respectable addicts.* Toronto: Quarter Books.

Killinger, B. (2007). *Integrity: Doing the right thing for the right reason.* Montreal/Kingston: McGill Queen's University Press.

Kirshenbaum, M. (2000). *The gift of a year: How to give yourself the most meaningful, satisfying and pleasurable year of your life.* New York: Dutton.

Kottler, J.A. (1999). *The therapist's workbook: Self-assessment, self-care and self-improvement exercises for mental health professionals.* San Francisco: Jossey-Bass.

Kottler, J.A. (2003). *On becoming a therapist.* San Francisco: Jossey-Bass.

Kubassek, B. (1997). *Succeed without burnout: Proven strategies to move your life from burnout to balance.* Ayr, Ontario, Canada: Eagle Press.

Larson, D.G. (1993). *The helper's journey: Working with people facing grief, loss, and life-threatening illness.* Champaign, IL: Research Press.

Martinez-Inigo, D., Totterdell, P., Alcover, C.M., & Holman, D. (2007). Emotional labour and emotional exhaustion: Interpersonal and intrapersonal mechanisms. *Work and Stress, 21*(1), 30–47.

Maslach, C. (1982). *Burnout: The cost of caring.* Englewood Cliffs, NJ: Prentice-Hall.

Maslach, C., & Leiter, M. (1997). *The truth about burnout: How organizations cause personal stress and what to do about it.* San Francisco: Jossey-Bass.

Maslach, C., & Leiter, M.P. (2008). Early predictors of job burnout and engagement. *Journal of Applied Psychology, 93,* 498–512.

Maslach, C., Schaufeli, W.B., & Leiter, M.P. (2001). Job burnout. *Annual Review of Psychology, 52,* 397–422.

Mate, G. (2003). *When the body says no: The cost of hidden stress.* Toronto: Alfred A. Knopf Canada.

Mayeroff, M. (1971). *On caring.* New York: Harper and Row.

McGillicuddy, P. (2006). *Understanding the stories we hold: An exploratory study of vicarious traumatization in Canadian health care workers.* Paper presented May 25, 2006, Toronto, Ontario.

McKenna, E. (1998). *When work doesn't work anymore: Women, work and identity.* New York: Dell.

Milgram Mayer, L. (2005). Professional boundaries in dual relationships: A social work dilemma. *Journal of Social Work Values and Ethics, 2*(2), 2–12.

Miller, B. (2005). *The woman's' book of resilience: 12 qualities to cultivate.* York Beach, ME: Conari Press.

Milner, M., & Criss, P. (2006). *Use of spiritual practices and classroom rituals of connection to reduce the impact of stress in social work students.* Paper presented at the NACSW conference, October, Philadelphia.

Morrissette, R.J. (2004). *The pain of helping: Psychological injury of helping professionals.* New York: Brunner-Routledge.

Norcross, J.C., & Guy, J.D. (2007). *Leaving it at the office: A guide to psychotherapist self-care.* New York: Guilford.

Papadatou, D. (1997). Training health professionals in caring for dying children and grieving families. *Death Studies, 21*(6), 575–600.

Papadatou, D. (2006). Caregivers in death, dying and bereavement situations. *Death Studies, 30,* 649–663.

Pearlman, L.A., Saakvitne, K.W. (1995). *Trauma and the therapist: Countertransference and vicarious traumatisation in psychotherapy with incest survivors.* New York: W.W. Norton and Company.

Peske, N., & West, B. (2001). *Bibliotherapy: The girl's guide to books for every phase of our lives.* New York: Dell.

Peterson, M. (1992). *At personal risk: Boundary violations in professional-client relationships.* New York: W.W. Norton.

Rabin, S., Saffer, M., Weisberg, E., Kornitzer-Enav, T., Peled, I., & Ribak, J. (2000). A multifaceted mental health training program in reducing burnout among occupational social workers. *Israel Journal of Psychiatry and Related Sciences, 37*(1), 12–19.

Radey, M. & Figley, C.M. (2007). The social psychology of compassion. *Clinical Social Work Journal, 35*(3), 207–214.

Rothschild, B. (2006). *Help for the helper.* New York: W.W. Norton and Co.

Schon, D. (1983). *The reflective practitioner.* New York: Basic Books.

Secretan, L.H.K. (1996). *Reclaiming higher ground: Creating organizations that inspire the soul.* Toronto: Macmillan Canada.

Simmons, P. (2002). *Learning to fall: The blessings of an imperfect life.* New York: Bantam.

Skovholt, T.M. (2001). *The resilient practitioner: Burnout prevention and self-care strategies.* Boston: Allyn & Bacon.

Smith, D. (1997). *Care giving: Hospice-proven techniques for healing body and soul.* New York: Simon and Schuster.

Sommers, E.K. (2005). *The tyranny of niceness: Unmasking the need for approval.* Toronto: Dundurn Press.

Sprang, G., Whitt-Woosley, A., & Clark, J.J. (2007). Compassion fatigue, compassion satisfaction and burnout: Factors impacting a professional's quality of life. *Journal of Loss and Trauma, 12*(3), 259–280.

Sutton, A.L. (Ed.). (2007). *Stress-related disorders sourcebook* (2nd ed.). Detroit: Omni Graphics.

Tennen, H., & Affleck, G. (2002). Benefit-finding and benefit-reminding. In C.R. Snyder & S.J. Lopez (Eds.), *Handbook of positive psychology* (pp. 584–597). Oxford, UK: Oxford University Press.

Weiss, L. (2004). *The therapist's guide to self care.* New York: Brunner-Routledge.

Wicks, R.J. (2008). *The resilient clinician.* Oxford, UK: Oxford University Press.

Wogrin, C. (2007). Professional issues and thanatology. In D. Balk (Ed.), *Handbook of thanatology.* Northbrook, IL: Association for Death Education and Counseling.

Wolin, S.J., & Wolin, S. (1993). *The resilient self: How survivors of troubled families rise above adversity.* New York: Villard Books.

Young, R. (2007). Boundaries. *Journal of the American Medical Association,* 29(4), 343–344.

Zlotnick Shaul, R. (2006). Are ethical issues weighing you down? The challenge of moral distress in Social Work. AAPOSW conference, May 9–11. Ontario, Canada.

Section *IB*

Relational Losses

6

Navigating Intimate Relationship Loss
When the Relationship Dies but the Person Is Still Living

DARCY L. HARRIS

INTRODUCTION

When I began to explore the topic of the ending of intimate relationships, I found a plethora of literature and popular readings. Indeed, this loss is probably one of the most common and deeply distressing experiences that individuals in our society endure. This chapter discusses the layers of loss that occur when one loses an intimate partner through separation or divorce. I have also identified areas of social change that I believe give insight into this experience, which might provide a framework for supporting individuals who experience a true loss where something has indeed died but there is no funeral or wake.

In this loss experience, the very fact that both individuals continue to live and may have ongoing contact through shared events that surround their children, family, friends, social gatherings, public outings, and even the workplace creates a very difficult scenario for adaptation and accommodation. In essence, it is the relationship that dies, but the individuals continue living. This idea is in stark contrast with the continuing bonds theory of bereavement that describes the ongoing relationship between individuals that may continue even after death and is often summed up in the phrase *death may end a life but not a relationship* (Silverman & Klass, 1996). Hence, the very crux of this loss immediately differs from the loss of an intimate partner through death. The fact that one partner usually chooses to leave the other or there has been a "leaving" of the partners of each other before there is a physical separation actually fits the criteria for our earlier discussion of an ambiguous loss, as the partners are still physically present but psychologically and emotionally absent to each other.

That the relationship ends through some form of intentionality rather than an act of fate sets up significant secondary losses related to self-esteem, self-worth, and one's views of the world and others (Grych & Fincham, 1992; Yarnoz Yaben, 2009). Complicating these losses is the discomfort of many individuals with the "messy" process that may be involved with relationship dissolution, so loss of support or the diminished support that is available may cause further difficulty to both partners. Widowed individuals often find there are offers of support and assistance, whereas individuals whose relationship ends by separation or divorce may find a significant lack of support as they lose many of the friends and family members who were affiliated with their former partner or who are uncomfortable with their situation or their perceived part in the dissolution of the relationship.

Current statistics on divorce in industrialized nations vary somewhat, but the general understanding is that approximately 50% of all marriages in these societies will end in divorce (Amato & Irving, 2006). This statistic is problematic by its exclusion of individuals who cohabit and do not marry and for individuals in same-sex partnerships whose relationship status is not recognized legally. I have intentionally not titled this chapter to include only divorce after marriage. The grief of the loss of an intimate partner is dependent not on the status of the relationship but on the attachment bond that is formed between the partners that exists whether the relationship is legally recognized (Hazan & Shaver, 1992; Weiss, 2006; Yarnoz Yaben, 2009). The issue of attachment in intimate dyadic relationships is discussed later in this chapter. However, there is some difficulty in drawing on the available literature for such an inclusionary approach, as most information pertaining to the dissolution of intimate relationships is written about married heterosexual couples. I therefore attempt to navigate through this topic to provide a broader approach while recognizing that there may be limited literature and research on which to draw for some of this discussion.

THE INFLUENCE OF SOCIAL CHANGES

Even though divorce is now more accepted in industrialized societies, language that reflects blame, stigma, and shame is still frequently used to converse about those whose marriages end. In my clinical practice, dealing with the damage caused by negative social messages on top of the pain of the loss of one's relationship is often a very challenging task. The use of the term *failed marriage* or the need of others to assign blame to one of the partners often causes a great deal of secondary pain to individuals who are already struggling with a great deal of personal angst and hurt (Grych & Fincham, 1992; Martin, 1989). It is common for the partner who initiated the separation process to experience considerable grief with the realization that the relationship could no longer continue as she or he had hoped from the beginning. It is important to keep in mind that partners who initiate the ending of the relationship often do so after a long and painful process of negotiation, attempts to reconcile difficult issues, and feelings of guilt for causing pain to the other person when he or she finally decides to leave (Emery & Dillon, 1994).

The influence of the media tends to magnify feelings of guilt: Public figures, popular media psychologists, and religious leaders talk about the need to return to family values, yet their call to do so carries the implication that it is possible to reverse the social changes that have led to the current practice and exploration of intimate relationships in this same society. I would like to propose that perhaps we are not in a "crisis" of moral values, nor is there something wrong with the rate in which intimate relationships dissolve; the current state of how intimate relationships form and are dissolved is a natural outgrowth of many social and demographic factors that would be impossible to change without unraveling the social fabric on which our current lives are now woven.

Many significant changes in the social structure of industrialized societies have had a profound impact on how intimate relationships are viewed. Until the early part of the 20th century, marriages tended to be formed within the backdrop of rural farming communities. Families tended to stay close together, and the family unit was structured along the division of labor according to prescribed gender roles and practicality. Men were stronger and performed the required heavy labor. Women tended to the children and the maintenance of the household. Families often had strong ties to formal religious beliefs and practices, which reinforced the maintenance of the dyadic marital relationship. In addition, the average life expectancy in the early 20th century was between 40 and 50 years. Infant mortality rates were high, and it was not uncommon for women to die in childbirth. Life was difficult, and most of daily life was consumed by basic functioning to ensure safety, security, and the things necessary to live (Amato & Irving, 2006; Toth & Kemmelmeier, 2009).

By the 1920s, the industrial revolution had begun. People moved away from their rural farms to find work in large urban areas where large companies established their manufacturing centers. The initiation of public health and sanitation measures, along with the discovery of how many communicable diseases were spread, led to a better quality of life for many people and an increase in life expectancy. Women also had entered the work force when men had gone to serve in the wars, and the early discussion of women's rights began with the women's suffrage movement in the 1920s in the United States. By the 1950s, the use of antibiotics to treat infections, along with the rise of allopathic medicine, led to greater possibilities for individuals to live longer and with a better quality of life than in the past (Amato & Irving, 2006; Toth & Kemmelmeier, 2009).

Currently, the average life expectancy for women in Canada is 84 years, which is double that from just over 100 years ago (CIA, 2009). The ideas of leisure and self-discovery became commonplace—ideas that were barely in conscious awareness for most individuals prior to this time. The 1960s brought a new wave of idealism and social awareness to the forefront. The universe and the physical world were explained in scientific terms rather than in religious ones, and an accompanying secular and humanistic view of society and social institutions followed. Sexual intimacy was no longer confined to marriage for the purpose of procreation. The introduction of the birth control pill and effective forms of contraception gave women choice in the planning of pregnancy and the timing of sexual intimacy (Fine & Harvey, 2006). By the end of the 20th century, the majority of women were working outside of the home and were able to achieve economic independence from men (Statistics Canada, 2009).

CHANGING RELATIONSHIPS

In reviewing the social changes over the past 50 years, it has become apparent that we can make the following statements regarding expectations and assumptions in industrialized societies:

- People live longer and with a higher quality of life than in the past; it is highly likely that one would outgrow a life partner instead of outlive one.
- The nuclear family is now the basic unit of a community rather than the extended family system.
- People generally have time to pursue leisure activities and personal fulfillment; however, people also spend less time at home due to work-related responsibilities.
- The focus is on individual accomplishments and independence rather than on the community and shared accomplishments.
- Sexual intimacy is no longer tied strictly to pregnancy and procreation.
- There has been an increased secularization of social norms, with an emphasis on individual rights and choices over the principles espoused by formal religious traditions.
- Women are able to live economically independent from men.
- Women no longer define themselves strictly by their marital status, as there are many more opportunities for social status that they are able to achieve through work and personal pursuits.

Thus, to expect that the way marriage is viewed would remain the same over this period of time in the face of these significant changes would be unrealistic.

In addition to these social changes is the undercurrent of individualism and achievement for both men and women in industrialized societies. It makes sense that living longer with a high standard of living and quality of life would lead to a greater ability to achieve self-actualization over that time. The purpose of marriage has changed accordingly, from one where marriage was accepted as a social obligation designed mainly for security and procreation to the present expectation that marriage is a joint partnership in which the purpose is to advance the personal growth and fulfillment of each of the partners. This change is sometimes referred to as the *deinstitutionalization* of marriage (Amato & Irving, 2006). Marriage is seen no longer as a social institution necessary for social definition and survival of the community but as a support system for the self-actualization of each person in the relationship, which is often referred to as the *companionate* model of marriage (Burgess, Locke, & Thomes, 1963). In light of this view, staying in a marriage that interferes with the personal growth and achievement that are strongly valued in a highly individualistic and achievement-oriented culture would be very difficult.

My wish in exploring these social changes is to move away from the tendency to look at the dissolution of intimate relationships in Western industrialized societies as a result of individual self-centeredness and narcissism to one that exposes the natural outcome of a society where the majority of individuals' basic needs for safety and security are met and where the push for personal and professional achievement is highly prized and lauded.

If one in two marriages ends in divorce and the trend in relationships is toward serial monogamy, the obvious question is whether marriage is relevant to current social trends (Amato & Irving, 2006; Toth & Kemmelmeier, 2009). Why would individuals choose to marry, or risk another partnership, even after a previous marriage ended in divorce? Weiss (2006) offers an answer to this obvious question. Drawing from attachment theory, he posits that the dyadic partner relationship is one that carries significant value as an attachment relationship for adults. Since the attachment system in humans exists mostly outside of conscious awareness, the choices that are made to satisfy the attachment system may also stem from an unstated but known need for humans to identify feeling safe, secure, and more content when in a dyadic intimate relationship. In his descriptions of clients who were separated or divorced, Weiss noted difficulties in daily functioning, high levels of anxiety, irritability, and depression. He found an explanation for his clients' symptomatic manifestations while attending a lecture on attachment given by Dr. John Bowlby. Weiss applied Bowlby's theory of attachment to adult relationships, finding in his clients the very same types of behaviors initially described by Bowlby in children who were separated from their attachment figures.

Weiss (1975, 2006) later postulated that adults form dyadic relationships as part of their attachment system, satisfying a deep, unconscious need to feel safe and secure by partnering with and maintaining a proximal bond to another person. Based on this work, it would appear that dyadic partnering and marriage will continue to be pursued in a society that now focuses on individual growth and achievement. Marriage as it was once understood as a social institution has been replaced by a consensual partnership. Unfortunately, the laws that hold marriage as a social and legal entity do not reflect the current state of social norms and understandings; therefore, the ending of a marriage or intimate relationship may be normative given the aforementioned social changes, but the legal and emotional ramifications of the ending are certainly anything but painless.

It is highly apparent that there is a split in how marriage and partnering are perceived from a social standpoint versus the legal and structural issues that surround these partnerships. Although socially women and men may no longer need the institution of marriage in the way that individuals of 50 years ago may have for self-definition and stability, there are structural pressures that continue to favor marriage. For instance, it is often impossible or extremely difficult to name a common-law or same-sex partner as the beneficiary of insurance, extended medical benefits, or a pension supplied by a workplace. Laws that govern the distribution of property and support after the end of a marriage may not apply to common-law relationships, with the possibility that one of the partners may be more vulnerable in a nonmarital relationship should it end. Decisions regarding health care, funeral choices, and the disposition of the body are left to a spouse, relatives, or next of kin unless stipulated in a legal document, and laws regarding common-law relationships are often inconsistent or nonexistent. Part of the controversy over the ability of same-sex partners to marry pertains to these issues, as the legal recognition of the union through marriage affords these benefits to the partners, which might be otherwise denied. It is also a painful reality that the dissolution of a relationship is not considered by many to be as significant if a couple was not married. Since the response to loss is determined by the attachment bond formed between the partners and not the legal definition of the relationship, it is important to recognize the presence of profound grief when any intimate dyadic relationship ends for whatever reason.

There is also a dichotomy in popular thinking regarding intimate relationships. Ideas of romance, idealized love, and unrealistic relational hopes and expectations continue to abound in popular movies, television shows, and fiction. One variation of this theme is the twist on wounded people who are either cynical about relationships or considered poor souls "reborn" when they meet the "right person." Popular culture sets up an idealized notion of the intimate partnership that is far removed from the realities of day-to-day existence. Whether the longing for this type of romantic love is a form of denial or hope, the loss of an intimate relationship when expectations have been shaped by popular culture toward idealized romantic love is a harsh reality.

Hagemeyer (1986) refers to the loss of the dreams associated with an intimate relationship as "the fall." Because of the flux in the social views of intimate relationships, there is a mixture of public opinion toward the dissolution of these same relationships. There can be judgment for leaving a relationship, and there can also be judgment for staying in a relationship. Individuals who leave a relationship may be judged for their lack of commitment or for being self-centered. Negative assumptions and attributions about the partner who initiates the ending of the relationship are often pointed and severe. These negative commentaries can place highly sensitive and private information about the person into a public forum of scrutiny and shame. However, the person who stays in a relationship may also be subject to criticism. Hagemeyer discusses the dilemma of individuals who remain in relationships in which they are unhappy or unhealthy. For example, individuals who stay in a relationship that is not meeting their needs may be viewed as dependent or stunted in some way, as there is an expectation that you are responsible for your own happiness and the master of your destiny. Thus, if you are unhappy in a relationship, the message is to stop whining and do something about it. There is also very little understanding of those whose sense of self and safety have been so undermined from living in an abusive relationship that they are afraid to leave. Social supports for these individuals are often burned out due to tendency of the victimized partner to return to the relationship repeatedly, even after incidents involving threat and harm.

DIVORCE VERSUS DEATH

Yarnoz Yaben (2009) compares and contrasts the dissolution of a marriage through divorce versus death. Unlike widowhood, divorce is a voluntary process, and, despite similarities in the grieving process between divorce and the death of a partner, it is my view that the adjustment to divorce is more difficult than adjustment to widowhood. Death is seen as a fact of life, and in death there is often an idealized view of the deceased. However, divorce brings forth the ambivalent feelings that were present in the relationship, and there is often a long-standing pattern of conflict, attachment, hurt, humiliation, and shame that complicates the grieving process after the relationship ends. Emery and Dillon (1994) describe divorce as a process of change that can extend over long periods of time. Divorce is not a one-time event but a culmination of many losses and pain typically over an extended period of time. Furthermore, death does not require a renegotiation of boundaries and relationships, as the deceased individual is gone and there is generally much sympathy extended to the widow or widower. However, after divorce, many boundaries must be renegotiated with family members and friends from both partners as well as with children who were a part of the family system. There are also issues with loyalties that others may feel toward one partner and not another who are not present when a relationship ends through the death of one of the partners. Boundaries must be renegotiated in the midst of uncertain normative expectations, intense and painful emotions, incompatible desires, limited contact, and difficult communication. There is often a discrepancy between the partners, as the one who decides to formalize the end of the relationship may have already withdrawn emotional investment, whereas the partner who has not initiated the process will most likely be experiencing fresh and intense emotions in response to the news. The result is often a protracted period of intense interpersonal conflict and inner distress (Emery & Dillon). You will not run into your deceased spouse in a grocery store, but you may very well run into not only your former spouse but also your spouse's new partner in the same venue; the possibility of ongoing contact can be very difficult, triggering new feelings of pain, anxiety, and humiliation.

Layers of Loss

The losses associated with the dissolution of an intimate relationship can be very encompassing, consisting of both tangible and intangible losses. As mentioned previously, there is the feeling of "paradise lost" on the realization that the relationship is perhaps not all that was hoped for. Cynicism about relationships, the legal system, religious beliefs, and ultimately oneself are common in the aftermath of a lost intimate relationship. There is an assumption that persons initiating the actual ending of the relationship fare better because they have had time to absorb the ensuing reality and may already be looking to a better future once the relationship has ended. This view may be very short-sighted, however, as it does not take into account the existence of an anticipatory grief process that one may experience when letting go of the hopes and dreams regarding the relationship prior to any action taken to bring the relationship formally to an end (Hagemeyer, 1986). Martin (1989) describes a strong sense of painful ambivalence when choosing to exit a relationship, played out by a desire to leave the difficulties and pain in the relationship, while experiencing a great deal of anxiety and fear about the unknown and being alone.

Loss of self-esteem and identity are common after the dissolution of an intimate relationship as well. These losses carry a sense of shame and humiliation with them; even though divorce is generally viewed as an unfortunate necessity and a more common occurrence in industrialized societies, there is still an assumption that one of the partners caused the "failure" of the relationship (Fine, Ganong, & Demo, 2005; Grych & Fincham, 1992). The implication is that there must be some flaw in one of the partners for the relationship to have ended. In my counseling office, a good deal of the work that occurs with clients who have lost an intimate relationship is the rebuilding of their sense of self without the partner as a key reference point for their identity and self-worth. Ironically, it is this deep sense of loss that often leads to a desire to repartner quickly after the ending of a relationship. Weiss (2006) describes this behavior as the activation of the attachment system, which draws individuals to seek out relationships that will enable them to feel safe and secure. The need to feel safe again in another relationship may be a very strong part of this desire, even in the presence of the previously described conflicting emotions about intimate relationships.

The more tangible losses may include the financial ones that occur with the division of property and assets, payment of legal fees, and no longer having the benefit of one living arrangement for two people. Earlier in this chapter, it was discussed that women are no longer financially dependent on men as they were in the past; however, they tend to fare worse financially after the ending of an intimate relationship in which they cohabited. Women are still paid less for their work than men, and many women have taken time off work to raise children or have fewer options for choosing work due to the need for flexibility related to child-care issues. Ironically, it is women who now tend to initiate the ending of marriages more than men, even though they are more likely to lose financially in the process (Amato & Irving, 2006; Sayer, 2006).

Although the scope of this chapter does not include the experiences of children after their parents separate, the ongoing conflicts that can occur through attempting to coparent in a situation where even basic communication has become very difficult adds to the stress of this process. Children's general standards of living tend to decline after their parents separate (Sayer, 2006). There are often ongoing losses associated with raising children in an environment of mistrust and conflict, and for parents who are in high conflict long after the relationship has ended the emotional and financial exhaustion can take a heavy toll on both the parents and children alike.

CLINICAL IMPLICATIONS

Supporting individuals after the loss of an intimate relationship can pose many challenges for clinicians. This is an area where social change in the past 50 years has had a direct impact on peoples' lives and where individuals feel a great deal of ambivalence and vulnerability. It is important to find ways to assist individuals to piece together what happened in their relationship and to validate the many losses that occurred during the relationship and after it ended. Clinicians need to recognize the tendency for there to be ongoing grief after the loss of an intimate relationship, due to intentionality of the decision ultimately to end the relationship, and the possibility of recurring contact with the former partner. Individuals may describe a sense of being lost as well as feelings of emptiness and abandonment. It is important to remember that these feelings are common manifestations of an attachment bond that has been broken and are not signs of weakness or overdependence.

Individuals who leave the relationship may have had more time to plan for their departure and to make new living arrangements, but they may need to sort through feelings of guilt and responsibility for their choice and possible repercussions from friends and family members for being seen as the one who is causing pain to the remaining partner. Partners who are on the receiving end of the news of the dissolution of the relationship may be in shock and be disadvantaged in making decisions because they have not had time to absorb the news. As a result, clinicians may need to offer practical support in the form of referrals to resources as part of their therapeutic work with these individuals. Reviewing the social changes and how they have had an impact on the experience of relational dissolution may help individuals to move away from feelings of shame and humiliation that cripple their ability to move forward after this loss. Clinicians who work with individuals who seek help due to intimate relational loss need to accept the "new normal" of the diversity in beliefs about marriage, divorce, and what constitutes a family system and to be able to work within many different belief systems and frameworks to fully support their clients.

It is important for clinicians to be very familiar with resources that are available for individuals facing the ending of their intimate relationships. It may be helpful to become familiar with the family law practitioners in your area and some of the basic legal jargon and procedures that surround marriage, cohabitation, separation, and divorce. This is the world in which your clients are now trying to navigate, and your awareness of this aspect of their experience may allow you to be very specific and understanding in your support and work with them at this time. It is very difficult to grieve the loss of the relationship while you are embroiled in a legal system that can add an incredible amount of stress to the situation. Many individuals find their feelings of grief must be set aside until after there is a settlement or resolution of the outstanding material or child-care issues, which carries implications for a "second wave" of assistance and support at a time when the social expectation might be to move forward because "it is over."

We run the risk of minimizing the experiences of individuals whose intimate relationships end because this loss is no longer uncommon. However, for individuals who face the loss of a partner through separation or divorce, the pain is not diminished just because many others have shared the same experience. It is very possible, and even likely, that this loss can lead to a great deal of personal growth and depth once these individuals have been able to reflect on what has happened and can allow the adaptive aspects of the grieving process to heal the wounds that have been opened. Our role as clinicians is to validate the complex and painful aspects of this experience and to support the healing aspects of the grieving process for these individuals.

REFERENCES

Amato, P. R., & Irving, S. (2006). Historical trends in divorce. In M. A. Fine & J. H. Harvey (Eds.), *Handbook of divorce and relationship dissolution* (pp. 41–57). Mahwah, NJ: Erlbaum.

Burgess, E. W., Locke, H. J., & Thomes, M. (1963). *The family: From institution to companionship.* New York: American Book.

Central Intelligence Agency (CIA). (2009). *Life expectancy by country.* Retrieved December 6, 2009 from https://www.cia.gov/library/publications/the-world-factbook/geos/ca.html

Emery, R. E., & Dillon, P. (1994). Conceptualizing the divorce process: Renegotiating boundaries of intimacy and power in the divorced family system. *Family Relations, 43,* 374–379.

Fine, M. A., Ganong, L. H., & Demo, D. H. (2005). Divorce as a family stressor. In P. C. McHenry & S. J. Price (Eds.), *Families & changes: Coping with stressful events and transitions* (pp. 227–252). Thousand Oaks, CA: Sage.

Fine, M. A., & Harvey, J. H. (2006). Divorce and relationship dissolution in the 21st century. In M. A. Fine & J. H. Harvey (Eds.), *Handbook of divorce and relationship dissolution* (pp. 3–14). Mahwah, NJ: Erlbaum.

Grych, J. H., & Fincham, F. D. (1992). Marital dissolution and family adjustment: An attributional analysis. In In T. L. Orbuch (Ed.), *Close relationship loss: Theoretical approaches* (pp. 157–173). New York: Springer.

Hagemeyer, S. (1986). Making sense of divorce grief. *Pastoral Psychology, 34*(4), 237–250.

Hazan, C., & Shaver, P. R. (1992). Broken attachments: Relationship loss from the perspective of attachment theory. In T. L. Orbuch (Ed.), *Close relationship loss: Theoretical approaches* (pp. 90–108). New York: Springer.

Martin, T. L. (1989). Disenfranchised: Divorce and grief. In K. J. Doka (Ed.), *Disenfranchised grief: Recognizing hidden sorrow* (pp. 161–172). Lexington, MA: Lexington.

Sayer, L. C. (2006). Economic aspects of divorce and relationship dissolution. In M. A. Fine & J. H. Harvey (Eds.), *Handbook of divorce and relationship dissolution* (pp. 385–408). Mahwah, NJ: Erlbaum.

Silverman, P. R., & Klass, D. (1996). Introduction: What's the problem? In D. Klass, P. R. Silverman, & S. L. Nickman (Eds.), *Continuing bonds: New understandings of grief* (pp. 3–30). Washington, DC: Taylor & Francis.

Statistics Canada. (2009). Labour force characteristics by age and sex. Retrieved December 6, 2009 from http://www.statcan.gc.ca/subjects-sujets/labour-travail/lfs-epa/t091204a1-eng.htm

Toth, K., & Kemmelmeier, M. (2009). Divorce attitudes around the world: Distinguishing the impact of culture on evaluations and attitude structure. *Cross-Cultural Research, 43*(3), 280–297.

Weiss, R. (1975). *Marital separation.* New York: Basic Books.

Weiss, R. S. (2006). Trying to understand close relationships. In M. A. Fine & J. H. Harvey (Eds.), *Handbook of divorce and relationship dissolution* (pp. 605–611). Mahwah, NJ: Erlbaum.

Yarnoz Yaben, S. (2009). Forgiveness, attachment, and divorce. *Journal of Divorce & Remarriage, 50,* 282–294.

7

Adoption
*A Life Begun With Loss**

SHERRY R. SCHACHTER and JENNIFER A. SCHACHTER

INTRODUCTION

When researchers or clinicians discuss adoption, there seems to be unanimous consensus that adoption involves a triad of grief. No matter how well or smoothly an adoption is executed, it is always accompanied by loss and grief (Wolff, n.d.). Generally, there are at least three parties intimately involved, and all parties experience loss and grief—perhaps one could say even traumatic loss (Johnson, 2002). The three parties of the triad are the relinquishing birthparents, the adoptee, and the adoptive parents (Cooper, 2002; Leon, 2002).

The fact is that adoption is founded in loss, and, without that loss, there would be no adoption. To gain anything someone must first lose something: a child, a family, a dream. The experiences of these losses do not end; they continue throughout the life cycle for each member of the triad. The adjustment is ongoing and remains a part of life's narrative. Understanding the connection between these losses can assist clinicians in helping those involved cope in healthy ways and successfully navigate the experience of adoption.

This chapter is narrow in its focus and specifically looks briefly at the losses experienced by adoptive parents and more deeply at the losses experienced by adoptees adopted in infancy. This chapter does not attempt to address the complexities of such issues as cross-cultural adoptions, the challenges of foster care, or the debates related to open versus closed adoptions.

---

* As an adoptive mother and adopted daughter, the authors of this chapter are intimately familiar with adoption. The chapter is both a sharing of personal experiences and a look at some of the relevant research.

THE ADOPTIVE PARENT

Adoptive parents have numerous losses to grieve. Many adoptive parents grieve the loss of their wanted biological child (Reitz & Watson, 1992; Rosenberg, 1992); often, this is compounded by losses related to infertility, failed pregnancy, stillbirth, or death of their child. Adoptive parents, because of issues related to infertility, may feel betrayed by their body that has left them barren, may feel "punished for misdeeds" (Giuliani, 2009, p. 216), or may feel rejected by God and their physician's inability to help them medically. Kalus (2006) stresses that childless families are often stigmatized whether childlessness is intentional or due to infertility and that "real families" are nuclear families consisting of a heterosexual couple and their biological children. Kalus also notes that because the adoptive parents are not biologically connected to their children their parenthood is often questioned and not considered to be "real," further stigmatizing them. Johnson (2002) describes a comprehensive U.S. study where 90% of those surveyed viewed adoption positively; however, half noted that adopting a child was "not quite as good as having your own child," and 25% noted that it is sometimes harder to love an adopted child than one's own child. Cooper (2007) further adds that adoption was viewed as a second best way to create family, but better than no family at all (p. 5).

One adoptive mother noted that becoming a mother was not the same thing as overcoming infertility (Wilson-Buterbaugh, n.d.) and that although adoption cures childlessness it does not cure infertility. Although every loss needs to be grieved and supported, this is not always the custom in Western culture. Losses related to infertility are not generally recognized and increase the risk that the griever will become disenfranchised in their grief (Doka, 2002). Although diminished self-worth resulting from infertility was thought to contribute to poor parenting (Leon, 2002), longitudinal studies have dispelled this myth, suggesting that adoptive parents are warm, nurturing, and accepting of their children. Adoptive parents function as well as or better than childbearing parents (Leon), implying that genetic ties are less important for family functioning than the strong desire for parenthood (Golombok, Cook, Bish, & Murray, 1995).

For women who have been unable to become pregnant or carry to full term, there may be a consistent pain and jealousy when spending time with pregnant friends or family. It is difficult and painful to listen to others discuss pregnancy and childbirth without thinking of their own loss. After having a miscarriage, Pam wrote, "I have long been aware of societal pressures to have children, but had not appreciated how strongly the 'ability' to bear children is linked to your own self-image as a woman. Your definition of success and confidence depends far more on biology than is ever realized" (Moulder, 2001, p. 1). This can be experienced as a personal attack and can further exacerbate an already diminished sense of self-worth leading to self-induced isolation from others as a way of self-protection. However, ironically, this behavior simultaneously prevents them from receiving the potential support of others.

Even after successful adoption, women may grieve the loss of not having a biological child—someone who looks like them or other family members and has familiar characteristics (Kalus, 2006). In addition, the adoptive parents might grieve any medical issues that may have arisen from the child's prenatal care. In some adoptions, the child might not have received adequate (or any) prenatal care. Other children might have been exposed to drugs or alcohol while in the womb. The adoptive parents might experience grief in seeing the medical or emotional consequences as their child has to deal with these issues arising from these consequences.

Until an adoption becomes finalized, adoptive parents can be almost paralyzed with fear: that "something" will happen and that the adoption papers will not be signed and finalized; that the courts or others involved in the ultimate decision will not think that they are suitable to become parents; that perhaps they are not smart enough, rich enough, or young enough to become parents (Mather, 2001). Indeed, the process in traditional closed adoptions is such that the prospective adoptive parents are scrutinized by the adopting agency to see if they are good enough to become parents (Silverman, Campbell, & Patti, 1994). I (srs) remember when the social worker from the court was coming to our house to look us over prior to going to court; I cooked and baked and cleaned the house—you would have thought the president was coming. I was so crazed with thoughts of what might happen if the social worker thought I was not a "perfect mother" and fit to keep Jenny. When the social worker came the next morning, I was beside myself. He was young—just out of graduate school—and all I kept thinking, as I was serving him coffee and homemade apple pie, was that he was going to judge and determine my fate.

The adopted parent must also recognize and acknowledge that growing up as an adopted child will differ from growing up as the biological child in a family. Clearly, trauma and loss will greatly influence adoptive children's general development and how they view themselves and their world. Life crises and emotional distress impacts and challenges these individuals' coping abilities (Calhoun and Tedeschi, 1999).

PERSONAL REFLECTIONS OF AN ADOPTEE

Sit in a room with a dozen adoptees at a support group meeting, and the feelings shared by the adoptees will vary dramatically. There is no one way to experience being adopted. Similar to one's journey in bereavement after a death, every adoptee's journey is uniquely his or her own. One adoptee might express an overwhelming gratitude for the parents who raised him; another may share her eternal ache for something missing; yet another may offer descriptions of a life spent feeling different, feeling other than. For all, the feelings are ever changing and evolving throughout their lives, and the sense of loss resurfaces at various points in their life.

For me (J.A.S.), an adoptee, it has been nearly 40 years since I was brought from the West Coast and adopted into the Schachter family on New York's Long Island and 16 years since I was reunited with my birth mother* and birth family. Coming to terms with how I fit in with either family is a work in progress. I

---

* There is some debate among triad members about the terminology used to describe the different parental relationships. Throughout this chapter we chose to use the terms birth parents and adoptive parents. We apologize to readers who may feel that these terms dehumanize them or devalue the relationships. Additionally, we chose to deal with the awkward issue of gender-neutral pronouns by using the neutral term adoptee.

continue to uncover the impact being adopted has had on every aspect of my life: from how I form personal relationships to the choices I have made throughout my life and to how I judge myself and move in the world.

I, like others adopted in infancy, knew no family other than the one in which I was raised. I do not have any concrete memory of my birth mother. There were no cameras rolling, capturing images of a sobbing child torn from her mother's arms. But even without the conscious memories of the separation, I grew up with an ever-present ache to connect with the woman who gave me life. I felt it was integral to my journey and that to know where I was going I needed to know where I came from.

Until the age of 10 I do not remember struggling with the knowledge that I was adopted. My parents had told me so young that to this day I do not recall "the adoption conversation"; it was simply a fact. And because they had made the conscious decision to be open with me and others about that fact, I never felt ashamed of being adopted, but I definitely had an internal struggle. As a child I did not have the words to make sense of, let alone express, my feelings. Even as late as the 1970s and 1980s adoption was not something openly discussed at dinner tables or widely covered in mainstream media. So although my parents were open at home, outside sources did not reinforce this, and I felt very much alone with my feelings of being adopted.

When I was 9 our family took a cross-country camping trip, and we visited the hospital where I was born. The picture of my parents and me in front of the hospital is etched in my memory as the first glimpse of where my life started. This memory later became the foundation for dreams of the day when I, in a hospital like that one, would have a child of my own—someone who for the first time in my life others would say "looks just like you, Jennifer."

The winter following that camping trip, I had a sleepover party for my 10th birthday. As we were spread out on the living room floor in sleeping bags in the dark, some of the girls started bickering. I felt anxious and was overcome by feelings of intense sadness, and I started to cry—on my birthday, in front of my friends. Why I was sad and crying did not make sense to me, let alone to the other girls. I am sure that they must have thought I was crazy. What child cries on her birthday? I think that birthday is when I started to comprehend that to be chosen first I had to be unwanted. My birthday was the ultimate reminder that I was abandoned, and the day carried a cloud of pain until I reunited with my birth mother in my 20s.

As I moved closer to adolescence, curiosity emerged, and a strong desire to know where I came from developed. I sensed that my longing conflicted with how others expected me to feel. Most gave me the impression that they thought I should be grateful for the life I was given, honored that I was "chosen," and satisfied to be the "princess" in a family of boys with parents who adored me and raised me in a comfortable middle-class family filled with love. Alongside those very strong external messages I could not reconcile the internal longing to meet the woman who abandoned me. Why would I even care about her, given the wonderful life I had been "chosen" into? However, logic never quieted the internal curiosity and wishes to know where I came from.

Maybe it was the regular reminders that continually underscored that I was physically different from my family that led to my grappling with my sense of self: from the family photos where it was like the Sesame Street game of "which one of these is not like the others"; or the confused faces of friends when they were introduced to a member of my family for the first time; or the simple fact that I was the only left-handed one in the lot of us. Maybe it was that any questions about family medical history at doctor's visits were quickly answered with one word scribbled across a page: "Adopted." The emotions that swirled around being given away never got the chance to settle and gather dust. Either life's events or my own nature has a way of bringing me back to it to understand the present.

We moved when I was 13. I had just come through that really awkward stage, and the move was an opportunity to start fresh. My older brother had gone off to college. I was in middle school, and my younger brothers were both in elementary. I was no longer following my older brother, and teachers did not have anyone with whom to compare me. I made friends easily and settled into this new hometown effortlessly. But in the second school year, I pulled away from my first group of friends and started to hang out with new friends. The third year, I had a new group, and in the fourth year I was hanging out with yet another group. I did not realize until my 20s that this was a pattern and that I was incapable of maintaining intimate relationships. What is ironic is that I so desperately wanted them. I yearned for connecting with people but always ran when I started to feel vulnerable.

Throughout my teenage years, the pain of feeling different shadowed my life, and at times I wallowed in it, lashing out at my parents and seeking solitude away from my family. My mom and my dad tried to connect with me and get me to open up, which backfired because I was struggling with guilt and self-loathing around my wish to know the woman who had given me away while right in front of me were two people who "chose" me, who wanted me, who took care of me and loved me unconditionally. I learned to cope with the pain and shame by detaching myself from my feelings and continuing my pattern of self-limiting intimate relationships, by making close friends and then inexplicably pulling away from them, and, worse, by pulling away from my family.

During my senior year in high school, while applying for my passport to go to Paris, I got to see my birth certificate for the first time. The document was marked with the word "Amended" and an issuance date more than a year after my birth. It was as if my beginning on Earth had been annulled. I felt robbed of continuity in life. I knew then that as soon as I was on my own I would start my search. I could never undo being adopted, but I wanted to be able to answer the doctor when I was asked, "Is there any history in your family of …?"

I graduated from high school in 1988 and was off to college, where I had my own mailing address. I subscribed to the Concerned United Birthparents (CUB) newsletter and submitted my information to their registry. The first newsletter was eye-opening. For the first time I read about reunions and other adoptees' stories. I started to feel a sense of belonging and of peace; soon, it was not a matter of "if" I found my birth mother but confidence in "when."

The summer before my senior year in college, my parents gave me my adoption records, and at 21 I learned not only my birth mother's name but also that she had actually given me a name. I was not just Baby Girl X at birth. I had first and middle names and carried her last name. If she named me, she must have cared about me even if she knew she was not going to keep me. It was a nudge to keep going. I wanted to regain what my amended birth certificate had stripped from me—that is, knowledge of what came before my first breath, my genetic history, as well as an understanding of why I was given up.

As soon as I got back to college, I started searching. My roommates helped me in my quest. My parents had told me they wanted to help when the day came, and I knew they meant it but could not bring myself to tell them, let alone ask them to help. I was too young then to articulate what I was feeling, but I know now that having them involved in my search would have brought an internal conflict of worrying about their feelings versus my own. This was a journey back to self, and one I needed to make independently.

As it was, I got nowhere, and, worse, I was completely distracted from my studies because the search was all consuming. So I decided to shelve it until I was more equipped emotionally and financially to deal with it. I believed that knowing my birth mother and how I came to be would help me make more sense of myself, so I knew that someday my search would be renewed.

Eventually, rather randomly and suddenly, I found my birth mother. Within two weeks from deciding to attend a support group meeting at Adoption Crossroads in New York City, I had my birth mother's name, her husband's name, their four daughters' names and ages, an address, and a phone number. I had no time to tell my parents. There was so much for me to process that I decided a letter was how to make contact. I thought it offered the most opportunity for sorting out my emotions. Writing is how I manage my thoughts and feelings, and writing that letter helped me to articulate for the first time to myself and my birth mother why I wanted to find her and what I wanted in terms of a relationship. It also helped me to consider and accept the various "what if" scenarios that could play out. Ultimately, it allowed me to come to peace with letting go of the expectations I had and embracing "what would be, would be." Then, I called my mom and dad and made a plan to head home to talk with them about it.

Against the odds, what I actually found was a complete family. My birth parents married 4 years after I was born, and I had four full-blooded sisters. I jumped into bonding with my birth family and planning a 2-week visit. But I came to the reunion with my emotions at arm's length, the same type of behavior that kept me from maintaining continuous friendships. The 2 weeks were event filled, from meeting cousins to experiencing my first earthquake and living with my birth family without electricity and water for a week. It was a quick initiation into the family dynamic, one that was at the same time both odd and familiar. I quickly bonded with the oldest of my sisters and adored my younger sisters. I was positive about the future of my relationship with my birth mother, although a bit skeptical that I would be able to connect with my birth father.

One thing was certain; I found exactly what I had been looking for all those years: faces that looked like mine. I could see in both my birth mother and birth father the physical resemblance, and in my sisters I finally had siblings who looked like me. I even sounded like the oldest and shared some of the same mannerisms—two of the four were left-handed.

That first meeting was a turning point; it ushered in a new phase of personal growth. My need to have a child of my own began to fade; I had the physical connection to another living being that I had so desperately wanted. Knowing where my life started allowed me to stop looking at my (adoptive) family though the filter of the differences between us and what they were not and to see them for the amazing individuals they were and how they shaped me and where the similarities were. Ironically, in the wake of the reunion I grew closer to my family.

I would like to say the road since the reunion was without pain, but that is not the case. There have been disappointments. My birth mother is very different from my mom, and in the beginning I struggled with this. I kept expecting my birth mother to take an interest in my life, but that never came to be. I have not spoken with my birth mother more than once in nearly 3 years. At this point, sadly, we have no relationship. She gave me up when I was born, and as an adult she did not put in the effort to build a relationship with me. In essence, she abandoned me twice. This has been at once heartbreaking and cause for introspection. I cannot help but ask myself if my behavior in relationships—the running from them—is a function of who I am genetically and not that I was adopted. Regardless of the why, the questions remains: What am I going to do about it?

THE PSYCHOLOGY OF BEING ADOPTED

While adoption does not automatically lead to psychopathology as once believed, clearly, as the author's personal story expresses, adoptees are vulnerable and face unique challenges (Nickman, 1985) in learning to cope with the adoption experience (including rejection and loss) at an early age (Smit, 2002). We currently believe that it is "normal" behavior for adoptees to think about their birthparents and to be preoccupied with the events around their adoption and original family (Nickman, 1985, 1996). As adoptees determine how and what the experience of adoption and loss means specifically to them, the specific issues (e.g., guilt or shame, identity, intimacy and relationship) and unique challenges must be dealt with (Smit).

Loss

Just because children may have no knowledge or memory of their adoption or the separation from their family of origin does not necessarily mean that they have not suffered because of the separation (Robinson, 2001). Loss is a major issue for adoptees. The knowledge that their mother did not want them when they came into this world is a primary loss that can affect their experience of self-worth and can contribute to feelings of being devalued as a person (Nickman, 1985).

Nickman (1985, 1996) describes the experience of loss in adoptive children as being similar to the experience of loss from parental divorce or death. He describes these losses as being either covert, overt, or loss of status. Covert loss can damage self-esteem, with confusion about one's identity; it includes an inner reflection on why the child was not kept ["Was I not good enough? Not lovable or cute enough?

(Moran, 1994)]. Overt loss represents many losses including birthparents, a family history (e.g., Who are my relatives? Where were my ancestors born?), and family traditions including religious and cultural rituals. Questions about medical background and genetic predispositions can also create a sense of loss for adoptees as well as questions about possible siblings and other family members and relationships. Nickman (1985) further describes status loss as the experience of being perceived as different from others, whereby children feel stigmatized about their birth or status and are singled out as looking different from their parents and family members.

For adoptees, these losses continue throughout the life cycle, as birthdays, Mother's Day, or Father's Day are celebrated (Smit, 2002). Although the losses are numerous, there are no predescribed rituals or ceremonies to acknowledge them (Smit), and adoptees can become disenfranchised if their loss is not openly acknowledged or supported (Doka, 2002).

Miller-Havens (1996) argued that one of the challenges facing adoptees is that they are "suspended" in their grief because they do not have the vital information they need to allow the natural grief process to proceed. Questions regarding their birth parent remain unanswered: Is my birth mother still alive? If so, does she want me? Whereas all children and adolescents, at times, use make-believe and fantasy to boost their self-esteem, adoptees' fantasies about their birth parents may encompass feelings of loss in closed adoptions (Leon, 2002) and often sustain the plan to search for their biological parents (Nickman, 1996): Is my birth mother a princess? Is she rich? Is she looking for me? Is she a movie star? Is she going to come for me and take me to Hollywood? Nickman (1985) notes that "every reference to a fairy godmother in children's stories, every exposure to myths or news items about parents and children taking leave of one another, every arrival of a new sibling, every separation from the parents takes on special meaning for adopted children" (p. 374).

Miller-Havens's (1996) study focused on the dual identification of adopted females with both their birth mother and adoptive mother through the usage of birth-origin fantasies. A total of 84 female adoptees were contacted and asked (1) to write out fantasies about their birth origin and (2) to record what they had been told about their birth parents. Of the 84, all were closed adoptions, and 32 women had completed their search for their birth parent. Results of a study taken from a total of 1,954 responses revealed that, contrary to previous empirical studies, 70% of the women did not search because they were unhappy; rather, they were searching for "sameness" (i.e., someone who physically looks like them, acts like them, or has similar personality traits). Researchers found that the women who searched were not filling a void but instead were trying to find a way to reconnect with someone who had been lost. Individuals who were adopted before 2 months of age had no mental representation of the loss of their birth mother but were often left with a vague sense of loss.

Birth-origin fantasies of adopted females were split into two themes: fantasies involving why the adoptee was relinquished, and fantasies involving who the birth mother was (e.g., characteristics, physical appearance, what she thought or did over time). The study argues that unsuccessful grieving at any age can increase fantasy production and "that grieving does not resolve loss without the expression of positive and negative feelings for the lost one" (Miller-Havens, 2006, p. 285). Furthermore, researchers found that the women did not wish to know their birth mother to have a better mother. In fact, although there was the hope that the birth mother would be found alive and well, there was often concern that the adoptive mother would get hurt in the process. Miller-Havens concludes that birth-origin fantasies contribute to grief resolution by keeping the lost one alive as well as illustrating the basic human desire to stay connected.

Grief

Verrier (1993) describes the "primal wound" as the devastation—even during the first few days of life—that infants feel because of separation from their natural mother. This is a deep, permanent feeling of abandonment infants will feel for the rest of their life. Children may feel guilty and even inadequate if they have not resolved their grief (Robinson, 2001). However, some adoption researchers and clinicians disagree and do not believe that infant adoption constitutes an immediate loss that will disrupt early attachments (Leon, 2002). Some claim that the emotional attachment between child and mother is not biological but rather the "day-to-day attention to the child's needs, nourishment, comfort, affection and stimulation" (Leon, p. 653) and that toddlers and preschoolers adopted at birth demonstrated no significant differences in attachment and development (Singer, Brodzinsky, Ramsay, Steir, & Waters, 1985).

Adoptees might experience grief in learning that they did not "grow in mommy's tummy." As their understanding changes and develops with age, grief may turn to the realization of what they, the adopted children, really lost—their biological family (Smit, 2002). Secrecy and denial contribute to the difficulties in resolving adoption-related grief as adoptees may feel inadequate, helpless, and powerless. Bereaved children can exhibit symptoms of distress including pain, sadness, anger, confusion, sleep disturbances, and an inability to focus on schoolwork (Corr, 2000; Dowdney, 2000; Lohan, 2006).

Adoptees may grieve not only their initial separation from birth parents—their first loss—but also other aspects of themselves including separation from biological heritage and a sense of who they are (Leon, 2002). "Even if the loss is beyond conscious awareness, recognition, or vocabulary, it affects the adoptee on a very profound level. Any subsequent loss, or the perceived threat of separation, becomes more formidable for adoptees than their non-adopted peers" (Silverstein & Kaplan, n.d.).

Rejection

Adoptees might grieve feeling "rejected" by the birth family and being placed for adoption. Questions may arise such as, "Why didn't my mother want me? Did I cry too much? What was wrong with me?" It would not be unusual for children to view their adoption as anything but a rejection by their birth parents. Even the concept of being "lucky enough to be chosen" by their adoptive parents is eventually deconstructed, and they recognize that to be chosen means that at first "I was unchosen" (Silverstein & Kaplan, n.d.).

Identity

For adoptees, missing important genetic and medical information can have an impact on their sense of continuity and link to their past (Silverstein & Kaplan, n.d.), and the replacement birth certificate can raise feelings of worthlessness. Robinson (2001) notes that by creating a replacement birth certificate for children we are saying that we do not value their actual heritage and identity. A new birth certificate fosters the assumption that the birth parents do not exist and creates a permanent legal separation for adoptees.

When parents adopt infants they can wrongly assume that their life begins with them and the adoption. In families where there was a blend of biological and adoptive children, parents often strive to treat the children the same, not acknowledging the differences. This was generally the thinking previously when many adoptive parents, including the author, believed that growing up as an adopted child did not differ from growing up as a biological child. "We were aware of the many obstacles facing us but naively believed our love and affection for this child would overcome any major problems we might encounter. We thought adopting a child from infancy would be easier for there would be no past memories making the process more difficult" (Schachter & Schachter, 2007, p. 9). This understanding has since evolved to a greater understanding of the loss and how it impacts adoptees, regardless of their age at the time of adoption.

Intimacy and Relationships

Silverstein and Kaplan (n.d.) note that the multiple losses in adoption, together with feelings of rejection, shame, and guilt, can impede the development of intimacy. For adoptees, this can manifest itself with impaired relationships with members of the opposite sex and partners, related to issues about adoptees' conception, biological and genetic concerns, and sexuality. Leon (2002) suggests that perhaps it is not adoptees' learning of being adopted that is traumatic but rather the clash between their attachment to their parents and the new understanding of "real" biological parents that creates the turmoil and trauma.

Children who have had many experiences with multiple losses are frequently fearful of developing and fostering new relationships in anticipation of those relationships terminating. These children may present as having a low self-esteem and poor self-image, often becoming detached and aloof to protect themselves (Brockhaus & Brochkaus, 1982). It is not unusual for adult adoptees to cope by finding comfort in alcohol or drugs (Cooper, 2007). Continually seeking the approval of their adoptive parents, children may often appease their parents at their own expense by not being honest about their own needs—for example, their desire to search for their birth parents.

Control

Adoptees may feel helpless and powerless because they were never a part of the decision-making process and therefore had no control over the loss of their birth parents or the family that adopted them. This can be especially true if they are unable to connect with their birth families. As a result, adolescent adoptees may engage in power struggles with their parents and other authority figures (Silverstein & Kaplan, n.d.): "They may lack internalized self-control, leading to a lowered sense of self-responsibility. These patterns, frequently passive/aggressive in nature, may continue into adulthood" (p. 3).

Reunions

It has only been since the 1980s that reunions* in the United States between adoptees and birth parents have become popular and almost commonplace (Campbell, Silverman, & Patti, 1991; Silverman et al., 1994). Prior to that time reunions were thought to occur because of a failure of the adoptive families or a sign of pathology in adoptees (Campbell et al.). Campbell et al. note that the literature on reunions was drawn mostly from autobiographical reports of adoptees who had searched and found their birth parents. A research study by Triseliotis (1973) studied adoptees whose reunions were arranged through a registry. It was believed that adoptees who searched for their biological parents seemed to be dissatisfied with their adoptive families. This theme has been repeatedly suggested by others who, for example, viewed the adopted teenager as being more vulnerable than nonadopted teens (Sorosky, Baran, & Pannor, 1990); adoptees struggled with having a poor self-image and were unhappy with their adopted parents (Aumend & Barrett, 1984; Triseliotis). Similar studies found that adoptees searched to satisfy an existential need to know their origins (Burgess, 1989; Kowal & Schilling, 1985; Sorosky et al.; Sachdev, 1989).

Unlike these earlier studies, the study by Campbell et al. (1991) of 133 adoptees found that 114 had reunions with at least one birth parent. Most of them (n = 101) had actively searched for their birth parent, and 13 were "found" as the result of the birth parent searching for them. The study described the adoptees as not being unhappy with their adopted family and, in fact, indicated that their families were loving, supportive, and communicative. The study described a variety of responses in the way that families discussed the adoption and how that discussion changed over time as the children matured. Most of the individuals in this study described a "need" to conduct a search resulting from four different motives: (1) life-cycle transition (e.g., after the birth of their own child); (2) desire for information (e.g., medical or genetic information); (3) hope for a relationship with the birth parent; and (4) a wish for self-understanding (a curiosity of who they looked like; peace within themselves). During their search for their birth parent, some adoptees described feeling guilty, and a small percentage (4%) kept their search

---

* Reunions, in this context, differ from the current common practice of open adoptions and of planned contact between children and their birth parents.

and their reunion a secret from their parents. Once contact had been made, most adoptees acted quickly to arrange a reunion, and by 6 months everyone had made contact. Most of the reunions were jointly planned by the adoptee and the birth parent. Researchers noted that reunions did not seem to disrupt the lives of those involved, that almost no negative effects were reported (either for the adoptees or their adoptive family), and that the adoptees' self-esteem was greatly improved.

Moran (1994), a counselor who is also an adoptee, describes her two reunion experiences: the first, with her three siblings, was a favorable experience; her other reunion 15 years later with her birth mother was unfortunately not so favorable. Moran describes different stages adoptees go through after attempting the reunion: (1) paralysis, where the shock of the initial encounter leaves the adoptee paralyzed; (2) eruption, the second stage where adoptees' emotions become explosive as they wrestle with their long-standing fantasies and the reality of what actually is; (3) loss and grief, as adoptees recognize that the foundation on which they have built their lives has crumbled and that bonding cannot be recaptured (p. 258); and (4) empowerment, which can lead to new growth, a sense of self-knowledge and self-awareness, and a sense of accomplishment.

THERAPEUTIC INTERVENTIONS

Just as nonadopted children grieve the death of a loved one, adopted children will also grieve their loss. For all children, the understanding of that loss will change over time as the child grows and develops. With each new milestone in these children's lives (e.g., graduation from school, marriage, having children of their own), new questions will emerge as adoptees grieve the loss and gain a different understanding of what that loss means to them. Consistency and truth are the foundations of any trusting therapeutic relationship that would be important in helping them feel secure. Therefore, open communication and shared information between parents and children are correlated with better psychological outcomes for bereaved children (Christ & Christ, 2006). Questions and discussions about adoption should be an ongoing process, with more details given as the children grow. Being honest and forthcoming with information in an age-appropriate way provides a safe environment that will encourage adoptees to continue to ask questions and explore their emotions.

Young children are able to feel the pain of separation, sadness, anger, and fear, but they may not necessarily know how to verbalize these feelings. Additionally, they may not be aware of how their feelings affect their body. Children need help in learning how to explore and give voice to these feelings as they learn to develop healthy ways to express them—particularly the more difficult ones such as anger, fear, and regret (Schachter & Georgopoulos, 2010). Strategies to help both younger and older children can include art, music, and therapeutic play (Smit, 2002). The use of expressive arts encourages children and teens to communicate difficult feelings and thoughts using various artistic modalities (Schachter & Georgopoulos; Moon, 2006). Some children are socialized to believe that they should not express their anger. We need to teach them that anger, like any other feeling, can be safely expressed in different ways. One healthy way is to have children write everything that makes them angry on a balloon and then to use a stickpin to do a ritual balloon popping. Other therapeutic interventions encouraging children to express their anger include doing something physical, such as punching a pillow or throwing a soft ball.

Recognizing special dates (e.g., birthday, Mother's Day, the day the adoption papers were finalized) allows adoptees to ritualize the event and gives it further meaning as they process their grief. These anniversaries or specific dates are similar to those after the death of a loved one. Encouraging rituals to help children grieve their loss is therapeutic and can facilitate the expression of angry or sad feelings (Smit, 2002). If true, remind adolescents that they have strengths that have helped them cope in the past in positive and meaningful ways. Becoming more aware of these strengths and of their own self-worth can help adoptees function well in spite of challenges and adversity (Brockhaus & Brockhaus, 1982).

Nickman (1985) advocates that the only way we can help adoptees grieve their many losses (e.g., not being wanted or kept, confusion about their biological and adoptive parents, the role they occupy in their family) is through dialogue and open communication. He cautions that this is not a one-time conversation but rather one that is ongoing and continues throughout children's development. An older study by Stein and Hoopes (1985) found that adopted children who perceived that their families were frank and talked openly about the subject of adoption had a positive sense of self-worth and self-esteem. It is important that adoptive parents teach their children that it is okay to be sad about the losses in adoption. Parents need to show their children how to grieve those losses and how to cope with loss and disappointment in life. People who learn how to grieve their losses are able to function in life without their losses overshadowing every other aspect of their lives.

As much as adoptive parents would like to spare their children from pain and suffering, we know that they cannot. However, the more open and communicative adoptive parents are with their children, the more their children will feel supported, validated, and understood, thus assisting them in their grief (Smit, 2002). A study by Keefer and Schooler (2000) indicated that when adoptive parents had an awareness of their own sense of loss history (e.g., miscarriages, infertility) they were more empathetic to the needs of their adopted child. Building on this concept, adoptive parents must have a comprehensive awareness and understanding of who they are, what their own issues of loss are, and how that loss impacts their lives and relationships including their marriage. The implications of this greater self-analysis and self-awareness will impact child rearing and parenting. This process can be facilitated with the help of professionals in individual therapy.

FINAL THOUGHTS

The emotional effects of adoption for both adoptees and adoptive parents are unavoidable, and there is still open debate about what is the right course of action and treatment. What is clear, both from our personal experiences with adoption and those reported in the research, is that striving to foster open, honest, and ongoing communication is central to triad members gaining the coping skills to understand

and grieve the many adoption-related losses that will emerge throughout their lives and the losses that may not otherwise be recognized as an effect of the adoption experience.

REFERENCES

Aumend, S., & Barrett, M. (1983). Searching and non-searching adoptees. *Adoption and Fostering, 101*, 23–31.

Brockhaus, J., & Brockhaus, R. H. (1982). Foster care, adoption and the grief process. *Journal Psychosocial Nursing Mental Health Service, 20*(9), 9–16.

Burgess, L. C. (1989). *Adoption: How it works.* Tilton, NH: Saint Bani Press.

Calhoun, L. G., & Tedeschi, R. G. (1999). *Facilitating posttraumatic growth: A clinician's guide.* Mahwah, NJ: Lawrence Erlbaum.

Campbell, L. H., Silverman, P. R., & Patti, P. B. (1991). Reunions between adoptees and birth parents: The adoptees' experience. *Social Work, 36*(4), 329–335.

Christ, G. H., & Christ, A. E. (2006). Current approaches to helping children cope with a parent's terminal illness. *CA: A Cancer Journal for Clinicians, 56,* 197–212.

Cooper, R. (2002). Unrecognized losses in child adoption. In K. J. Doka (Ed.), *Disenfranchised grief: New directions, challenges and strategies for practice* (pp. 265–274). Chicago: Research Press.

Cooper, R. (2007). When the professional is personal. *Forum, 33*(4), 5–6.

Corr, C. A. (2000). What do we know about grieving children and adolescents? In K.J. Doka (Ed.), *Living with grief: Children, adolescents and loss* (pp. 21–32). New York: Hospice Foundation of America.

Doka, K. J. (2002). *Disenfranchised grief: New directions, challenges and strategies for practice.* Chicago: Research Press.

Dowdney, L. (2000). Childhood bereavement following parental death. *Journal Child Psychology Psychiatry and Allied Disciplines, 41,* 819–830.

Giuliani, J. (2009). Uncommon misery: Modern psychoanalytic perspectives on infertility. *Journal of American Psychoanalytic Association, 57,* 215–226.

Golombok, S., Cook, R., Bish, A., & Murray, C. (1995). Families created by the new reproductive technologies: Quality of parenting and social and emotional development of the children. *Child Development, 66,* 285–298.

Johnson, D. E. (2002). Adoption and the effect on children's development. *Early Human Development, 68,* 39–54.

Kalus, A. (2006). Childlessness and adoption: The experience of loss as a source of suffering. *Journal of Physiology and Pharmacology, 57*(4), 175–181.

Keefer, B., & Schooler, J. (2000). *Telling the truth to your adopted or foster child: Making sense of the past.* Westport, CT: Bergin & Garvey.

Kowal, K. A., & Schilling, K. M. (1985). Adoption through the eyes of adult adoptees. *American Journal of Orthopsychiatry, 55,* 354–362.

Leon, I. G. (2002). Adoption losses: Naturally occurring or socially constructed? *Child Development, 73*(2), 652–663.

Lohan, J. A. (2006). School nurses' support for bereaved students: A pilot study. *Journal of School Nursing, 22*(1), 48–52.

Mather, M. (2001). Retrieved June 29, 2001 from http://bmj.com/cgi/content/full/322/7302/1556

Miller-Havens, S. (1996). Grief and the birth origin fantasies of adopted women. In D. Klass, P. R. Silverman, & S. L. Nickman (Eds.), *Continuing bonds* (pp. 273–293). Washington, DC: Taylor & Francis.

Moon, P. K. (2006). Reaching the tough adolescent through expressive arts therapy groups. Retrieved December 29, 2009 from http://www.counselingoutfitters.com/Moon2.htm

Moran, R. A. (1994). Stages of emotion: An adult adoptee's post-reunion perspective. *Child Welfare, 73*(3), 249–260.

Moulder, C. (2001). *Miscarriage: Women's experiences and needs.* London: Harper Collins Publishers.

Nickman, S. L. (1985). Losses in adoption: The need for dialogue. *Journal of the American Psychoanalytic Study of the Child, 40,* 365–398.

Nickman, S. L. (1996). Retroactive loss in adopted persons. In D. Klass, P. R. Silverman, & S. L. Nickman (Eds.), *Continuing bonds* (pp. 257–272). Washington, DC: Taylor & Francis.

Reitz, M., & Watson, K. W. (1992). *Adoption and the family system.* New York: Guilford Press.

Robinson, E. (2001). *Adoption and loss—the hidden grief.* Presented in Toronto at the ASK …about reunion and the Canadian Council of Birthmothers. Retrieved September 22, 2009 from http://www.adoptioncrossroads.org/Adoption&Loss.html

Rosenberg, E. B. (1992). *The adoption life cycle.* New York: Free Press.

Sachdev, P. (1989). *Unlocking the adoption files.* Lexington, MA: Lexington Books.

Schachter, S. R., & Georgopoulos, M. (2010). How the Calvary Model of Non-Abandonment facilitates open communication in bereavement. *Journal Pediatric Hematology Oncology, 32*(1), 25–29.

Schachter, S. R., & Schachter, J. S. (2007). Adoption: Stories from a mother and daughter. *Forum, 33*(4), 9–10.

Silverman, P. R., Campbell, L., & Patti, P. (1994). Reunions between adoptees and birth parents: The adoptive parents' view. *Social Work, 39*(5), 542–549.

Silverstein, D. N., & Kaplan, S. (n.d.) Lifelong issues in adoption. Retrieved September 22, 2009 from http://library.adoption.com/articles/lifelong-issues-in-adoption.html

Singer, L. M., Brodzinsky, D. M., Ramsay, D., Steir, M., & Waters, E. (1985). Mother-infant attachment in adoptive families. *Child Development, 56,* 1543–1551.

Smit, E. M. (2002). Adopted children: Core issues and unique challenges. *Journal of Child and Adolescent Psychiatric Nursing, 15*(4), 143–150.

Sorosky, A. D., Baran, A., & Pannor, R. (1990). *The adoption triangle* (2nd ed.). Garden City, NY: Anchor/Double Day.

Stein, L. M., & Hoopes, J. L. (1985). *Identity formation in the adopted adolescent: The Delaware family study.* New York: Child Welfare League of America.

Triseliotis, J. (1973). *In search of origins. The experiences of adopted people.* Boston: Beacon Press.

Verrier, N. N. (1993). *The primal wound: Understanding the adopted child.* Baltimore: Gateway Press.

Wilson-Buterbaugh, K. (n.d.) Adoption: Not by choice. Retrieved September 22, 2009 from http://www.adoptioncrossroads.org/NotByChoice.html

Wolff, J. (n.d.) You don't have to be perfect and other adoption myths. Retrieved September 22, 2009 from http://www.childadoptions.com/adoptions/you-don't-have-to-be-perfect-and-other-adoption

SUGGESTED RESOURCES

Adoption Crossroads: www.adoptioncrossroads.org/Adoption&Loss.html
Concerned United Birthparents (CUB): www.cubirthparents.org
Grief & Loss: http://poetry.adoption.com/poems/grief-loss-2.html

Considering adoption in the midst of infertility: http://library.adoption.com/articles/considering-adoption-in-the-midst-of-infertility.html

Adoption—yours by choice: http://libraby.adoption.com/articles/adoption-yours-by-choice.html

Empty arms—the lonely trauma of miscarriage: http://libraby.adoption.com/articles/empty-arms-the-lonely-trauma-of-miscarriage.html

Infertility and aftershocks: http://libraby.adoption.com/articles/infertility-and-aftershocks.html

SUGGESTED READINGS FOR CHILDREN

A Bear Called Paddington by M. Bond. Mifflin Company, Boston, 1958. (5 to 8 years)

A Family for Jamie by Suzanne Bloom, 1991. (2 to 8 years)

A Mother for Choo by Keiko Kasza, 1992. (2 to 8 years)

Abby by Jeannette Caines. Harper & Row, New York, 1973. (3 to 8 years)

And I'm Stuck With Joseph by Susan Sommer. Herald Press, Scottsdale, Pennsylvania, 1984. (8 to 12 years)

Anne of Green Gables by L. M. Montgomery. Bantam Books, New York, 1979. (First published in 1908) (11 and older)

Another Mouse to Feed by Robert Kraus. Windmill Wanderer Books, New York, 1980. (4 to 8 years)

Being Adopted by Maxine B. Rosenberg. Lothrop, Lee & Shepard Books, New York, 1984. (5 to 12 years)

Edgar Allan by John Neufeld. New American Library, New York, 1968.

Families by Meredith Tax. Atlantic Monthly Press Book, Boston, 1981. (4 to 8 years)

Growing Up Adopted by Maxine Rosenberg (Lothrop, 1984)

Horace by Holly Keller, 1991. (2 to 8 years)

How It Feels To Be Adopted by Jill Krementz, 1988.

I Wished for You: An Adoption Story by Marianne Richmond, 2008.

Is That Your Sister? by Catherine Bunin and Sherry Bunin. Pantheon Books, New York, 1976. (7 and over)

Living in Two Worlds by Maxine B. Rosenberg. Lothrop, Lee & Shepard Books, New York, 1986. (6 to 14 years)

Lucy's Feet by Stephanie Stein, 1992. (4 to 12 years)

Our Baby: A Birth and Adoption Story by Janice Koch. Perspectives Press, Fort Wayne, Indiana, 1986. (5 to 8 years) Previously titled *Our Adopted Baby*

Pippi Longstocking by A. Lindgren. Viking Press, New York, 1950. (9 to 13 years)

Rosie's Family: An Adoption Story by Lori Rosove, 2001.

So You're Adopted by F. Powledge. Charles Scribner's Sons, New York, 1982.

Supporting an Adoption by Pat Holmes, 1986.

Susan and Gordon Adopt a Baby by Judy Freudberg and Tony Geiss, 1992. (2 to 8 years)

Tell Me Again About the Night I Was Born by Jamie Lee Curtis (3 to 8 years), 2000.

That's One Ornery Orphan by Patricia Beatty. William Morrow & Company, Inc., New York, 1980. (8 years and over)

The Adopted One: An Open Family Book for Parents and Children Together by Sara B. Stein. Walker and Company, New York, 1979. (3 to 8 years)

The Adoption Experience by Steven Nickman. Julian Messner, New York, 1985.

The Boy Who Wanted a Family by Shirley Gordon, 1982.

The Chosen Baby by Valentina P. Wasson

The Day We Met You by Phoebe Koehler, 1990. (0 to 5 years)

The Face in the Mirror: Teenagers Talk About Adoption by Marion Crook, 2000.

The Mulberry Bird: Story of an Adoption by Anne Braff Brodzinsky. Perspective Press, Fort Wayne, Indiana, 1986. (4 to 7 years)

Twenty Things Adopted Kids Wish Their Adoptive Parents Knew, by Sherrie Eldridge, 1999.

Why Am I Different? by Norma Simon. Albert Whitman & Company, Niles, IL, 1976. (4 to 8 years)

Why Was I Adopted? By Carole Livingston. Lyle Stuart, Inc., Secaucus, NJ, 1978. (9 and over)

Zachary's New Home: A Story For Foster and Adopted Children by Geraldine M. Blomquist and Paul Blomquist, 1991.

8

Loss Related to Developmental Milestones
An Analysis of the Postparental Transition

LAURA LEWIS and EUNICE GORMAN

INTRODUCTION

Our life journey is unique to each of us, and the twists and turns along our individual pathways are initially unknown. Along our paths, however, there are certain life events that may unfold almost predictably. We call these events human developmental milestones, and they are simply the events or markers along life's way that sculpt, define, or enrich us as we each live out our lives. These socially ascribed "milestones" of living are woven into the fabric of social norms that surround us and cover us in a blanket of social messaging that can unconsciously or consciously influence our own desires and aspirations for ourselves. Therein, many people feel compelled to experience these milestones and actively pursue them as their own lives unfold, believing that they give life a certain richness and definition that is worthy of their realization.

Developmental milestones are evidenced in transitions to nursery or formal schooling when the world apart from the security of early life caregivers is experienced for the first time. Milestones may present again in transitions to adolescence and first experiences related to emerging puberty, personal freedoms, and beginning sexual expressions. Transitions to early adulthood and the world of work or college requires for some a leaving of the nuclear family home and a moving into the world as an independent adult. This developmental milestone may evoke a "postparental" transition for parents where parenting suddenly takes on a radically different form in the absence of everyday contact with one's children.

Other early adult transitions occur when individuals leave their family of origin to consolidate a love relationship, whether through marriage or a cohabitating arrangement. This particular developmental milestone solidifies the intimate commitment inherent in couples' relationships and moves individuals beyond family and friendships as their sole source of relational sustenance and guidance. If couples are able and decide to conceive or adopt a child, then, again, the developmental milestone of parenthood is experienced along with all that accompanies the assumption of this responsibility and joy. A life transition of advancing age is revealed when individuals take on care-giving responsibilities for their parents. In later adulthood, they may also experience moving off employment's center stage to a position of semi- or full retirement. Indeed, many possible developmental milestones influence and define people's experiences—life transitions that powerfully shape and define our experiences of ourselves and those we love.

Socially, these developmental milestones provide opportunities for celebration that may be marked by elaborate ceremonies or rituals. First days of kindergarten, bar or bat mitzvahs, graduations from institutions of higher learning, weddings, births and baptisms, and retirement gatherings are all opportunities that publically acknowledge the social importance of these life milestones and allow for those gathered to communally support and celebrate with the individuals involved. We all know, however, that these same events of transition and celebration are also occasions that may elicit feelings of sadness and loss. One has only to attend a wedding and look about at the people in attendance to witness not only feelings of happiness in celebration of union but also those whose tears express something other than joy. It may be that those who weep are experiencing feelings of loss and sadness for a family structure that will be forever altered by the introduction of a new member: Though welcoming a new member is always an occasion for celebration, it does forever alter the family's prior form and ways of being and thus is also about losing ways of being and the family that was.

It is this sadness, the "bittersweet" parts of moving forward in life, that merits consideration, for sadness as an affective response in these transitions is a response that is less openly acknowledged or discussed and is thus less understood. For some, developmental transitions present deeply held and often silently acknowledged feelings of loss and upheaval and internally constructed demands for personal adaptation. The presence of such feelings deserves fuller elucidation in a search for greater understanding. For the purposes of this chapter, the developmental transition of the postparental transition—what some would call the empty nest—is reviewed in depth. It is beyond the scope of this chapter to analyze all the aforementioned developmental transitions for their unique characteristics, although some of what will be revealed in a deeper analysis of the postparental transition may be applicable in content to a deeper understanding of the other life transitions as well.

POSTPARENTAL TRANSITION (EMPTY NEST)

It is important to define what is meant by the postparental period. This is a phase of the adult life cycle that unfolds when parents' children are all grown and permanently leave their home; this usually occurs when parents are in their midlife phase. The terminology *postparental period* (Borland, 1982) is more neutral in its meaning and less sexist than the more common lexicon of barnyard language that terms this same phase *the empty nest* (Harkins, 1978). Using the term postparental transition is also more inclusive of both the mother and father's experiences and as such allows for a fuller elaboration of the phenomenon from the perspective of both genders. It is a time in the family life cycle that can usher in feelings of eager anticipation and long-awaited freedom, and, for many, this time is experienced as a highly positive transition (Mitchell & Lovegreen, 2009). It can also be a time fraught with feelings of anxiety, where striking a balance between closeness and autonomy can be a balancing act between parents and their children and where feelings of sadness and loss present and demand recognition.

GENDER

For those who experience sadness and loss in this phase, it is important to note some of the sociocultural factors that may be viewed as influencing or contributing to this emotional response. Many parents devote nearly two decades of their lives to the parenting role, which is a substantial portion of time in an adult's lifespan. This time, however, seems to affect men and women differently, such that the loss experienced seems to be influenced by different sociocultural gendered factors. For women, a contributing factor relates to the concept of *role investment*. Women, in particular, still receive social messages suggesting that "good" mothers subjugate their needs to those of their children and that the role of mothering should become a central force in the construction of their self-identity. For women who internalize these socially constructed dictates, the loss of such a role may usher in a crisis of identity and an anxiety born of concern for the reassignment of day-to-day time previously devoted to raising children. Women who are deemed as overly involved in the mother role and who have subjugated their needs to those of their children appear to be most susceptible to maladaptive responses to the postparental transition (Black & Hill, 1984; Borland, 1982; Cooper and Gutmann, 1987).

Another feature of women's sadness may be related to *power*. The maternal role is the only role where some women are able to exercise their own desires for power—a power that has the capacity to influence and control the lives of other human beings (Oliver, 1977). This loss of power for some women, often in the only area of life where they have been able to exert some power, may leave them bereft, empty, and helpless. The postparental woman is "retired" as it were, without her permission or consent, to again meet the socially sanctioned requirements of the "launching" chapter in her children's lives. Of course, this is paradoxical in the social messaging that emerges at this transition. For close to 20 years or so, socially sanctioned messages have put her in charge and tell her that her children's life outcomes are, in part, a reflection of her competence in her maternal role. Yet, at the apex of her offspring's launching in Western culture, a mother is supposed to release her children from her power and influence. At this time, women are expected to retreat, back off, cease and desist, keep all of their opinions and directions to themselves, and allow their emerging adults to direct their own course from here on. Anything less than this is socially stigmatizing. Indeed, some of the sadness for women may be related to this essential loss of socially sanctioned power that is essentially irreplaceable.

And then there is what to do about the socially sanctioned messaging that calls for a subjugation of a mother's needs to the needs of her children, which then radically changes into a demand for learning to come to terms with her own needs rather than receiving gratification through sustaining the physical and emotional needs of others. Fixing a focus on their inward lives and needs and desires, especially when some mothers have spent decades ignoring these internal messages for the sake of dependent others, can be tricky at best. Yet if they are unable to shift the focus from the child to themselves and the demand for a reconstruction of need gratification, the potential remains for a vigilant overinvolvement in their children's lives. At this stage, demands for involvement often create conflict between mother and adult child, which may deepen if she is unable to reshape her role gracefully. Barring this, her behavior may be experienced as interfering and controlling and has the potential to fuel conflict between her and her child. This potential increase in conflict may intensify feelings of sadness and depression in her demonstrated inability to make the required shifts. Feelings of resentment build on both sides—her for feeling abandoned and undervalued in her overall contribution to the child's life and the adult child for feeling undermined in one's own autonomous functioning and being subjugated to scrutiny and criticism that at this stage is horribly misplaced.

Studies have found that *work* is a significant factor affecting adjustment to the postparental period for women. Powell (1977) found that women employed full time are least susceptible to intense sadness associated with this life transition, followed by women employed part time. Unemployed women were most at risk for maladaptive responses. The impact of the work role has much value as an alternative to the mother role and may be highly facilitative of adaptive emotional responses to this midlife transition.

The *experienced feelings of loss for fathers* appear to have different sociocultural and emotional antecedents. This is a time in human history when fathers' involvement in the direct provision of care for their children is highly variable, with a wide variety of care being enacted. At one end of the spectrum there is the "stay-at-home dad," a man who essentially provides all of the day-to-day care for his children and enacts his parenting responsibilities in a manner similar to mothers who remain at home. The other end of the spectrum reflects a more traditional father role, one that has very little to do with the day-to-day parenting of offspring and is exclusively and heavily invested in the role of breadwinner and family provider. Such wide variation in male parenting involvement is in part attributed to the unprecedented numbers of women in the workforce and the familial need for an equal distribution of parenting tasks in response to women's employment. The amount of direct and instrumental care provided to children by their fathers seems to influence the intensity of men's emotional responses, with involved men experiencing a greater emotional loss response to this transitional time (Karp, Holmstrom, & Gray, 2004). The experience of loss for fathers seems related to their assumption of caring roles throughout their children's lives.

Our society still promotes emotional constriction, autonomous functioning, and the need to appear strong and unmoved by challenging life events as social features that shape male functioning and behavior (Scher, 1992). As such, men may be more ill-equipped to manage the plethora of feelings that emerge when their children leave home. Scher suggests that the emotional straightjacket in which men are socially encased may lead to inappropriate acting out in an attempt to deal with the powerful but unidentified or unconscious feelings of abandonment, loss, fear, and despair that this postparental transition may elicit. Such acting out may be evidenced in failed marriages, which crumble following the departure of children. Essentially the children's presence provided the glue that held the marriage together, without which there emerges a realization that the pursuit of career aspirations has left the marriage untended, neglected, and unsatisfactory. Other means of acting out may be evidenced in the existence of extramarital affairs. Such affairs may foster and support desired feelings of potency and desirability, keeping feelings of mortality and emerging physical limitations at a safe distance (Scher). In summary, the postparental transition demands much emotional integration of varying feelings for men, which may be responded to through acting out. For some men, the demands of such emotional work are perhaps too great given the emotional constriction that has shaped current male socialization processes.

Whether men's presenting behavior in response to this life transition consists of sadness, depression, compulsively driven escapes into work, or acting-out scenarios, at the root of the behavior may be the realization that time is unyielding, that the time ahead in life is less than the time behind, and that one is essentially on a trajectory toward nonbeing. Scher describes his own experience of the postparental transition as what got him in touch with wanting to have his life back. This transitional time harbored an inextricable altering of life's promise. "Having a child around provided the promise of future – … young children are optimistic and faithful and endlessly full of the joy of living" (p. 198). He suggests that when children leave some of life's promise leaves too and that there is an intense desire to return to what is replete with the joys of life instead of being in the presence of the passage of time with mortality in full view. He acknowledges his sadness as honoring his connection to his child and their lives together while also being in the presence of the emerging limits of his life.

CULTURE

A second factor that merits consideration of this life transition is that of *culture and cultural influences.* Mounting evidence suggests that sociocultural processes are particularly salient to understanding how families and their individual members negotiate the postparental transition (Mitchell & Lovegreen, 2009). Some cultural groups do not expect that their children will ever leave home to sustain themselves independently of their nuclear family or marital arrangements (Singh, 2005). Therefore, children who challenge these cultural dictates may be the source of duress for their parents. Cultural expectations and meaning about the timing of and reasons for leaving home are significant factors in shaping parental emotional response.

Mitchell and Lovegreen (2009), in their study of parental health and well-being in relation to the postparental transition, found distinct variations by cultural background. In their research analysis of four cultural groups—British, Chinese, Southern European, and Indo/East Indian—several interesting facts emerged. Parents across cultures were more like to identify negative affect associated with the postparental transition if the parents were in poorer health and had more ambiguous relational attachments and moderate face-to-face contact after children left. Indo/East Indian cultures reported higher negative feelings associated with the postparental transition due in part to shame felt from the larger Indo community because of the violation of normative expectations, which included daughters leaving home to seek independence rather than to marry or their eldest son choosing not to remain at home as is their cultural custom. Conversely, Mitchell and Lovegreen found that Chinese parents reported low levels of emotional distress at the time of the children's leaving. This may be reflective of the cultural dictate in Chinese families to discourage displays of emotion and the formality imbued in role relationships (Lim & Lim, 2005). Despite being an equally strong family-oriented culture, distress levels were significantly reduced for Chinese parents, and one might assume this is linked to sociocultural influence that shapes and guides norms regarding identity and emotional response.

In summary, cultural backgrounds profoundly shape the meaning and expressions of child-launching experiences. Parental emotional reactions, experienced as being positive, negative, or ambivalent, are seemingly influenced by whether the unique and distinct cultural norms of launching are being achieved.

ATTACHMENT AND ATTACHMENT THEORY

A third consideration in the experience of loss is associated with the constructs of *attachments and attachment theory*. Hobdy, Hayslip, Kaminski, Crowley, Riggs, and York's (2007) study of the role of attachment style in coping with empty nest in adulthood reveals several important findings. The first relates to securely attached individuals, according to the features developed by Bowlby (1973, 1982) and Ainsworth (1989). While it is beyond the scope of this chapter to detail the features of these categorical constructs, suffice it to say that securely attached individuals found it less necessary to engage in active efforts to cope with the postparental transition and were generally more equipped to meet the developmental life challenges of adulthood. Owen (2005) also echoed this finding, citing that securely attached women faced the highest levels of adjustment to this transitional phase. The results of Hobdy et al.'s study suggest that individuals who are securely attached fare better in adjusting to life transitions, particularly those that represent either the potential dissolution of valued relationships with others or role changes that are central to one's adult identity. In contrast, study participants with an anxious, ambivalent, or avoidant attachment style saw varying degrees of distress associated with this developmental transition. This research is reminiscent of the importance of attachment constructs in determining and evaluating emotional responses, with the suggestion that secure attachments determine positive affective responses to this developmental transition (Hobdy et al.).

In summary, a comprehensive understanding of this developmental milestone cannot be achieved apart from the various sociocultural influences that contribute to presentations of distress, sadness, and loss. These can be more deeply understood when considering the complexities influencing this transition that are specific to gender, culture, and attachment history. True understanding is elusive; however, attention to these dimensions ensures, at the very least, an acknowledgment of this complexity, and at best, a helping effort that leads to greater understanding, meaning making, and affective relief.

CASE STUDY INFORMATION

Barb (48) is the single mother of one son, Alex (22). She has raised her son with very little involvement from her ex-husband, Bob (50), since Alex was an infant. Bob is Alex's biological father. Bob's numerous extramarital affairs were cited as the reason for the couple's separation shortly after Alex was born. His occupation as a construction worker meant he frequently crossed the country in search of work and could not commit to predictable visitation or summer vacation schedules with his son. Bob did not oppose sole custody being awarded to Barb at the time of their separation and subsequent divorce. Bob has financially supported his son through monthly child support payments since their separation.

Barb has taken her parenting responsibilities very seriously throughout Alex's life. She suggests that working full time as a nurse and raising Alex consumed her time and describes the past two decades of her life as the decades of feeling personally "overwhelmed" and "exhausted." She cites never having become romantically involved with anyone else after her marriage ended as she did not want to expose herself to further possible hurt and betrayal. She states that no apparent activities in her life support her own personal interests or desires or from which she derives pleasure.

For the past years Alex had been pursuing and recently achieved an undergraduate degree at a local university. He livied at home for the duration of his undergraduate studies. Three months ago, he left to pursue graduate work overseas in Australia. Since his departure Barb has felt very lethargic and tearful. She cries at melancholic songs on the radio, e-mails her son daily, and calls him weekly. The intensity of her feelings of sadness have surprised her, and she states that these feelings have the capacity to be physically immobilizing. This is evidenced when she comes home from work and simply falls asleep on the couch for the rest of the evening. This exhaustive pattern occurs at least three times per week.

Along with her sadness, Barb suggests that she feels happy for and proud of her son's academic pursuits. She sees the past decades as having been about laying the foundation for his eventual departure to self-sustaining independence and is proud that her parenting guidance has brought him to this point in his life. In her worst moments she thinks about moving her life to Australia so that she can be closer to him and then recognizes these thoughts as irrational. She seeks an alleviation of her current symptoms and some greater understanding of her feelings of profound loss.

Suggested Clinical Recommendations

The following are broad recommendations that will guide clinical work with families experiencing a post-parental transition. Not all of these points apply to the described case study.

1. Our Western society is increasingly characterized as an ethnic mosaic that is seeing increasing influence from cultures across the globe. Cultures that are family centered require a differential assessment and intervention response that values and respects the cultural norms that shape the family's cultural beliefs and actions. It is important to thoroughly understand the cultural expectations, norms, and values that dictate and influence responses to the postparental transitional phase.

2. For women who self-identify as overly involved in the maternal role, it is important to identify ways they may be able to invest in other roles that replace the need gratification once met through mothering. Exploration of other possible avenues for the expression of their maternal care is suggested.

3. There may indeed be parental gender variation in the felt experience of loss. This may be linked to whoever provided the most amount of instrumental "hands-on" care to the child throughout childhood and adolescence. Given that more men are contributing to instrumental care of their children and may be contributing equally to the material, physical, and emotional provision of child care, the loss experiences of fathers needs to be acknowledged as a possibility and validated in a manner that respects the need to assess gender experiences related to postparental transition from the construct of emotional attachment and investment.

4. It is important to obtain comprehensive background information to assess and understand the meaning of this transition to clients. Factors to consider include the depth and personal identity tied to the parental role, parents' investment in roles outside of their parental role, levels of marital satisfaction, their opinion regarding their children's success or lack of success with independence, and their personal levels of self-esteem. Information such as this is crucial in determining potential intervention strategies.

5. Knowledge of the variables that affect adjustment can be important. Ethnicity, health status, and the kind of bond experienced with the child (attachment) are all knowledge bases that will inform assessment and subsequent intervention. Keeping informed of the current literature and emerging research is a requirement so that clients can be informed not only of the normative features of their experiences but also of the emerging strategies that will assist them to acknowledge, honor, and manage their underlying feelings of sadness and loss.

6. Losses that result from a life transition phase may bring up feelings of loss that not only are associated with the present loss (whatever that may be) but also that reveal prior losses, associated with and connected to the

present loss, that demand another introspective look. The transitional situation may reveal another layer of emotional processing for a related or unrelated loss that needs tending to. For example, the feelings of loss associated with an adult child's leaving home may also reveal feelings of loss associated with a prior divorce from the child's father. Not dissimilar to our understanding of grief and an ongoing acknowledgement and renegotiation of grief feelings at different stages of life development, it is suggested that loss and sadness at one developmental transition may also reveal prior losses that are in ways associated with the current transitional loss.

7. Coping skills are of great significance in determining adaptation in the postparental period. Therefore, recognition of existing coping styles and abilities, along with education and training in new or alternative ways of coping with major life stressors and transitions, may be necessary. People cope differently, and as such what works for some may not work for others. An exploration of current coping styles to assess whether they facilitate adaptation is necessary, along with suggested alternatives if current coping strategies seem lacking.

8. Counselors should be aware of reactions in the postparental phase that are indicative of severe emotional distress, including long-standing depression that colors daily functioning and contributes to a failure to invest in new life roles that provide pleasure and meaning. While psychopathologizing terminology such as the "empty nest syndrome" is not advocated, it is important to be able to distinguish between reactive depressions that result from transitional loss and chronic depressive symptoms that defy amelioration. Particular attention should be paid to depressive affect, sexual drive, sleep disturbances, extreme fatigue, crying spells, weight loss or gain, and an inability to concentrate.

REFERENCES

Ainsworth, M. (1989). Attachments beyond infancy. *American Psychologist, 44*, 709–716.

Black, S. M. , & Hill, C. E. (1984). The psychological well-being of women in their middle years. *Psychology of Women Quarterly, 8*, 282–292.

Borland, D. (1982). A cohort analysis approach to the empty-nest syndrome among three ethnic groups of women: A theoretical position. *Journal of Marriage and the Family, 44*, 117–129.

Bowlby, J. (1973). *Attachment and Loss: Vol. 2. Separation: Anxiety and anger.* New York: Basic Books.

Bowlby, J. (1982). *Attachment and loss: Vol. 1. Attachment.* New York: Basic Books.

Cooper, K., & Gutmann, D. L. (1987). Gender identity and ego mastery style in middle-aged, pre- and post-empty nest women. *Gerontologist, 27*(3), 347–352.

Harkins, E. (1978). Effects of empty nest transition on self-report of psychological and physical well-being. *Journal of Marriage and the Family, 40*, 549–556.

Hobdy, J. Y., Hayslip, B., Kaminski, P., Crowley, B., Riggs, S., & York, C. (2007). The role of attachment style in coping with job loss and the empty nest in adulthood. *International Journal of Aging and Human Development, 65*(4), 335–371.

Karp, D. H., Holmstrom, L., & Gray, P. (2004). Of roots and wings: Letting go of the college-bound child. *Symbolic Interaction, 27,* 357–382.

Lim, S. L., & Lim, B. K. (2005). Parenting style and child outcomes in Chinese and immigrant Chinese families—Current findings and cross-cultural considerations in conceptualization and research. In S. K. Steinmetz, G. W. Peterson, & S. M. Wilson (Eds.), *Parent–youth relations: Cultural and cross cultural perspectives* (pp. 21–42). New York: Haworth.

Mitchell, B., & Lovegreen, L. D. (2009). The empty nest syndrome in midlife families. *Journal of Family Issues, 30*(12), 1651–1670.

Oliver, R. (1977). The "empty nest syndrome" as a focus of depression: A cognitive treatment model, based on rational emotive therapy. *Psychotherapy, Theory, Research and Practice, 14*(1), 87–94.

Owen, C. (2005). The empty nest transition: The relationship between attachment style and women's use of this period as a time for growth and change. *Dissertation Abstracts International, Section B: The Sciences and Engineering, 65*(7-B), 3747.

Powell, B. (1977). The empty nest, employment, and psychiatric symptoms in college educated women. *Psychology of Women Quarterly, 2*(1), 35–43.

Raup, J., & Myers, J. E. (1989). The empty nest syndrome: Myth or reality? *Journal of Counseling and Development, 68,* 180–183.

Scher, M. (1992). The empty nest father. *Journal of Men's Studies, 1*(2), 195–199.

Singh, J. P. (2005). The contemporary Indian family. In B. N. Adams & J. Trost (Eds.), *Handbook of world families* (pp. 129–166). Thousand Oaks, CA: Sage.

9

Grief and Caregiver Turnover in Nonfamilial Communities
Left Behind but Not Bereft

PAMELA CUSHING and CARL MACMILLAN

By late summer, Pamela had been living and working in a L'Arche home for 7 months. The house had a great if eclectic team—lots of differences had to be worked through, but they'd also had fun. While she knew that various assistants in the house were considering what to do next, it was only at a house meeting that the full extent of the changes came into focus. First Carly, then Linda, Frank, and Sian—each of them had come to a decision to leave Preston House: Carly to lead another community home, Linda to live in her own apartment, Sian to move back to Germany, and Frank to pursue a relationship. Only then did Pamela realize, with some surprise, how strong her sense of connection to them had become and how much she would miss them. She could not imagine enjoying it anymore with such an altered landscape in the home, and she wondered about how the people with intellectual disabilities* could cope with these regular but difficult changes every year.

INTRODUCTION

People in transitional communities of belonging such as schools, camps, and human service settings experience ongoing grief due to the regular turnover in staff or other participants. Chronic turnover disrupts or ends relationships, making people reluctant to invest in getting to know new colleagues or clients, even where this is vital to the work or residential setting. Knowing that recurrent loss is structurally inevitable to the field can mitigate but not eliminate people's grief and hurt. Alongside the hurt, however, grief can become meaningful with the right supports and rituals.

---

* In L'Arche, people with intellectual disability who live there are referred to as the "Core members of the community" partly as a way to avoid medical terms as well as to underline their central role. Here we use the term *people with intellectual disabilities* as a more specific subset of *developmental disability* to be consistent with the mainstream terms in Canada and the United States (Fujiura, 2005).

This chapter explores these concepts using the case of L'Arche, an international network of intentional communities of belonging where people with intellectual disabilities and those who support them live and work together. We draw parallels with other kinds of *transitional communities* and workplaces where many participants' tenure is limited. We describe various people's experiences with such changes in their workplace relationships. We then articulate principles and rituals that L'Arche has developed to help people to live these passages well and to recognize in them opportunities for growth and personal transformation. These practices have a broad application in other settings.

Staff Turnover as a Source of Grief

There are certain work settings where grief in some form is largely unavoidable since change and loss are intrinsic to the work or the setting. Hospitals, funeral homes, and jails come to mind as places inherently predisposed to grief as they trade continuously in illness, death, and deviance. One important but overlooked work-related type of loss is the change in or loss of valued relationships with colleagues and clients due to the turnover of staff. When we conceive of turnover as a normal workplace occurrence, it is easy to miss the meaningful relationships entangled with or disrupted by it, and we often underestimate the significance of the associated sense of loss.

All work settings have turnover, but in some fields turnover is a central feature of the organization of work and a regular source of emotional labor and loss as the people who stay must repeatedly train others and build essential relationships with new people, only to see many of them depart. This factor creates a sense of the workplace as a transitional community since valued professional and personal relationships are regularly disrupted by either default or design.

While so-called professional etiquette may adjure us to avoid friendships with colleagues or clients, the social and interactive dimension of many jobs means that strong work-based relationships are a reality for most people. Such relations can be a pleasure but can also be complicated when, inevitably, loss due to job transitions occurs. Knowing that such recurrent loss is a structurally inevitable part of the environment may do little to diminish people's grief. As the introductory story suggests, Pamela was surprised by the strength of her initial reaction to her colleagues' leaving, but this response was eased by experienced L'Arche members who helped to contextualize her experience in the potential generative dimensions of these inevitable losses.

This chapter explores how one organization has developed intentional ways of creating a culture in which grief due to turnover is woven into the fabric of everyday life; it is thus normalized within this community. While grief is acknowledged as painful, it is also a sign of the fruitfulness of what people have lived together and of the potentially meaningful personal growth for those who leave and those who stay.

TRANSITIONAL COMMUNITIES

We use the term transitional community to refer to two aspects of how people experience these organizations. By calling a workplace a *community*, we simply mean a place where people work together (work is what they "share in common" [L.

communis]) but also where they feel some sense of belonging. In such a workplace community, people come to know their colleagues and those who are served there on a personal level. By *transitional* we mean that the people in that setting change more often than an average workplace by either design or default. Combining the two, we aim to evoke the types of settings where people often develop relationships and a sense of belonging in spite of knowing that they will not all be together for long.

Examples of transitional communities that have high turnover *by design* include schools and universities, summer camps, and emergency aid teams in crisis locales. In these cases, the whole community is not meant to stay together forever—students graduate, summer ends, a crisis abates. Work communities that are transitional *by default* are sometimes that way due to features of the work that most people cannot live with for extended periods, such as low pay, no job security, poor or dangerous working conditions, burnout, inadequate regulation, or primarily entry-level work such that most people move on to other things eventually. Frontline primary care settings are infamously transitional due to high staff turnover when they work with people with intellectual disability, mental health issues, or the elderly (Braddock & Mitchell, 1992).

LOSS AND OPPORTUNITY

Whether by design or default, turnover is a costly challenge for many organizations due to the constant need to recruit and retrain people (Braddock & Mitchell, 1992). It also leaves less obvious but nevertheless upsetting emotional marks on people—often for both those who depart and those who remain. Humphrey and Zimpfer (1996, p. 1) wrote that while "loss is an integral part of life," often death is the "only loss that is validated as a legitimate grief experience." We echo their concern based on our experience and research in L'Arche, where the loss of valued working relationships through turnover (i.e., non-death related) can instigate significant and often unexpected grief.

Simply put, grief is "the reaction to loss," and this includes a "complex amalgam of painful affects" (Raphael, 1984, p. 33, cited in Murray, 2005, p. 23). Individual perception is influential since a change is not always perceived as a loss or can be experienced differently if it is a surprise or was anticipated (Murray, p. 25). Pamela's response would have been less pronounced had she lived in L'Arche longer and anticipated the regular changes that come at the end of every summer. You learn that in a transitional community, no team persists intact for long. One helpful definition states that "loss is produced by an event which is perceived to be negative by the individual involved and results in long-term changes to one's social situations, relationships or cognitions" (Miller and Omarzu, 1998, p. 12). While some people in L'Arche communities are not bothered much by recurrent turnover, the next story illustrates how central individual perception is to whether and how much grief the changes will occasion. Importantly, we also see the ripple effect of one person's grief on others.

Susan is a middle-aged woman who has lived in a L'Arche home for more than 25 years. Dually diagnosed with both an intellectual disability and a mental health disorder, Susan has both cherished and challenged many caregivers over the years. For a time, she would get up and dressed in the morning only if one of her two preferred assistants—Cynthia or Ingrid—was there to support her. Susan had developed close attachments to them. While Cynthia and Ingrid did their utmost to be available for Susan, there were inevitably days when neither was available. This created difficulties for many people on the team, not the least Susan, who could not express her desires verbally but who emanated a deep sadness and frustration around the unpredictability of her relationships with primary support people. It also meant that her support people tended to feel guilty for wanting to have time off, knowing that it would be so disruptive for her. Aside from Susan's frustration and the extra work for the team, those choices also had indirect effects such as creating barriers to developing meaningful ties with new assistants. Over time, the house team learned how important it was to actively support Susan to develop comfortable working relationships with a variety of assistants.

Susan's experience paints a dark picture of how such grief can color a person's perspective on all aspects of life, beyond the particulars of one relationship. Her experience of being stuck in the negative of her situation is not universal, however; these intrinsic losses due to turnover need not be as disruptive as we have so far implied. In this chapter, we consider the cultural norms and rituals that L'Arche has developed to encourage people with and without disability to both grieve a loss and to consider the opportunity or gift that a loss engenders. As Harris (2010, p. 1) notes in her introduction, grieving and loss are important to "shaping who we are" and are part of the "normal dynamic of human existence." Extending Harris's point, we emphasize that people do not always emerge from this "shaping" satisfied; personal growth stemming from hardship and loss is certainly possible, but not inevitable or even the norm.

Some research suggests that the focus on mental illness in relation to loss "has meant that positive aspects associated with the integration of loss have often been overlooked" (Thompson, 1985, cited in Murray, 2005, p. 28). Still, a number of studies indicate that being able to discern and focus on a positive interpretation of loss can be quite adaptive. For instance, people who can "identify benefits in the face of adversity" develop high resilience and "positive life stories" as well as competence and maturity (Murray, p. 29). Other evidence shows that "the spiritual dimension of holistic care" enhances people's "ability to reframe a situation" in more positive ways (Murray, p. 29).

L'Arche culture and practices equip its members in just this way to diminish the default negative optic on loss and to draw on alternative interpretations. We outline the nature of ongoing relational losses in transitional communities through this case.

L'ARCHE AS A SALIENT CASE

L'Arche is an international network of intentional communities that was formed in the mid-1960s in France and Canada by Canadian Jean Vanier (L'Arche Canada, 2009). Vanier's varied career pursuits included World War II military training, theological schooling and reflection, and a doctorate in philosophy (Spink, 1990). Vanier's later exposure to the deplorable midcentury conditions in institutions

(Trent, 1994) led him to seek out an alternate, more fully human model of living for those in the institutions (Vanier, 1995).

While this model was in many ways in synch with the contemporary movement toward "normalization" and independence for people with intellectual disabilities (Wolfensberger, 1973), Vanier's faith inspired him to put greater emphasis on relationships and *shared living* than the more typical work skills focus (Cushing, 2003). *Life-sharing* meant that most assistants (i.e., staff or caregivers) lived in the homes with the people with intellectual disabilities all the time—they did not keep separate homes. The idea was to move people with intellectual disabilities away from remote, austere, professionalized institutions to smaller groupings of people in settings on a more human scale, communities where people could be known. Vanier (1989) promoted the inclusion of people with intellectual disabilities in social life by reimagining their support needs as being on the same spectrum with the needs of all human beings.

We chose L'Arche for our illustrative example as it fits the criteria of a transitional community where there is an experience of grief in both those who stay and leave. We hypothesize that L'Arche has a more developed approach to dealing with this issue because of its emphasis on the importance of personal growth for people of all abilities. While many people experience grief due to turnover in their transitional workplace community, most people hide their grief from others and deal with it (or not) privately. Often, people with intellectual disabilities are less likely to mask their response to loss. Since their emotional response tends to be more public and raw, L'Arche has had a more compelling incentive to grapple with this experience than most workplaces. Ultimately, though, their efforts to face grief and loss directly benefit all members of L'Arche, not just those with intellectual disabilities.

Both authors are very familiar with L'Arche. Following graduate studies in social policy and human services management, MacMillan lived in L'Arche communities for over 20 years, including many years as a live-in assistant. He is currently the community leader of L'Arche Daybreak near Toronto. Cushing has done extensive ethnographic and other qualitative research with L'Arche communities across Canada and internationally since 1999 and lived in for a year. Narratives in this chapter source from both empirical research and personal experience.

THE LANDSCAPE OF TURNOVER IN L'ARCHE

Jean Vanier never imagined L'Arche growing to more people than could fit in a single van, yet since its founding in 1964 in France L'Arche has become a movement that has expanded to 135 communities in over 30 countries around the world (L'Arche Canada, 2009; Vanier, 1995). While the debate over group homes versus independent living is ongoing, few people question the value of Vanier's contribution to reimagining the way people with intellectual disabilities can contribute to society when given the opportunity (CBC Radio, 2004; Cushing, 2010; Spink, 1990).

This growth of L'Arche comes alongside the reality that, over the long term, the life-sharing model is not for everyone. In time, shared living can be a challenge for anyone and that includes the people with intellectual disabilities who live there

(Cushing & Sumarah, 2008; Cushing, 2003). While technically the core members are as free to leave as assistants are, in reality their choices are much more limited in terms of what they can afford, what is available [most options have waiting periods of years (Brown & Percy, 2002)], and what works given their specific support needs. As such, in this chapter, the experiences of those with intellectual disability are mainly characterized from the side of those who stay and must grapple with the fallout of the ongoing turnover. Harold's story is not uncommon:

> Harold is a dignified older man who has lived at Preston House at L'Arche for 35 years. Innumerable current and former assistants count Harold as their favorite person in the community and are always quick to share their stories. For a new person, this might be hard to believe—Harold has a nervous, guarded character that is especially reserved around new people. However, as he gets to know new assistants, Harold often develops a close attachment of trust. Assistants who have gotten to know Harold report that the feeling is mutual and that they learn a lot from him. While this mutuality is on the whole beneficial for both parties, it is also a regular and ongoing source of sadness.
>
> With long-term assistants in his home, Harold has welcomed and oriented dozens of young assistants—some for the summer or a year, a few for several years. The "changing of the guard" seems eternal. For Harold, learning to adjust and cope had a lot to do with learning how to grieve: naming feelings, developing rituals, and claiming the important role he has played in the formation of the young assistants who have lived with him. There have been so many assistants for Harold that he cannot remember them all by name. Not one of them will forget his name.

Assistants' grief experiences with relational change will be described from both the perspective of staying and leaving. The chapter's story is representative of many assistants' first experience of the grief that can be associated with turnover when others leave. There are other dimensions of grief to such stories as well: the assistant who is leaving will likely also grieve the loss of routines and relationships that have become part of the everyday; the remaining assistants must find ways to support their housemates with disabilities in their grief, and all will need to welcome new assistants, even in the wake of their own grief. Each L'Arche community has a coordinator dedicated to supporting the assistants in their roles, including hiring, changing houses, and leaving. Bob is a coordinator and his reflection illustrates the complex vectors of turnover-related grief as he experiences it.

> Raoul is the assistants' coordinator (human resources) for a Canadian L'Arche community. Bob explains that one challenge of his role is that he is constantly in front of the deliberations of other assistants about whether to stay. The majority of assistants live in L'Arche for less than two years and this is also the group with the highest turnover and greatest felt need whether to stay or not. When you plan to stay in the community, as Bob does, it can be hard to listen to people's internal pro–con debates with an open mind. Others' reflections feel like a constant reminder of the challenges of living in community. In his role, Bob also hears fallout after these kinds of conversations take place informally amidst the house teams, after compounding anxiety.

Add to all of this the fact that the expression of the grief by some people with disabilities may be ambiguous or indirect, especially if their capacity for verbal articulation is limited, as in the case of Susan. It should be noted of course that not all assistants will be missed by those who remain, nor is every person who leaves sad to be gone; sometimes personality conflicts or professional differences mean that staff change is welcomed. Still, everyone who was interviewed reported feeling grief because of staff turnover on some occasions.

CULTURAL NORMS

Supporting the value of mutual relationships among all its members is one of the central tenets of the culture of L'Arche. On arrival, one immediately notices a quality of welcome and familiarity. The impact of ongoing disruptions to relationships in this transitional community is noticeable only when one spends more time there. Most experienced staff become adept with managing their personal boundaries; while they still welcome newcomers, they generally avoid overinvesting personally in many new relationships, knowing that most will not likely extend past a year or two.

People with intellectual disabilities who live in the homes have a variety of responses ranging from avoidance to embrace. One such man, Rainer, refused to acknowledge the new assistants who were assigned to support him. Rainer might simply ignore them for a time or could intermittently actively reject them. People who knew Rainer for many years surmise that perhaps he was simply tired of opening up to new people after decades living in institutions prior to L'Arche. His story is similar to that of Susan, who also resisted most new assistants in her home. Others see the arrival of new people as an occasion to give, to teach, and to feel useful—opportunities that can be rare for people with intellectual disability in the wider world. We provide a few brief examples to dimensionalize our point. Bastien, for example, loves to initiate new assistants or dinner guests with a litany of jokes, whereas Don enjoys giving people a tour of his shared home. Dillon interrogates new people about their knowledge of local clergy, whereas Jacob prefers to acquire the business card of newcomers and ask, "Where's your home?"

Vanier often argues that the mission to transmit life is part of being fully human (Cushing & Sumarah, 2008, pp. 33–34, 65, 72; Valente, 2006; Vanier, 1998). People with intellectual disabilities are often shut out of typical life-giving opportunities such as parenthood and career success. Vanier believes, however, that there is a rich window for them to transmit life through their gift of welcome to new assistants. As they spend time together, they also effectively train new people to begin to grasp and appreciate the distinct, idiosyncratic ways each and every person has of being in the world. Assistants are encouraged to find ways to facilitate these occasions, especially at transitional times. Vanier argues that the steady stream of new assistants brings prospects for new life that outweigh the eventual grief sometimes associated with their departure (Vanier, 1989, pp. 265–73).

While others in this book address how people deal with grief and loss that does not fit with their assumptive notions about how the world works (Murray, 2005, p. 32) we show that L'Arche seeks to prepare people for the predictable types of loss like staff turnover by changing their assumptive worldview ahead of time. As such, the grief of loss is somewhat mitigated through crafting an alternative, meaningful cultural context for loss due to turnover. This is conveyed through orientation, mentoring, and ongoing accompaniment as elaborated herein. These preemptive occasions for reflection and growth provide community members with a framework of interpretation that counters our society's typically negative reaction to unexpected changes in relationships.

CULTURAL DIMENSIONS OF SUPPORT FOR GRIEF

There are four key dimensions of how L'Arche moves to moderate individual and collective grief due to staff turnover. Each of these contributes to the creation of a sociocultural environment wherein this phenomenon is acknowledged as normal and is even valued for its potential to stimulate personal change and growth. The four dimensions attempt to (1) normalize turnover, (2) make space for reflection, (3) articulate what good has been lived, and (4) nurture a focus on generativity over stasis.

Normalize and Foreshadow Grief Due to Turnover

A primary dimension of the L'Arche approach to dealing with grief related to staff turnover is to normalize the phenomenon early and often. They create a sense that both turnover and its related grief are natural parts of the cycle of transitional communities and not necessarily problematic. Right from the initial series of orientation sessions for first-year assistants, the reality of staff turnover, and the resulting grief, is usually named as endemic to L'Arche. The orientation includes the facts on how predictable turnover is in L'Arche, as in most human service settings. Stories are told of how individuals have found it hard to leave, or to stay, amid these changes. New assistants are also helped to understand that people in their new L'Arche home may still be grieving for the assistant who has just left and how the same cycle of grief might be repeated for them later on.

Being aware of such undercurrents of loss can sensitize new people and ensure that they do not interpret the house's initial reluctance to reengage relationally as their issue. They learn that change and grief are normal and not something that they could or should have "prevented." As noted already, while being able to anticipate these inevitabilities does not make them disappear, it can at least diminish the surprise factor associated with loss. Echoing these insights, research suggests various factors that "affect individual grief reactions: anticipation versus suddenness, the presence of trauma, perceived preventability, and the chronicity of the loss (Harvey, 1998)" (cited in Murray, 2005, p. 31).

The default response for most of us when someone leaves our workplace or community of belonging is often to wonder what was wrong with us, or with the setting, that made the person want to leave. L'Arche reframes that impulse by emphasizing the way that the grief of both stayers and leavers can instead be understood as signaling the value of what was lived together. Since those who leave are also often sad at the prospect of going, this is easy to convey. Some former assistants keep up phone and e-mail contact with community members and even come back for extended visits from as far as Japan, Germany, and Brazil. Normalizing turnover and loss at a general level through stories and departure rituals is a key resource for people faced with the departure of a friend as discussed under "Reframe Loss."

Make Time for Reflection and Mentoring

Personal relationships are among the most compelling and anchoring elements of L'Arche, but this trait is true for many workplace or educational settings. While L'Arche does not list grief as one of the guaranteed thrills of community life, the culture of L'Arche helps people to recognize that an experience of grief is a sign of the depth of the relationship that will be—or has been—interrupted, lost, or in some way changed. The sting of grief becomes a passage to growth rather than something to be endured. While it in some ways seems a paradox, encouraging relationships that have meaning can engender grief.

When people have a sense that others have a genuine interest in them, they are encouraged to grow by taking the risk to get to know others and to be known. This does not mean that we should be expected to befriend everyone in our workplace or school. It may be valuable, however, to recognize the opportunities for personal interaction and engagement. This can happen in a broad variety of ways. Most of us can imagine how helpful it would be for a beginning doctor to be mentored by a seasoned, caring physician, yet that kind of experience may be more the exception than the rule. While most people work with others, many people feel alone in their work. Taking time to listen to people can seem like an enormous luxury, even an inefficiency, yet the most dynamic environments are where people feel that they are growing personally as well as professionally.

L'Arche is exceptionally intentional about giving its members time and space for reflection, mentoring, and personal accompaniment. These practices help to strengthen bonds in a community of belonging such that even in transitional communities, people can feel centered and supported. When people feel listened to and held by their colleagues, they are better able to deal with loss maturely. We outline two examples of practices inspired by this insight that could be applied in other settings.

Orientation Groups for New Employees or Students Bringing together small groups of newcomers is a personal way to impart information, give instructions, learn about an organizational culture, and encourage personal sharing among the group. This is an ideal juncture to name the common dynamic of people arriving in a new situation feeling some grief about the place that they have just left—and entering a role that was just vacated by someone else, someone whom others may miss. People are often surprised to hear about this ubiquitous "double grief" phenomenon in L'Arche and express relief that their sense of angst around these issues is not unique. "Naming the gremlin" helps to tame it.

One-to-One Mentoring Many L'Arche communities have recognized the value of pairing each new assistant with an experienced assistant for mentoring. This formal mentoring relationship continues for the first year of the assistant's experience. The mentor role is in addition to both the human resources director and the assistant's work supervisor who supervises the assistant in his or her duties. Mentors are not ready-made friends, but they are there to listen to the experience of the new assistant, to ask questions, and to challenge the new assistant when appropriate. Roughly once every month, mentors offer a willing ear and the experi-ence of someone who was once new to community life too. These mentoring links tend to be as interesting, and sometimes as challenging, for mentors as for the new assistant.

While the L'Arche mentoring model demands a significant commitment of time, other mentoring models are also possible. Retired professionals in many fields have often welcomed the chance to lend their expertise to people who are "learning the ropes." In some organizations, an important dimension of the human resource department is mentoring new recruits. Experiential education intern-ships in universities have also found creative ways for experienced workers to men-tor new students.

Reframe Loss: Emphasize the Gifts Already Present

One of the key themes in the previously mentioned reflection time is to encour-age all community members to live in the present and to become more attuned to and grateful for what is given here and now. This simple, but not easy, idea is par-ticularly powerful in a transitional community where people could easily fixate on potential future changes. In L'Arche, there is considerable time given to storytell-ing and celebration, both of which encourage people to attend to the present. All community members regularly engage in informal storytelling about everyday life, which draws attention to the simple pleasures of sharing time together. L'Arche also creates a positive emphasis on the present by prioritizing the celebration of milestones such as birthdays, anniversaries, spiritual and other holidays, and even people's departures.

The celebration of a departure can be a time for people to express gratitude and grief in relation to the person being fêted. It can also be a time to acknowl-edge something that person has done or made possible. Such acknowledgments are usually very moving both for the speaker and the listeners. In L'Arche, the traditional medium for these petitions is in the context of prayer, often at the con-clusion of a meal, but it is important to note that even people who do not consider themselves religious tend to find the ritual meaningful and affirming. These rituals help people to celebrate what has already been given rather than focusing on an unpredictable future.

Such rituals also help unearth the positive growth that lies beneath the inevi-table sorrow of loss. For instance, turnover is characterized as largely good for the work community since new assistants and people with disabilities offer renewed energy and they help keep longer-term people from getting stuck in static routines. Instead of seeing each new assistant as "yet another" person, they have to train and adjust, and the long-term assistants and core members try hard to treat each new person as a valued individual who is worth every bit of their effort. Here again, Vanier's point is relevant: There is an intrinsic opportunity for people with dis-abilities to grow in the continual cycle of new assistants. He writes that to be fully human is to transmit life and that to become complete we must discover a way for each of us to transmit life to others, for instance, through child rearing, leadership, or teaching (Cushing & Sumarah, 2008, pp. 33–34). Our society has not always recognized that people with intellectual disability can transmit life or even that they would feel that need. Vanier argues that many people with disabilities in the L'Arche homes are especially gifted in the art of welcome, perhaps because they know how hurtful it is to be rejected and undervalued. This cultural practice helps refocus people from what will be lost to celebrating what is given in the present.

Develop Rituals That Focus on Generativity

During a visit from Jean Vanier to a Canadian L'Arche community, members were invited to ask him questions. Camilla, an elderly, frail, long-time member with intellectual disabilities asked boldly, "Why do people go?" The grief that underlined Camilla's question was clear to all. Why do so many assistants leave just when things become consistent and familiar?

Vanier was unhesitating in his response: "I know what you are talking about, and it's very hard, but I also want to say that you have formed many assistants here; you have taught them how to live with others, how to create home, how to claim their humanity. This is incredibly important work, and I am sure that it is work you do well. When that assistant is ready, though, we need to let go. As hard as it is, we need to send them forth—to love the world."

Camilla had listened intently and replied, simply, "Thank you, Jean." Camilla's grief had been honored and given new meaning and purpose.

Celebration is a central element of L'Arche culture. People come and go in transitional communities in a predictable and relentless way. Amid the inevitable grief of loss, it is helpful to find some purpose and goodness and to create occasions to celebrate them. L'Arche began in the Roman Catholic milieu of France (Vanier, 1995). While the spiritual dimension of L'Arche is still vibrant, internationally L'Arche is nondenominational and nonsectarian. L'Arche welcomes people of all spiritual traditions as well as many without one. Still, prayerful practices are a constant, such as blessing the meal at the start and taking time for a thoughtful reflection after the meal. Various common L'Arche rituals that began as spiritual practices have evolved in ways that have broad application in other settings. For instance, the reflection after dinner may take up a passage from the Bible or an entirely secular song or story that has spiritual or moral import for the person sharing it with the group.

One generativity ritual is to thoughtfully "send forth" those who leave. The aim is to focus on how the person's experience of community will continue to bear fruit as he or she moves on. The cultural emphasis is to look on those who leave as ambassadors for L'Arche and people who, because of an intense lived experience, will in some way continue to herald the value of people with intellectual disabilities.

In the small setting of the L'Arche homes, there is a send-off dinner when someone leaves that concludes with the presentation of a card and a special gift— often something made in the community like a candle, a mug, or a T-shirt. This is followed by the ritual of passing the candle around the table. The candle is a symbol of the person's "light." Each person in turn holds the candle and shares something that he or she appreciates about the person departing. Often there are funny stories, or treasured memories, words of gratitude, or sometimes tears. The honoree is the last one to receive the candle. It is a chance to offer thanks, or stories. Sometimes the emotion is so immense that there are no words, only tears. The ritual ends with an upbeat song. This rite can easily be adapted for other settings like a special coffee break or a farewell lunch. The hallmark of this circle is its relative intimacy.

With a big group, going around the circle would take too long and become tedious. When there is a gesture of "sending forth" in larger L'Arche settings, the person leaving receives a blessing, often in a spiritual context or service. The person appointed to convey the blessing calls the person who is leaving to the center of the gathering. People who have lived or worked directly with that person are invited to gather around, sometimes placing a hand on the person's shoulder during the blessing and words of thanks. In a secular context, a friend or boss can accomplish something akin to this sending forth by offering thoughtful remarks or a toast at a celebratory occasion.

It is noteworthy that this ritual affirms those who are doing the "sending" as much as those who are being sent. In naming what has been generative, both parties are able to claim their vital role in the relationship. Recognizing our lack of control in the world and learning to let go can paradoxically create fertile ground for personal growth (see also Harris, 2010, p. 2). For instance, a change in the house team provides people the occasion to step back and reflect on what was good or difficult in the team relationships. The creative power of loss has the potential to transform our worldview depending on how we choose to interpret it.

CLOSING THOUGHTS: THE NECESSARY ILLUSION OF CONTINUITY

A central challenge of living in a transitional community is clearly how to strike a sustainable balance between the necessary welcoming of new people and crafting sustainable personal boundaries. As the spiritual writer Henri Nouwen (1996, pp. 59–61) eloquently wrote, opening oneself to new relationships enriches one's life and can contribute to one's maturation and development, painful endings notwithstanding. On the other hand, members of transitional communities also find they need reasonable limits on how much they invest in new relationships to avoid the perpetual emotional turmoil of turnover. As one consultant to L'Arche advised, "L'Arche is a community that grieves. Each member must choose to work at transcending this or it will take them down fast" (B. Herman, personal communication, 1993).

In spite of the complications, it is difficult, and probably not healthy anyway, to avoid relationships in primary care settings (Ungerson, 1999). Since turnover-related grief is intrinsic to transitional communities, people have had to develop ways to cope. One way is to allow themselves to imagine their community and relationships as more permanent than they are likely to be. Engaging in this illusion of continuity facilitates getting on with everyday life. Harris (2001, p. 1) echoes our need for such pretenses: "We attempt to function as if there is certainty and stability in everyday life...." "Positive illusions" are people's attempts to perceive a situation in positive ways even when they realize the negatives. Research has shown that these "are instrumental in enabling people to overcome adversity in their lives" and function effectively (Taylor, 1989, cited in Kearney, 2009). This kind of illusion can serve people well in any transitional community by discouraging them from becoming closed to new relationships just because some are transitory.

The insights and ritual practices of L'Arche offer the contours of how one transitional community has reshaped the inevitable grief caused by staff turnover into opportunities for personal and organizational development.

REFERENCES

Braddock, D., & Mitchell, D. (1992). *Residential services and developmental disabilities in the United States: A national survey of staff compensation, turnover, and related issues*. Chicago: American Association on Mental Retardation.

Brown, I., & Percy, M. (Eds.). (2002). *Developmental disabilities in Ontario*. Toronto: Ontario Association on Developmental Disabilities.

CBC Radio (2004). Jean Vanier (12). *100 great Canadians*. Accessed February 10, 2010 from http://www.cbc.ca/greatest/greatcanadians/

Cushing, P. (2003). *Shaping the moral imagination of caregivers: Disability, difference and inequality in L'Arche*. PhD dissertation, McMaster University, Hamilton, Ontario, Canada at L'Arche.

Cushing, P. (2007). Story-telling it like it is: How narratives teach. In V. Raoul et al (Eds.). *Unfitting stories: Narrative approaches to disease, disability, and trauma*. Waterloo, ON: Wilfrid Laurier University Press (pp. 159–169). Available at http://info.wlu.ca/~wwwpress/index.shtml

Cushing, P. (2010). Disability attitudes, cultural conditions and the moral imagination. In H. Reinders (Ed.), *What can we learn from the disabled? Responses to Jean Vanier from theology and the sciences* (pp. 71–88). Eerdmans Press (forthcoming), http://www.templeton.org/humble%5Fapproach%5Finitiative/Learning%5Ffrom%5Fthe%5FDisabled/

Cushing, P., & Lewis, T. (2002). Negotiating mutuality and agency in care-giving relationships with women with intellectual disabilities. *Hypatia Journal of Feminist Philosophy, 17,* 137–160.

Cushing, P., & Sumarah, J. (2008). *An anthropology of L'Arche: Being and becoming human*. Internal Report for J. Vanier, L'Arche Canada & USA.

Fujiura, G. T. (2005). Developmental disabilities. In G. Albrecht (Ed.), *Encyclopedia of disability* (Vol. 1, pp. 394–397). Thousand Oaks, CA: Sage.

Harvey, J. (1998). *Perspectives on loss: A sourcebook*. Philedelphia: Brunner/Mazel.

Humphrey, G. M., & Zimpfer, D. G. (1996). *Counselling for grief and bereavement*. London: Sage.

Kearney, P. (2009). *Lecture 10—Chronic grief (or is it periodic grief?)*. Lecture Notes for Course: Grief in a Family Context - HPER F460 at Indiana University. Accessed March 3, 2010 from http://74.125.93.132/search?q=cache:FDsHjRL91hEJ:www.indiana.edu/~famlygrf/units/chronic.html+olshansky+chronic+sorrow&cd=2&hl=en&ct=clnk&gl=ca

L'Arche Canada. (2009). *The story of L'Arche*. Accessed February 15, 2010 from http://www.larche.ca/en/jean_vanier/the_story_of_larche

Miller, E. D., & Omarzu, J. (1998). New directions in loss research. In J. H. Harvey (Ed.), *Perspectives on loss: A sourcebook* (pp. 3–20). Philedelphia: Brunner/Mazel.

Murray, J. (2005). A psychology of loss: A potentially integrating psychology for the future study of adverse life events. In A. Columbus (Ed.), *Advances in Pscychology Research*, 37 (pp. 15–46). Nova Science Publishers Inc.

Nouwen, H. (1996). *The inner voice of love*. Doubleday.

Raphael, B. (1984). *The anatomy of bereavement: A handbook for the caring professions*. London: Hutchinson.

Spink, K. (1990). *Jean Vanier and L'Arche: A communion of love*. New York: Crossroad.

Sumarah, J. (1988). L'Arche from a participant observer's perspective: The creation of universal community. *International Journal of Special Education, 3*, 185–196.

Taylor, S. E. (1989). *Positive illusions. Creative self-deception and the healthy mind*. New York: Basic Books.

Teel, C. (1991/2006). Chronic sorrow: Analysis of the concept. *Journal of Advanced Nursing, 16*(11), 1311–19. http://www3.interscience.wiley.com/journal/119355218/abstract

Thompson, S. C. (1985). Finding positive meaning in a stressful event and coping. *Basic and Applied Social Psychology, 6*(4), 279–295.

Trent, J. W. (1994). *Inventing the feeble mind: A history of mental retardation in the United States*. Berkeley: University of California Press.

Ungerson, C. (1999). Personal assistants and disabled people: An examination of a hybrid form of work and care. *Work, Employment & Society, 13*, 583–600.

Valente, J. (2006). An interview with Jean Vanier. In *Religion & Ethics Newsweekly*. May 26, Episode 939. Accessed November 15, 2009 from http://www.pbs.org/wnet/religionan-dethics/week939/interview3.html

Vanier, J. (1989). *Community and growth* (Trans. J. Vanier, 2nd rev. ed.). New York: Paulist Press.

Vanier, J. (1995). *An ark for the poor: The story of L'Arche*. Toronto: Novalis.

Vanier, J. (1998). *Becoming human*. Toronto: Anansi Press (CBC Massey Lectures).

Wolfensberger, W. (Ed.). (1973). *A selective overview of the work of Jean Vanier and the movement of L'Arche*. Toronto: National Institute on Mental Retardation (now the Roeher Institute).

Section *II*

Loss of Meaning or a Sense of Justice in the World

*I*n this section, we explore losses that affect our sense of justice or meaning in the world. As part of this section, consider how loss experiences are often framed—someone *deserved* what happened due to their actions, the events are part of *God's will*, or they make us stronger, or we have learned something significant. It is common for us to have certain assumptions about justice and meaning in the world based on the code of conduct that was shared with us in our formative years. Experiences that defy these assumptions and beliefs throw us into a place of imbalance and disequilibrium, and these authors acknowledge the turmoil that can occur after such experiences and also propose that these same experiences may also provide us with an opportunity to reevaluate what is most important in life as well.

In a chapter that explores the concept of existential suffering, Thomas Attig reviews that the mere awareness of our mortality and our vulnerability in the face of the many aspects of life that we cannot control leads us to a struggle to find meaning and value in our lives. In the face of significant losses and life events, we are no longer able to hold onto the perception that we are invulnerable and in control; this throws us into a place of distress that he describes as a unique form of suffering.

Similar to the previous chapter, Brad Hunter takes a philosophical approach to the losses that are inherent when an individual comes to terms with the multiple uncertainties in life. This chapter explores what happens when we have to let go of the ideas and beliefs that we have held about the constancy and predictability of the world, ourselves, and others—and somehow accommodate to the reality that we actually have very little control over events that carry profound significance for us.

Doug Harvey examines the difficulties encountered by individuals who lose a sense of belonging with their original faith community. Individuals may have come to a place of reckoning if their experiences can no longer be accommodated within the tenets of a specific faith community or belief system. Some of the losses associated with the loss of one's faith community may not be ideological, such as the description of the loss of a faith community when a church building closed its doors. However, for those who leave the faith community because of disillusionment or disenfranchisement, the pain can be intense and far reaching.

10

Existential Suffering
Anguish Over Our Human Condition

THOMAS ATTIG

INTRODUCTION

Existentialist philosophers distinguish between objective and subjective truths. Objective truths are abstract, general, and statistical truths about the way things are in the world and in broad populations of human beings. Subjective truths are about the particular ways individuals experience the world and life in the human condition. To grasp the distinction in an elementary way, you can write out the following simple, valid arguments. Both are valid in the strict sense that their premises are true, and the truth of their conclusions follows logically from the truth of the premises.

The first argument:

> All humans die.
> Socrates is human.
> Therefore, Socrates dies.

The second argument:

> All humans die.
> (Fill in your name) is human.
> Therefore, (fill in your name) dies.

For most everyone who does this simple exercise, there is a noticeable difference, however slight, in writing out the second argument. That difference is the experiential difference between the objective truth of the conclusion of the first argument and the subjective truth of the conclusion of the second. In the first argument, the truth of human mortality that applies to everyone is applied to someone else, namely, Socrates. But in the second, the truth of human mortality is brought home to you. You are reminded of the mortality that is part of what makes you who and what you are. You may even shudder as you spell out the conclusion.

Similarly, in the early part of the film *Shadowlands* (Attenborough & Eastman, 1993), C. S. Lewis is seen as the internationally known author and speaker on Christian theology, love, and suffering that he was. He knows the literature on the subjects, including many objective truths about Christian beliefs about the place of human life in the greater scheme of things and the powers of love and suffering to shape human lives. But he lives a sheltered life in his Oxford home, in the classroom, and on the lecture circuit, never experiencing anything that tests his faith and holding himself at a safe distance from both love and suffering in his own life. He meets American poet Joy Gresham and befriends her. When she falls ill with cancer, he realizes he loves her, and they marry in a Christian ceremony. For the first time since his mother died when he was a child, Lewis opens himself to both love and suffering. Joy lives for some time in remission, and Lewis comes to know the subjective truths of the power of love. When eventually Joy dies, Lewis comes to know the subjective truths of the power of suffering. Both love and suffering permeate the depths of his being and change Lewis irrevocably. In his grief journal, *A Grief Observed* (Lewis, 1976), Lewis records his deep questioning of Christian beliefs he had taken for granted and the meaning of his life in the aftermath of loss. He writes passionately of his discovery of the subjective truth of his religious beliefs about the place of love and suffering in human life and about his personal relationship with God.

We suffer existentially when (1) we meet subjectively with challenging objective truths about life in the human condition and (2) we anguish about whether we are up to the challenges the truths present. Among the most challenging truths are these: We have no choice about most, and precious little choice about the rest, of the circumstances of and events in our lives. We are embodied and mortal. We are small and insignificant. We are buffeted by unwelcome change. We are vulnerable. We are imperfect. We are uncertain, even about the very meaning of our lives.

We may define existential suffering more precisely as the distress and anguish we experience when limitation, change, loss, brokenness, and sorrow lead us to question our very existence, the value and meaning of our lives: "Why me? Why this suffering? What does this suffering mean for who I am and can or cannot yet become? Why am I living? What is the meaning of my life? Is it worth continuing to live? Can I live meaningfully with or beyond this suffering? Do I have what it takes within me to endure or overcome it? Will the world support or overwhelm me?"

OCCASIONS FOR EXISTENTIAL SUFFERING

The most obvious circumstances within which we may suffer existentially are those in which we encounter our *mortality*. Our lives may be immediately threatened by illness or accident. Criminals, gangs, armed forces, or oppressive regimes may menace us. Less immediately, we may feel our mortality in our bones in midlife crises. Or we may be reminded of it as we witness the dying and death of a loved one. Fears of death or being overwhelmed or annihilated by forces larger than we are may grip us. Encounters with mortality remind us of how attached we are to our bodies, how small and vulnerable we are, and how short our time on Earth is. We may anguish over the limited possibilities for living meaningfully in the time that remains. In serious life review, we may doubt whether we have lived a meaningful life. We may fear that we will not be remembered but instead disappear into oblivion.

Loss of a loved one through death and the grief that follows often lead to existential suffering. Bereavement penetrates to the core of our being. We realize how our ties with others make us who we are. When family members, life companions, or friends die, it can be as if we have lost a part of ourselves. Our lives can never be just as they were when those we grieve lived. We have lost their physical presence and all that it meant to us. In the grip of intense suffering, it can seem as if we do not merely *have* sorrow but that we *are* our sorrow and nothing more. We may wonder who we are or may become now that they are gone. We realize how vulnerable we are in caring about and loving others. We may doubt we can ever care or love as deeply again. We may fear that our life has lost its meaning.

We may suffer existentially in *loss of physical abilities* due to life-limiting injury, chronic illness, blindness, deafness, infertility, amputation, or paralysis. Profound changes in our bodies and our experiences of them carry broad-ranging implications for all aspects of our lives. Physical disabilities shatter our sense of invulnerability as we learn how physical health determines so much of what is possible in life. They intrude insistently as we both have, and are had by, them. In and through our bodies we inhabit the world, experience the things and places around us, pursue interests in activities and projects, express ourselves, engage with others, and orient ourselves in space and time. When our bodily functioning is severely compromised, taken-for-granted understandings of who we are and may become are undermined. We may no longer recognize ourselves in the mirror, may feel alienated from our bodies, and may doubt we are still the persons we once were.

We may suffer existentially in the throes of *mental illness or addiction*. We may be painfully aware of the limits of our control over the faculties that enable us to function in everyday life, contribute to others, and thrive in ways of living we find meaningful. We may feel profoundly not ourselves, at the mercy of internal forces that prevent us from being who we want to be. We may be all too aware that expressions and behaviors we cannot control alienate us from others, cost us cherished ties with those we love, and even drive away social support we desperately need. One of the most common forms of mental illness, clinical depression, is the leading cause of suicide, a refusal to remain in life as we know it. If we sense that we are falling into dementia, we may fear that we will one day no longer be the persons we have always thought ourselves to be and that we will continue to live without meaning.

Loss or change in relationships with others, through divorce, loss of child custody, alienation from parents or children, the ending of friendships, or tragedies in their lives that profoundly affect our access to their care and love (e.g., birth anomalies, mental illness, brain injury, or dementia) can also precipitate existential suffering. We may feel helpless in the face of choices or actions by others, or events in their lives, that we cannot control. When we lose relationships, we may sense that our life has lost its meaning or purpose if we can no longer give or receive care and love in ties with those who have mattered most to us. We may fear that we do not have what it takes to care or love again or to sustain meaningful ties with others. We may hold ourselves responsible for troubles and failures in relationships and doubt that we are worthy of love or care. When we cannot give and receive in ways we had anticipated we could, or had come to take for granted, we may fear that we lack the capacities to endure the chronic sorrow of distance from them and to witness their suffering and to continue to care and love when, tragically, they can give so little in return.

We may suffer existentially as we experience *loss of place in our physical and social surroundings* resulting from such things as natural disaster or fire, unemployment, financial calamity, forced relocation, or homelessness. We may feel helpless in the face of events beyond our control. We may feel profoundly vulnerable without the security and safety that home and work provided. We may doubt our abilities to be ourselves when deprived of familiar surroundings or the wherewithal to provide for our loved ones or ourselves. We may wonder if we have what it takes within ourselves to ever feel at home again in our physical and social surroundings. We may doubt there is a place where we belong in the world.

We may suffer existentially in *meetings with our own imperfection and fallibility*. We may be profoundly disappointed in our failures to live up to our own or others' expectations. We may fail to match our good intentions with appropriate actions. We may become caught up in scandal. We may dishonor our families or communities. We may fail to meet obligations, keep promises, follow through on commitments, or maintain covenants. We may neglect, threaten, abuse, or harm others. We may even commit crimes and experience imprisonment or other punishment. In all of these experiences we come short of being the persons we hope to be or become. We may doubt our abilities to change and reform our ways. We may feel unworthy of the care and love of others or God.

EXISTENTIAL SUFFERING, INTEGRITY, AND DIGNITY

All of the previously described experiences of existential suffering shatter whatever ego illusions we may harbor. They threaten or undermine the integrity that makes us who we are. And they challenge our dignity and self-respect. Encounters with mortality, losses of loved ones, losses of physical abilities, mental illness or addiction, losses or changes in relationships with others, losses of place in our physical and social surroundings, and meetings with our own imperfection or moral fallibility remind us of subjective truths about life in the human condition. Experiences of finiteness and extraordinary changes in our life circumstances or within ourselves challenge us to relearn our ways of being, acting, and becoming in the worlds of our experience. These experiences challenge us to transform our life patterns, enter unanticipated next chapters of our life stories, and find new places, or play new parts, in connections with things larger than we are—family, community, the great scheme of things, or higher powers. We suffer as we realize how daunting these challenges are, as we doubt our own abilities to bear or overcome adversity or sorrow, and as we fear there may be no hopeful paths to living meaningfully beyond the brokenness in our lives or the worst of our sorrow.

Our ego's illusions are shattered when we come face to face with the demanding realities of life in the human condition. We cannot control or manage these constants in life as if they were everyday problems that are easily fixed. We cannot change fundamental dimensions of life in the human condition; we can change only the ways we live within them and ourselves in response to them. We are not invulnerable. Ego flight-or-fight defenses cannot enable us to avoid or fend off indefinitely encounters with these realities. We are not separate, self-contained beings autonomously navigating on our own terms through a life untouched by these constant life companions. Rather, they define the limits of our choice. When illusions of control, invulnerability, and separateness fall away, we realize the full extent of what finite life demands of us.

In our daily lives we weave together interests, desires, cares, and loves in and with things, places, experiences, activities, and others into an integrated web of life. Experiences that lead to existential suffering shatter the integrity of our daily life patterns. We cannot live just as we had before. We may no longer be able to find meaning in experiences and activities as we had previously. Our experiences may affect our access to or compromise our ways of living with favorite things, places, nature, family members, friends, and community. We may be less able, or unable altogether, to contribute through work or nurturing others. What once required little effort may now be far more difficult or even beyond our reach. This shattering of our daily life pattern threatens or undermines whatever self-confidence, self-worth, meaning, and identity we may have found in former ways of living. Reshaping daily life and finding new integrity and meaning within it can be daunting, even with the able assistance of others.

Across time, from our past, through present living, and into the future, our courage, hopes, and faith enable us to change, grow, and come to terms with adversity and continually reweave the web of our life into a life story with integrity and meaning unlike any other. Occasions that give rise to existential suffering often change the content and trajectory of our life stories. The next and remaining chapters of our lives cannot be just as we had anticipated or hoped they would be. Our life stories as wholes will be inevitably different. Unexpected life events and their consequences may undercut the sense of who we are and can become and the meanings that are grounded in the unfolding of our life stories. Redirecting the courses of our lives and finding new integrity and meaning in them can also be daunting.

As we weave and reweave the webs of our lives, we find grounding and meaning in connections with, or as parts of, something larger than ourselves, in family, community, nature, or the greater scheme of things, or higher powers (however we may understand them). Events and changes that give rise to existential suffering often threaten or break such connections. We may be taken away from life contexts where we have felt at home, have accepted roles and responsibilities, have been nourished, and have contributed significantly. We may feel alienated, compromised in our abilities to still do our part, or unworthy of inclusion within these contexts. We may find it hard to commune with nature. We may feel distant from the ground of our being or abandoned by higher powers or may lose our sense of spiritual place in the great scheme of things. We may come to doubt the safety and security of the world, the fairness of it all, whether it is worth going on day to day, and whether we still belong anywhere. We may feel dislodged from the familiar and afraid of the unknown.

One fairly common understanding of dignity refers to matters of pride or style in a relatively narrow sense. Dignity in this sense is a matter of our maintaining appearances or reputation, carrying things off well, without embarrassment, even with a kind of flair. However, in a deeper and broader sense of the term, dignity refers to everything about us that makes us worthy of respect, including self-respect. Our dignity resides in part in our autonomy—our capacities to decide for ourselves, to set our own life course, to live on our own terms. Our dignity also resides in the full range of our unique capacities to live meaningfully and thrive, not only in our autonomy. Think of Viktor Frankl's (1984) ideas of finding meaning in achievement values (making contributions great and small), in experiential values (especially in connections with others and something larger than ourselves), and even in and through suffering. Our dignity also resides in our capacities to live with integrity in our daily life patterns, in the unfolding of our life stories, and in connections with larger wholes and higher powers; to maintain or achieve wholeness even in extreme life circumstances; to remain true to our deepest selves; and to resist temptation and do the right thing.

When the previously described occasions give rise to existential suffering, we may sense that our dignity in these senses is threatened or even lost. We may doubt that we are worthy of respect, from others, higher powers, or ourselves. But though our illusions may be shattered, our life patterns unraveled, our life stories undone, and our connections with wholes larger than ourselves threatened or compromised, all is not lost. We can overcome existential suffering when we draw upon what is not broken within us: the breath of life itself, our will to live, and our drives to find meaning in caring and loving connection and in change. These are always worthy of respect and can enable us to live with deep integrity, however difficult it may be to access them when we are caught up in existential suffering. We can also draw on what is not broken in family, community, nature, the great web of life, and the grace of the universe that provide life support from birth until death.

ALTERNATIVE APPROACHES TO EXISTENTIAL SUFFERING

Acknowledging the subjective truths of our human finiteness and fragility is a daunting task. We realize that all beginnings have endings, that all attachments bring eventual separations, and that all commitments come only with attendant risks. Stoics find these human limitations to be horrifying; resolve to begin little, minimize attachment, and systematically avoid commitment; and recommend detachment from life as a means to minimizing existential suffering and attaining

peace of mind. Existentialists accept the finiteness and fragility of human existence, embrace the limited opportunities for meaning and fulfillment that life
affords, and accept existential suffering as the price of realizing the values that
beginnings, attachments, and commitments can bring. The great faith traditions
acknowledge the possibility of existential suffering and provide beliefs and practices to enable adherents to minimize such suffering and find meaning and value
in living in the human condition.

REFERENCES

Attenborough, R., & Eastman, B. (Producers), & Attenborough, R. (Director). (1993).
    Shadowlands (motion picture). United States: Savoy Pictures.
Frankl, V. (1984). *Man's search for meaning.* New York: Simon & Schuster.
Lewis, C.S. (1976). *A grief observed.* New York: Bantam Books.

11

Relinquishment of Certainty
A Step Beyond Terror Management

BRAD HUNTER

> To let go is to lose your foothold temporarily. Not to let go is to lose your foothold forever.
>
> **Søren Kierkegaard**

> The difficulty is to realize the groundlessness of our believing.
>
> **Ludwig Wittgenstein**

INTRODUCTION

Terror management theory is derived from some of Ernest Becker's basic ideas proposed in his book *The Denial of Death* (1973). In brief, Becker states that all of our activities, our accomplishments, our hopes and dreams, our social and political institutions, and even the construct of the self act as buffers and insulation against the cold reality of constant change, uncertainty, and unreliability in daily life and the one certainty of death. If we look closely enough behind the protective veil of our experience, it is hard to argue with this conclusion. Yet can this very platform be the springboard for a different perspective altogether? Is there a way to swim upstream against the current of denial that might lead to another way of managing the terror, which indeed might lead to a path that deconstructs the terror itself?

What happens if we turn toward the very elements of death and loss that seem to frighten us most and ask their permission for us to look them in the eye, with a humble, gentle attention, supported by the right balance of compassion and courage?

What we first discover is that there is no monolithic, homogenous entity called *death* or *loss*. There are many aspects to this moment when presence evolves into absence, and there are several key sources for our anxiety. In workshops over the past few years, I have asked participants the question, "What is it that we are really afraid of when it comes to the constancy of change and, ultimately, dying and death?" Four major fears have emerged: pain and suffering, the unknown, loss of control, and loss of self/other. I humbly ask permission to investigate each of these fears in turn.

PAIN AND SUFFERING

Try this simple experiment. Locate a place of discomfort in your body right at this moment. (If you cannot find such a place, firmly but gently pinch one hand with the other.) Focus your attention directly into the raw sensations, and investigate and name different elements, such as pressure, heat, tingling, throbbing, and tightened. Note how the pain itself is not a fixed and solid reality, but it too is constantly changing. Now shift your attention from being narrowly focused on the discomfort to a more global awareness of the entire body. Scan the body for an area that is experiencing pleasurable, or at least neutral, sensations. Allow your attention to gather and focus into this area. How does that change your experience of discomfort? You can experiment further and try to direct thoughts and feelings of compassion into the area experienced as pain. You can try to "hold" the experience in wider fields of spacious awareness. Reflect on how habitually we shift away from any experience of discomfort and what this might mean in terms of our psychological and spiritual development—how quickly we move into avoidance or denial when difficult life situations arise.

Our conditioning, and certainly our marketplace, tells us to avoid or extinguish any discomfort at all costs. However, by changing our relationship to pain, we can modify our experience of it. We can relearn how resistance and denial tends to intensify the feelings of distress and pain, whereas compassionate acceptance can have the reverse effect.

THE UNKNOWN

If we carefully consider what it is that can be known with clarity and certainty, our collective body of knowledge shrivels remarkably. What piece of knowledge is not based on other accepted theories, conjectures, hypotheses, and assumptions? If we direct our attention to the primal knowing of our direct experience, we discover that even our cognition of moment-to-moment events arises after the raw experience has passed. This whole process happens in a nanosecond of course, but once again this points out how we are almost always out of sync with the direct unfolding of our lives. If we can focus our attention on this field of raw sensory and mental experience we find a vast and unfathomable universe within our own body and mind. But even this arena of direct knowing, unmediated by categories of intellection, is an incomprehensible mystery.

To paraphrase Fyodor Dostoevsky, we have the unfathomable and incomprehensible reality within reach, yet we distract ourselves with a "toy called God."

When faced with the great mysteries of existence before us, our default position is to go to abstract reasoning, to make a toy out of the absolute, or, worse, a belief. This is not to say that our beliefs cannot be helpful, useful, and inspiring, but only as long as we do not believe them too strongly. If we cling tenaciously to some fixed belief, we may not be able to see a greater truth when it passes before us, not to mention that there has likely been more human slaughter over conflicts in beliefs than there has been over land, resources, wealth, and power.

We are so disconnected from the mystery of being (which is closer than our own breath) that we either crave satiation of the senses or we comb the world over looking for traces of the divine or the supramundane: the face of a saint in a taco, a crucifix in the fur on a calf's forehead, a Tarot reading, or perhaps Lady Gaga played backward. Disconnected and disembodied in this way we become a James Joyce character: "He lived a short distance from his body, regarding his own acts with doubtful side glances" (p. 108).

CONTROL

By turning our attention again to our most intimate and immediate sensory and mental experience, we can ask the same questions about control. How much control do we really have over the things and the events in our lives? I cannot know or control the next thought that is going to arise in the mind or the next sensation or feeling that is going to arise in the body. If I have little or no control over even these most "personal" things, how and why do I expect to be able to control events far beyond the range of my influence and direct awareness? I have some limited control over how I respond to the things that present themselves to awareness and the events that unfold before me, but even for these responses to be anything more than automatic reactions requires the long and hard work of deconditioning my habitual patterns of reactivity.

LOSS OF SELF AND OTHER

What exactly is this "self" we are afraid of losing? If it is *just the body*, then we need to ask ourselves when this body belonged to us to begin with?

We have already "lost" our infant body and our adolescent body and the body of cells that ceased to be 7 years ago. And what about that person we were a week ago last Thursday at 2 p.m., with all of those thoughts, sensations, shifting moods, and feelings—where is that exact "person" now? If we closely examine this fear of loss of self, it entails more than just the fear of the body's disappearance; there is a deeper fear of existential annihilation—the void of a me-less universe. At the same time, though, none of us has ever been able to produce this "me," to point to it, or to demonstrate its existence in the first place. Yet who doubts his or her own presence?

To paraphrase a friend and teacher, we cannot hold onto anything, even as we hold it. It is our mistaken perception, our *delusion* in spiritual terms, that selves and others are fixed and permanent entities that creates so many of our problems and the lion's share of our suffering. We cling to what cannot even be grasped. We chase after constant *becomings* as if they were permanent beings who could provide us with ultimate satisfaction. But both self and other are conditioned processes in a state of constant change. Nothing is even itself for more than an instant. All nouns are verbs.

A REFUGE IN THE ABYSS

I allow the wave to fold me over into the shore. Gaining a kneeling balance in the shallow salt surf, I cup my hands and scoop up a double handful of drenched sand, countless grains of an infinite variety of colors, each grain a world unto itself inviting investigation and exploration. But before my eyes can blink away some salt spray, the next wave has washed over and through, leaving my hands wet and empty.

Each instant of experience is similar to this, yet we relate to the world through the moment-to-moment memories of the conceptualized traces of experience, even though these traces themselves are less substantial than the fleeting, ever-changing phenomena before us. In this life journey, memory itself may one day be washed away completely in the turbulent river of aging (and what happens at the moment of death and beyond is pure speculation).

Where is there constancy and reliability? Where can I find certainty and hope? Perhaps my hopelessness is not yet complete. There remains a longing to somehow get it all right. To adjust aspects of personality and the various elements of "my life" so that *then* I might be truly happy. However, can ultimate happiness and unshakable certainty ever be found in a world of compounded things, where each entity depends on incalculable causes and conditions for its own very existence?

So we search for beauty and meaning. We create the most wondrous arrangement of flowers whose beauty is so striking that it is almost painful. Then we are unexpectedly called away for a few days, and on our return what greets us? Even with a vase full of water we might be lucky to get the entire mass of smelly mush to the compost heap without much of it falling on the carpet. And the most handsome, gorgeous person we can imagine—what if the next breath just does not come? Instantly, there is a radical change. Within minutes there is evidence of stiffening and the beginning of decay. What about days later?

This is not just an optional, one-sided way of looking at life. It is the reality that we face moment to moment—if we are willing to *look*. If we happen to feel compelled to look beyond the appearance of certainty, solidity, and permanence, however, where does that place us in a world and culture where the pursuit of happiness is embedded in the psyche and, in the wealthiest and most powerful Western nation, in its very constitution? As long as the sights of this pursuit are aimed at material phenomena, we are condemned to a life, not of happiness but rather of frustration, disappointment, unreliability, unremitting grief—in a word, a life of *suffering*.

In this insatiable orientation of our materialism, how much would be enough? How long do we really want to live? How much money (sex, power, recognition, entertainment, distraction, pleasure) would be enough to provide an unconditional and lasting satisfaction? Is it not insane to even ask unpredictable phenomena, which in turn are conditioned by other unpredictable phenomena and subject to constant change and ultimate decay, to provide us with a reliable and permanent happiness, whether this "phenomenon" is a presidency, a partner, or a Porsche? Yet this is precisely what we do and how most of us live our lives. We lean with hope toward the promise of the next experience, racing, often franticly, from one pleasure or distraction to the next, addicts all. The promise itself is at best an illusion, a lie at worst.

At first glance, it might appear that turning our gaze toward the very sources of death anxiety opens a road leading to crushing depression, despair, and angst. To be sure, the choice to step forward to the edge of the abyss and to behold without blinking will be followed by more than one dark night of the soul and many smaller deaths of hopes, cherished concepts, and clinging attachments. As Rumi observed, though, "What have I ever lost by dying?" (p. xvii).

Loosening our death grip (pun intended) on our conceptually constructed reality is frightening at first. We might feel that the earth and sky are both in constant motion and that "the center does not hold." But this is akin to that hypnogogic state where we are unsure if the dream world or waking world is the Real. To begin to glimpse reality as it *actually is* requires rousing ourselves from the dream of permanence, fixity, and reliability of phenomena. This is a phase of disenchantment, of awakening from the spell cast by our own conditioning, confusion, and constricted worldview.

This journey results in permanent despair only if we do not go far enough and deep enough, if we continue to cling to the pretty lights of the passing show, knowing that it will not bring lasting peace yet grasping after the ephemeral twinkling nonetheless. With every movement of letting go, there is a little flavor of release and freedom. A new "ground" begins to rise up and meet our every step, a ground radiant with an eternal, deathless luminosity that we do not even have to name. Over the centuries, sages and seers have pointed to this formless ground beyond the material realm with a wide variety of signage, such as the soul, God, the Tao, true nature, mind, original consciousness. At the same time, some of these luminaries have simply maintained a thundering silence. To name is to define; to define is to make finite.

So here we sit together in the roaring surf, hands wet and empty, but there remains this *presence*, this *awareness*, that is greater than any definition of you and I, that suggests a peace and stillness before the waves arise or fall away, and just a hint that this absolute presence itself might not be subject to birth and death after all. We slowly learn to let go of "I" and come to know directly that we could not lose the "am" even if we wanted to.

> Out beyond all ideas of right and wrong
> There is a realm of luminous consciousness—
> I'll meet you there.
>
> Rumi

REFERENCE

Becker, E. (1973). *The denial of death.* New York: Free Press.
Bly, R. (1992). *What have I ever lost by dying?* New York: Viking Press.
Joyce, J. (1961). *Dubliners.* New York: Viking Press.

12

Wrestling With the Loss of One's Faith Community

DOUG HARVEY

Thank God for the Church. It is only by faith, the blessed power of God's Holy
Spirit, and the Christian Family that one moves on from the loss of someone
so special as my Mom. God is good. I'll miss you, Mom. Thanks for raising me
in the church.

Rev. David Wilson Rogers

*T*his was posted on Facebook by a colleague only weeks after his mother had
died. Based on that statement and other e-mails we shared, it was clear
that the congregation he served, and his congregation back home, played
important roles in his overcoming this critical loss. Folk like David often find the
church to be a place of solace and a true family that provides nurture and support
throughout one's faith journey but especially in times of great need. At times of
loss, be they by death or otherwise, the faith community often becomes that place
or instrument used to face, deal with, and reconcile those losses. Thus, to lose one's
faith community can be an existential loss that compromises and complicates grief
responses in other areas.

What happens then when individuals lose that faith community or affiliation
with a faith group that has been so instrumental in their social or faith development? To answer this question, consider the following stories from case studies. The setting is a long-term care facility, and I am the hospice chaplain on a
team responsible for introducing ourselves to a new patient. We were a close team
and worked diligently to make introductions together as a team with the patient
and family. As we approached the nursing station, we were told that the patient
declined chaplain services and that it would be best if I not even enter the room.
For chaplain services to be declined was not unheard of; however, suggesting that
we not even offer an introduction was a bit unusual. The nurse shared with us that

the patient was very angry about church-related business and that if a priest came anywhere near her she became so angry that it would take well into the next day to get her physically relaxed. The team social worker said she would find out what was going on.

Nursing home charts do not usually include a spiritual history or pastoral counseling consult notes. You can learn many things about a patient from a medical chart yet not much at all about their spiritual development and pastoral care needs. To learn this part of a patient's history takes a bit of investigative work. This particular patient had been at this facility for many years, and everyone on staff was well aware of her angst with the church. Without a spiritual care person on staff, most accepted her denial of spiritual care and steered clear of her anger. This was not in my philosophy of care as a hospice chaplain. If her anger could be addressed through reconciliation with the church, she would not die angry, and this was my hope for her.

Digging through her social history, talking with the nursing staff, learning from my team, and from conversations with the patient's son, I began to understand the source of her anger. The patient had lost connection with her church 40 years earlier and had been grieving that loss ever since. The details are not so necessary here, yet suffice it to say this existential loss created years of pain and unresolved grief. In short, a disagreement between her and her priest regarding the placement of her son in the education program affiliated with the church left her with an understanding that the priest's directive to her was that she could no longer be a part of that parish. The patient believed she had been excommunicated from the church. This was incredibly painful for her, and now with great angst she found herself nearing death in a broken relationship with God because she did not have a relationship with her church. She was grieving that loss still, and in light of her anticipatory grief related to her own death the experience was particularly taxing on her both physically and spiritually.

In another situation, I had a pastoral visit with a congregational member, Mrs. Wilson. I enjoyed great conversation and tea as we sat at a small table overlooking her back patio and the beautiful rolling hills of Kentucky covered with a healthy crop of tobacco. I listened to her stories of years gone by and influential people in her life. As she reminisced, it became increasingly clear that she was grieving the closing of her lifelong church. The church had closed its doors some 7 years earlier after many years of financial struggling and low attendance, and the few members had joined in the life of a sister congregation in town.

Mrs. Wilson remembered children growing up, baptisms, intimate counseling moments with several of the pastors, weddings, and even funerals in her beloved church. She also spoke of the incredible support of that faith family in times of trial and heartache in her own life. In addition, she so terribly missed being able to be a part of supporting others as a shared responsibility in their times of need. While she tried to visit and participate in the life of other congregations, she did not feel a "connection" to those places or people. She had lost not only a sacred place but also some very close relationships. This center of healing and consolation for her was now gone, and she was not able to replace that. "My purpose has been shaken," she said, and "I don't know how to handle this loss."

The encounter with Mrs. Wilson reminded me of a close friend experiencing a similar sense of loss when he and his family faced the closing of a historical Lutheran church in rural Kentucky. This church had been established by German immigrants generations ago and held within its memories were the hopes and dreams of grandparents and great-grandparents in a new world as well as the struggles and pains of that new world. In my friend's case, the building and adjacent cemetery are kept safe as a historical site. He and I made several visits to the small church building, and we walked through the cemetery as he spoke about his connection to that place and to the larger church. "This place is an incredible part of my faith development. Staying connected here helps me to stay connected to the church at large." My friend was concerned that since the church was no longer functional as a community he would risk his relationship with the larger church.

While it is not uncommon for people to be faced with such losses, the loss of a faith community that has been foundational in one's spiritual and social development is not commonly addressed. It seems to be understood that such a loss is commonplace enough that it could be dealt with in the same manner as changing jobs or moving from one apartment to another. Assuming that this should not be a "big deal," it is a loss that is held closely. While there may be attachment that is acknowledged, it is often considered superficial, so the ensuing grief is expected to be short-lived. This is not always the situation individuals face when losing their faith community.

In the case of the dying nursing home patient, she had lost a place for the faith development of her son; thus, the loss had an impact on not only her life but also the life of another. She also lost the ability to believe and trust in the very institution that taught her how to believe and trust. That loss had great influence on her mental and spiritual health, personal relationships, and even self-identity. The priest from that experience was no longer around. Yet with the help of the current priest at the parish for the nursing home and the local bishop, we were able to piece together the story and to offer a request for forgiveness on behalf of the church and begin the process of reconciliation for this patient. She then began to open up to an experience of relief as the priest and I were invited to share in her life. In her dying days she was able to feel joy as she let go of her grief and the guilt, shame, and the spiritual pain plaguing her all those years.

David and Mrs. Wilson both lost a community to which to return when the trials of life and other losses confronted them. Without that foundation, a place for their faith to be grounded, the fear was that they would not be able to appropriately deal with faith-challenging situations (and grief itself can often be such a challenge).

Reviewing Worden's (2009) determinants of grief, one can see how the various aspects of attachment demonstrate the power of grief at the loss of a faith community. His work recognizes the variables in manifestations that affect grief at the loss of a loved one. However, in focusing on grief due to the loss of a faith community, considering both the corporate and individual relationships and determinants such as the nature of attachment, mode of death (loss), and the historical experiences of loss may be essential when counseling.

Other instances of the loss of a faith community or faith foundations might include when someone is ostracized (by the community or self-imposed) because of life experiences that differ from the dominate doctrine such as of divorce, admittance of different sexual preferences (coming out of the closet), interreligious or interracial marriages, or change in understanding of doctrine and faith (dissatisfaction or disillusionment).

When assisting persons who are grieving the loss of a faith community, it is critical to recognize that a move toward apostasy (completely severed ties) may result in wrestling with the loss of their doctrinal or foundational grounding, leading to individuals being identified as outsiders. This move may result in feelings of being ostracized or excommunicated (self-imposed or otherwise), as with the nursing home patient mentioned earlier (Brinkerhoff & Burke, 1980). Such an experience can lead to delayed or suppressed grief that might later be exposed in an additional grief event due to the inadequate addressing of this as a true loss (Worden, 2009).

With the rug pulled out from under them now and a lack of a faith foundation or the complete disruption of their *Gemeinschaft* that grew out of a theological doctrine, the grieving person is now set up for complicated grief reactions with future loss experiences. This compromised ability to respond to other losses can be interrupted by counselors and responders who recognize the loss of one's faith community to be as devastating as any other significant loss. In addition, it has been shown that even after people are disconnected from a faith community and their practices they remain connected with the associated god figure in their consciousness (Jacobs, 1987). We then might journey alongside the grieving person in the following ways:

- By helping them to explore new rituals to find meaning in the midst of this loss
- By honoring their spiritual grounding beyond their past religiosity
- By focusing on hearing what the loss has been like, appreciating the faith wrestling
- By avoiding giving explanations or answers
- By validating this loss as significant and helping to explore the varied affects of this loss in their daily living

In his book *Stages of Faith*, James Fowler (1981) speaks of faith as a verb that indicates "an active mode of being and committing, a way of moving into and giving shape to our experiences of life" (p. 16). He also demonstrates that faith is always relational; it is not independent of another. With this in mind, assisting those grieving such a loss as a faith community or faith in their religious doctrines might include many of the traditional approaches to grief counseling and grief therapy while recognizing the unique circumstances and associated losses.

In an era such as ours where disillusionment and dissatisfaction with the church and other faith communities is on the rise and people are defecting from such communities, both emotionally and socially, there is much to learn about how to best assist them with the associated grief from this loss. There are also the experiences of explicit and subtle polarization of peoples today as religious groups attempt to redefine themselves or return to orthodoxy. We read about such experiences in

novels and biographies more and more often. The experiences are real and devastating and have implications in how one reacts to future losses. Mental health
professionals, pastoral counselors, grief counselors, end-of-life counselors, and
chaplains today might take notice of this significant loss, record their approaches
to care, and offer further thoughts and suggestions to the thanatology community
through more professional research and writing in this area.

REFERENCES

Brinkerhoff, M. B., & Burke, K. L. (1980). Disaffiliation: Some notes on "falling from the
    faith." *Sociological Analysis, 41,* 41-54.
Fowler, J. W. (1981). *Stages of faith: The psychology of human development and the quest
    for meaning.* San Francisco: Harper.
Jacobs, J. (1987). Deconversion from religious movements: An analysis of charismatic
    bonding and spiritual commitment. *Journal for the Scientific Study of Religion, 26,*
    294–308.
Worden, J. W. (2009). *Grief counseling and grief therapy: A handbook for the mental health
    practitioner* (4th ed.). New York: Springer.

Section III

Loss of the View of Self as Worthy or Valuable

*I*n this section, we look at examples of losses that have an impact on how we view ourselves. Many of the examples in this section demonstrate how views of one's self can be radically altered by changes in life circumstances and geographical displacement and by changes due to aging or health issues. Many of these experiences cause us to pause and question who we now are or to doubt our previously held ideas of how our basic worth and value may have been defined.

Jeffrey Kauffman provides a rich exploration through the presentation of a case study of the loss of self that is experienced in an ongoing manner as a result of the absence of his client's mother's ability to connect with her in a meaningful way as a child. In his description of the client's case study, he describes this type of loss as insidious—emotional neglect of a parent is often invisible to others and hidden from awareness but may have repercussions into adulthood as the individual with this type of childhood experiences a sense of self that is deeply wounded and lost.

Wanda Sawicki addresses losses that occur on immigrating to a new country. Through the voices of immigrants, she explores the layers of losses that include the loss of familiar countryside, language, culture, and identity. Although adaptation to a new country occurs, the ongoing sense of the loss of home and the realization that there is no ability to return and have things the way they once were create ongoing grief. She also discusses the unique losses of children of immigrants who exist betwixt and between worlds—not really a part of the country that was left behind but not completely belonging to the new country where their family has moved.

The loss of employment means the loss not just of income and security but also of a significant source of identity and self-esteem for many individuals. In a society that values productivity and independence, not being able to contribute to the workforce, not having an outlet for one's expertise, and being disconnected from belonging to a workplace community can have deep repercussions for how individuals view themselves.

The desire but inability in some women to have children creates a very deep wound for those who have attempted to conceive and have been unable to do so. So much of the feminine identity, both socially and personally, is tied to the roles associated with motherhood, and infertility is often experienced as a crisis, with a cascade of painful losses, both tangible and intangible, that will continue throughout a woman's life.

Derek Scott describes the dichotomies that are present for men whose exclusively heterosexual orientation is gradually replaced by the recognition of a homosexual orientation. While this recognition may involve relief and a positive sense of congruence and authenticity, there are losses incurred regarding now being identified with a stigmatized group, loss of rites of passage that are afforded to heterosexual men, and an ongoing sense of shame and alienation from the dominant culture.

Eunice Gorman looks at the ongoing losses for individuals who have chronic, degenerative conditions. A key aspect of being diagnosed with a condition that will never improve is the constant nature of the losses and the uncertainty involved with navigating around loss of functionality and ability. The losses are also far-reaching and myriad, affecting every area of a person's life. In addition to these losses is the stigmatization that occurs with conditions that cannot be cured by medical intervention and the chronicity of care, which tends to be devalued in a medical system designed primarily for the delivery of acute care aimed at cure.

Phyllis Kosminsky describes the after-effects of a traumatic brain injury on an individual's identity and capacity. She makes the point that every area of a person's life is affected by this injury and that grief will encompass not just the loss of the person's functionality but also the loss of the person's former self and ability to reenter the world in the same way as before.

Nieli Langer explores the changes that may occur with aging from the personal experience of loss of functionality and independence and the related loss of confidence and self-esteem that may accompany these changes. The loss of independence is seen as a key aspect of the loss of one's identity, as the ability to care for one's self, make one's own decisions, and feel like a productive member of society are vital components of what is valued in Western society.

Section *IIIA*

Loss of Identity

13

The Trauma of Neglect
Loss of Self

JEFFREY KAUFFMAN

A CHILD'S WOUND OF BEING
SLIGHTED BY HER MOTHER

*T*his chapter considers the psychological consequences of a child experiencing herself to be neglected by her maternal caregiver. The wound of neglect is often, but not always, subtle and pervasive. It can remain unhealed from childhood and persist and be relived interminably in relationships with others and in a person's own most intimate experiences of herself.

The fact of being disregarded or ignored is often called a "slight." This draws our attention to the minimal and sometimes covert action deployed in inflicting the wound of neglect. The indirectness of the slight of neglect and the minimal action involved in neglect makes it easy to disregard how great the wound can be. To be slighted is to be diminished, insulted, and shamed. The wound of being slighted by neglect occurs in many everyday ways to people, with and without causing pain, but when this wound is experienced by an infant or child in relation to a parent, it is, however, formative. And this is the circumstance we are concerned about in this chapter. In the case example presented we will see how intense or enormous the slight of neglect by a child's maternal caregiver can be.

The theoretical framework deployed here for covering and thinking about the psychology of childhood neglect is psychoanalytic object relations theory and self psychology. This means that in this chapter we will be thinking about what happens psychodynamically in people's experience of their internal world.

THE PSYCHOLOGY OF THE NEGLECTED CHILD, WITH SPECIAL ATTENTION TO THE CRITICAL SIGNIFICANCE OF SELF-BLAMING IN LOSS-OF-SELF ANXIETY

Neglect unleashes the self against itself and against internal representations of the neglecting mother, setting in motion intrapersonal as well as interpersonal destructive forces. The wound of experiencing oneself to be uncared for by one's mother operates both as a fragmenting negation of the self and as a stimulus for reckless self-blame. A most troubling complicating factor of neglect is that it is experienced to be one's own fault, not only for something unknown that one has done but also for *who one is,* even as one may, in one's relation with oneself, vigorously protest and oppose or dissociate this. The self may feel it has no place to exist and no right to exist. The self comes into being as a faulted self, unworthy and experiencing itself to be deserving blame, though self-blame is often very conflictual, complicated, and protected against by dissociated self-constructs. Neglect is experienced as a blaming act of emotional abandonment.

Loss-of-self anxiety occurs within the matrix of the child's experience of herself in the eyes of the maternal caregiver, which is the primary experiential context in which the self develops. The crux of this loss is an *invalidation* of self occurring in the very formation of the self's experience of itself, so that an internalized sense of deprivation of selfhood and negation of self-worth and safety along with a threat of attack or concern with impending oblivion come to exist at the core of the self's relationship to itself and others.

While some degree of loss-of-self anxiety is an inevitable consequence of the normal development of the self and its internal object world, sometimes the experience of neglect crosses the threshold of tolerability and violates or traumatizes the developing self. The consequence may be pervasive self-blaming and shaming trends, along with helplessness, anxiety, and heightened levels of dissociative thinking. When loss-of-self anxiety does not cross this threshold, it no less operates as a powerful force in a person's reflexive negotiations, affecting self and social relations. This sense of loss, whether it creates a disturbance in a person's consciousness, is a basic aspect of psychological life.

Problematic loss-of-self anxiety may be experienced by a child when the mother is preoccupied with grief or when she is addicted or too depressed, narcissistic, psychotic, or traumatized to be empathically available. Physical and sexual abuse also tend to be experienced as involving significant maternal neglect, independent of any specific ways she is neglectful. And, certainly, physical abandonment may cause the same type of devastation. This underlying anxiety about oneself due to childhood emotional abandonment takes a variety of forms, meanings, and intensities, but it has certain basic characteristics. These include a generalized heightened vulnerability to narcissistic injury with specific and generalized anxiety about being shamed and blamed.

Displaced out of itself and delegitimized, the neglected self experiences itself to be unsheltered, unsafe in a world in which the wound of neglect is always at hand. Angry at being spurned and insulted and at fault, now again for being angry, she experiences herself to be at fault for the destructive energy that is turned against herself and against the internalized mother with whom the person is identified. Identity with mother tends to organize around introjects of the *destructive* mother (cf. Klein, 1977) in her active mode and the empty mother in her passive mode as well as attempts to defend against this identity by the deployment of denial and dissociation and by self-protectively embracing split-off good mother constructs.

Childhood experience of neglect and abandonment establishes a psychodynamic and a disordered reflexive field in which relationship with self and other is experienced throughout life. Identity as well as aspects of the ability to integrate experience is developed through experiences of the self in its developmental relationship with primarily the maternal object. Loss-of-self anxiety engendered in this relationship is experienced (and defended against) as the emotional reality in which the self experiences itself to be invalidated.

From this object relational and self-psychological developmental perspective of the organization of emotional reality, we recognize the establishment, in those who have experienced childhood neglect, of a subjective and intersubjective experiential space in which loss-of-self anxiety (Gaddini, 1992) is a powerful and disturbing underlying emotional dynamic. The nonrecognition experienced in neglect becomes a core of self-experience in which deprivation shames (Kauffman, 2010a, 2010b) and blames, constituting a self-relationship with a dissociated core bound up with the self being turned against itself. Loss of self is not just a deprivation; it is also an indictment.

ZOE'S GRIEF

Zoe's presenting problem was that spring had lost its joy. She felt empty. With an intensely turbulent self-awareness highly aroused, she was shut down and depressed in trying to manage an eruption of narcissistic woundedness, rage, and guilt that was triggered by experiencing a seemingly innocuous comment from a trusted friend. Zoe experienced this as a rejecting and insulting criticism, betraying the friend's secret contempt for her. Desire for a sense of pastoral oneness with the sweetness of spring, expressed her wish for a sanctuary, which she had at times known, away from the storms of interpersonal injury, conflict, and grief that had affected her throughout her life. The sanctuary of treatment provided sufficient shelter for her to do what she called "nuts and bolts" work, which meant talk about vehement, violent, and extreme inner states and her struggle to manage this emotional severity and its unrelenting assault on her selfhood.

To tell you her story, I have brought Zoe here in her own voice, with a few selections from her therapy diary, which she has kindly allowed me to use. The selections provided here are from the time during treatment when we were just figuring out what the nuts and bolts were. Her descriptions of her experience of loss-of-self anxiety are particularly suited to illuminate the psychodynamics and existential anxiety of a person torn apart by loss of self due to traumatizing experiences of childhood neglect.

SELECTIONS FROM *ZOE'S THERAPY DIARY*

6/19

Went to see JK to talk about blame. Feeling blame and shame. Taking on blame when it doesn't belong to me. How did I learn this? Disturbing memories of tension and conflict in the family. I saw how absent Mom was, I see, traumatized by her own childhood, loneliness, isolation, not being good enough. Contacted the inner child and saw her damage, devastation and anger. Feel how my identity is violated and fragmented by mechanisms of taking on blame for others. A default mode to help me stabilize in an unstable family field. I took on blame to try to get closer to others in the family. Where will all this lead?

9/18

Intense work on blame and shame with J. Tears on leaving the office, guilt and sadness. Acknowledging my pain of being misunderstood, wanting to connect. Being desperate to unravel the confusion and pain of the isolation. Feeling like I can't connect to family, I am not understood. Sadness around Mom, not being able to free her, help her in her pain; betrayal of myself for others, failing myself or their expectations of me. Nothing is ever enough to fill the hole there in Mom. Giving personal power away to connect; wanting to reduce my needs to stay cheerful and in alignment for more love. My personal power would negate my "fitting in" if I displayed it, so I shelved it. Confusion about my personal power and owning it. Not wanting to piss others off, upset or alienate them. Easier to merge and fade— creates boundary confusion. Under this, rage. Feeling it, owning it. Vulnerability of child within, emptiness. Using blame to counteract feelings of abandonment and emptiness—too scary to face alone. Disowning self and needs to protect and preserve mom.

9/24

Rage, power. A box in a corner, what's inside? SHAME. The other side of shame is RAGE. Mom and Dad's ignorance or denial makes it hard to blame them; to them it's not happening, so I must be the one who is causing it. Invalidation of my intrinsic goodness that all kids feel. My guilt for having a sense of power when others don't. Mom setting us up to compete for attention meant using feelings wisely. Mom setting up family tensions by playing out her own. I want to challenge the family pattern of denial but the cost is too great; causes alienation and character assassination. Internalized denial. Keeping alliances to protect my parents from their own shame! Split, inner conflict. Rage at self for letting myself do it. Feeling responsible.

10/9

Punishing and blaming others for my guilt. What is it about A [her sister] I don't like? That is me. Deceit, greed, self-centeredness, falsity, manipulation, brutality, cruelty, duplicitous. Can't let her reign because it means being victimized by her. Loss of identity by games of manipulation and mockery; wanted acknowledgment from A, B and others. Won't ever happen; need to form my own justice system inside now; needing to identify myself with goodness and sweetness to compensate for the nastiness in the family. Coping mechanism; need to accept my own disappointment in family members. Abandonment cycle plays out again and again through retaliation cycle. Trying to fix it. Exposing myself over and over again to abandonment via others; I am not capable of being abandoned now as I once was. If I want others to take responsibility I need to do it for myself; reconciliation with abandoned parts of self. Give myself justice if others won't. What does this look like? Eliminate warring factions of self; blaming and punishing.

11/5

Feeling shame internally and externally, Mom no accountability, no responsibility. If others don't claim it, it's mine! See how I mirror M's martyrdom, family ritual? See how we defend and protect against powerlessness, helplessness. When you are a martyr you are unable to be accountable. I need to protect others to stay safe from attack. Self validation means attacking others. I could not stop the continual attacks, only animals and nature provided relief. Wound is now continual, continual trespass. A refuses to take responsibility. If this bothers me so much, how am I doing it, too? How do I take more responsibility in my family without martyrdom?

11/13

Part of my diffusion is shock and disbelief related to M's vacuity, abandonment and not being a mirror. Stunned. Traumatic response, opens self for attack by others. If I take on others' blame then I have to hide my shame at having it. Living a secret life of collusion with perpetrators who are internalized. Needing other people to define me keeps me susceptible and on the hook. I need self-validation, need to find true source for this. Shame based family. Addiction to shame.

Comments on Zoe's Therapy Diary

Zoe's diary is a highly focused narrative that provides a succinct and vivid phenomenology of her experience of loss-of-self anxiety. I will now comment on a few selected topics related to this.

Her use of the diary is not simply as a record of treatment. Zoe's diary writing is a reflective exercise, summarizing the therapy session, reflecting on her experience of herself and continuing the conversation between us in her mind. The integrative effort revealed in her diary writing, in a very basic sense, is a mourning process, a mourning process for the self lost in her mother's "vacuity." She is processing her grief over her mother's "absence," that is, the self-relational impact and meaning of her mother's absence, which, inwardly, exists as the *loss-of-self anxiety* of which she gives an account. This mourning process does not look like mourning processes we see after the death of a loved one. But it is an example of a mourning process that is common when, in the development of the self through its relationship with mother, a serious disruption of the bond is experienced.

Her mother, in her "vacuity," is always present within Zoe; in these diary entries, she is present as a threatening object of consciousness that Zoe needs *to do something* with but is helpless. She is helpless in her efforts to connect or to detoxify being rejected, and in her efforts to destroy her mother she is, by shame-riddled guilt, fused with her.

In the wake of a failure to connect to mother and a failure to experience herself as recognized and thereby validated, she is bound by an all-consuming dilemma of being unable to connect on this fundamental level with her mother and therein, at the crux of her dilemma, cannot secure her own sense of existence. Her self is lost in the trauma of her mother's emotional abandonment, and anxiety about this drives an intense, desperate, and anxious urgency to do something.

Experiencing herself to be disconnected, an outcast in her family, shamed and alone, she seeks to connect and restore herself by protecting her mother from her destructive, retaliatory rage, her talion justice. Her self-blame, inflicted in the first place by her mother's rejection, is then reinforced by her belief that she has, indeed, destroyed her mother. In faulting her own aggressive impulses and her power, she can then identify in herself something for which she can take responsibility. Her efforts to survive abandonment and self-blame involve conflicting intentions to repair her mother and to destroy her mother—with whom, however, she is identified. In this biphasic (repair–destroy) intentional stand against being annihilated by her mother's neglect, she resists her helplessness. This resistance staves off psychic annihilation but keeps her in turmoil. By taking responsibility she seeks to ground herself and end the roller-coaster ride. Taking responsibility protects her from being consumed by self-blame, emptiness, self-pity, and shame–rage, but the wound and injustice of her neglect does not dissolve. She, time and again, finds herself lost in the throes the deep psychic insult of being neglected. Nonetheless, her feeling of power (in her knowledge of the truth about her mother and her family)—a power she, in her disconnect, confirms within herself—is blazing and palpable. In the calm, in the eye of her stormy rage, Zoe constructs a clear and psychologically insightful, though grandiose, zone in which she is able to look with well-composed judgment on her mother and recognize her trauma, weakness, and ignorance. In this "knowledge" of her mother, however, she pities her and projects shame back into her mother—only to then again find shame and rage returning to her through the spurious love she gets back from her mother. In her safety zone "default position" Zoe is able to achieve a semblance of normalcy and connectedness; she has learned from painful experience and is able to use feelings "wisely" to be engaged and compete in the family. The denial she embraces in playing her mother's game is self-negating and dystonic. Living her mother's shame, which her mother induces in her by neglect, along with the shame–rage this ignites, and her protecting her mother from this rage leave her split against herself.

Like her mother, Zoe is a martyr who cannot be accountable because she is self-absorbed in her own victimization. She is nonetheless keenly aware of this and is prepared to relinquish her martyrdom should her mother be accountable and her loss be recognized. For her mother to take responsibility would relieve Zoe of the torment of having *to* blame herself. The finishing shame–blaming stroke of her mother's neglect is her not taking responsibility for not acknowledging the reality of Zoe's experience and Zoe's wound. Zoe's mania screams and takes arms against the despair of her abandonment.

In her diary entry of 10/9 she is able to recognize her guilt-based blaming of A, her sister, for despised attributes of her own, projecting them onto A, who behaves toward Zoe in ways that suggest these same or similar qualities are also present in her. Being able to recognize hated parts of herself through her relationship with A, without being ashamed or being a martyr, is integrative, but her experience of herself with A is predominately fighting back against anxiety that she is being subjugated and controlled by her competitive sister.

When she says, in the first diary entry, "I saw how absent Mom [was], I see [her], traumatized by her own childhood, loneliness, isolation, not being good enough," she is expressing her ambiguous identification with her neglecting mother. She takes her bearings here by stepping back from the feverish immediacy of her experience of herself to get a perspective on her mother, and we hear her lexographic stammer, "I saw how absent Mom, I see… "—seeing herself in her mother. "I see" expresses her stepping back to look, as she stammers, perhaps in reaction to a faint intrusion into her thoughts of being ill at ease in sympathizing with the aggressor, or a faint shutter at a glimpse of herself as the otherness of her mother.

With her next thought we may observe her seeing. Writing "contacted the inner child and saw her devastation and anger," she seems to shift attention from her mother back to herself. However, in using the word "the" not the word "my" ("contacted *the* inner child"), she makes the subject whose inner child she contacts ambiguously to be her mother as well as herself. Her "inner child" is identified with her traumatized, isolated, and not-good-enough mother. This "inner child" is desperate, confused, and in pain; she is not able to make bonding contact with her mother. In its place, Zoe's wound of traumatic neglect becomes her perpetual bond with mother, in which she has not just lost herself but very early in her development was unable to become herself. Her mother is a traumatizing mirror in which she comes to experience herself and in which she exists in a state of exposure to self-consuming shame–blaming, and an emotional inner-world vicious circle of blame and protection between herself and her internalized mother. Her mother's neglect is experienced as an accusatory assault that Zoe is compelled, by exposure and loss-of-self anxiety, to carry out against herself. Feeling she must take blame when she is wounded, she is always angry at others. Neglect prompts a primitive self-destructive energy, which we see in Zoe along with her intensive lifelong campaign to oppose it. She opposes the insult and humiliation of neglect with injured rage; she opposes rage at mother with protection of mother; she opposes self-blame with responsibility and with blame toward mother; she opposes isolation with "default mode" pseudo-connection.

The psychodynamics induced in Zoe by neglect are predominately manic, while frequently the psychodynamics initiated by neglect predominately depressive. Zoe's expansiveness and sense of power in this way contrast with the frequently seen inhibited dispositions of despairing powerlessness in loss-of-self anxiety.

Neglect is abuse in which there is no overt violence but that initiates inward violence against the neglected self. Neglect is often difficult to point out to others and to trust one's own experience. The contrast between the sometimes virtually invisible acts of neglect and the inward violence neglect causes can contribute to a person's sense of confusion and to complex feelings of invalidation. Zoe's very disturbing sense of unfairness in feeling blamed for what she is victimized by stirs deeply, complicated by her own emotional violence, shaming and blaming.

REFERENCES

Gaddini, E. (1992). *A psychoanalytic theory of infantile experience: Conceptual and clinical reflections* (A. Limantani, Ed.). London: Routledge.

Kauffman, J. (2010a). The primacy of shame. In J. Kauffman, (Ed.), *The shame of death, grief and trauma*. New York: Routledge.

Kauffman, J. (2010b). Making sense of being human. In J. V. Ciprut, (Ed.), *On meaning*. Cambridge, MA: MIT Press.

Klein, M. (1977). *Love, guilt, and reparation and other works: 1921–1945*. New York: Delta.

14

We Are Not Like Other People
Identity Loss and Reconstruction Following Migration

WANDA SAWICKI

INTRODUCTION

M y city slowly moves away from me, folding into the converging embrace of railway tracks that glide from beneath our train's last car. I am 8 years old and excited about moving to Ontario with my family, yet I feel worried to realize I may never see Saskatoon again. I press my palms to the window on either side of my face and try to inhale the memory of each escaping scene: the downtown buildings; the Saskatchewan River, where we picked luscious Saskatoon berries in summer; our neighborhood of wartime houses; the Canadian National Exhibition grounds that held so much excitement; my uncle's farmlands of sensory adventures; the scruffy woods where my grandfather showed me how to find mushrooms. *Remember this.* My body resonates with an urgency to preserve these memories, an urgency imbued with a sense of anxious and ancient sadness. It is 1959. Years later, I would understand how these feelings came to be part of me before I was even born.

Remember this. Pamiętaj o tym. These words accompanied the stories and life lessons imparted by my Polish parents, grandfather, aunts, and uncles for as long as I can remember. They were not fables or fairy tales but real stories of survival about their deportation to slave labor in Siberia on freight trains in 1940, their life in refugee camps on three continents from 1942 to 1949, and their subsequent exile (Dubinski, 2008). A tone of urgency accompanied these stories. It was understood that they were intended to teach my siblings and I about survival, but more imperatively they described the essence of who we are. It was made clear that a strong sense of identity, braided from generations of faith, nationhood, culture, and family, provided a lifeline that could strengthen one in the face of any peril. The ultimate test of integrity seemed to lie in the depth and performance of one's allegiance to God, nation, and culture when in the face of life-threatening danger or at great distance from the Motherland (Brodniewicz-Stawicki, 1999; Wright & Naszynska, 2001). *Pamiętaj. Remember. We are not like other people.*

The questions of identity arising from losses due to migration, exile, and acculturation not only affect those who experience it firsthand but also ripple to those close to them (Akhtar, 1999; Dunlop, 2005; Guzlowski, 2007; Halasz, 2001; Hoffman, 1989). In this chapter, I share insights from my experiences as a second-generation bearer of such loss and as an art therapist who has worked with immigrants and refugees for 19 years (Sawicki, 1991; Sawicki & Yepes-Millon, 1994; Sawicki & Zaczek, 2005). The reconstruction of personal identity follow-ing separation from all that has been familiar is a normal developmental task at times, such as moving away from home for education or work prospects. However, the task becomes more complex when faced as a result of systemic and traumatic circumstances. Increasing numbers of people are migrating due to political and economic strife, ongoing wars, and natural disasters. The personal, generational story and insights offered here are shared as a beacon of hope to others whose lives are affected by such turmoil and challenge.

WHO ARE YOU?

The question, "Who are you?" is often answered with one's name. Other quali-fiers may include an address, occupation, or statement of relationship such as "son of," "partner of," or "friend of." Indigenous peoples may identify themselves more broadly by describing their place in natural, spiritual, and social ecologies. They name the land they are part of by birth and give their spirit name as divined through ceremony. Their tribal, clan, family, and common names are then shared to fill out the description of their identity. All of these modes of introduction require a shared language and some familiarity with the context of the responses that are offered for a good understanding to take place between inquirer and respondent.

IDENTITY AND CULTURE

Each culture defines parameters of identity through relationship between the self and all else. Our family, community, nation, natural environment, and even our relationship with the powers—nameable or unnameable—greater than the life we lead all hone elemental facets in our sense of self (Bowden, 2001; Corey, 2005). We begin to absorb cultural attitudes before we learn to speak (Akhtar, 1999; Levine, 2003). When we first receive food in response to our wail and first gaze into another's eyes, we rejoice in validation and consequently begin to construct a sense of worth. Thus begins the dance of striving to belong to thrive—physically, emotionally, and spiritually (Levine). Culture becomes a blueprint for survival that has been refined by the many who lived before us, those who live with us in the present, and even those not yet born, through the hopes we carry for them (Akhtar; Kisiel Dion, 2006). Whether we choose to follow, stretch, or break the bounds of culture, it remains a vital element of our life schema. Like water that shapes the stones of a river's bed, culture flows through our life and forms the shape of who we are.

The depth of our cultural imprinting may not make itself known until we enter the realm of a new, unfamiliar culture. Surprised or perhaps shocked to find that our life schema is not shared in this new place, questions of survival suddenly glare before us. Food may appear different or be difficult to procure; our mode of dress or movement may be offensive to others; attitudes toward gender may restrict what we do; language may be strangely incomprehensible. In such a situation, how do we convey what we need or who we are? How do we learn who others are? It may feel threatening to realize we need to change our ways to live well among others. Will our self-identity change as well? When we no longer walk among the familiar markers of our identity such as family, language, and landscape, it becomes easy to lose our sense of belonging—and our sense of self (Dunlop, 2005). How will we know where to turn for affirmation and support?

John Guzlowski, a retired professor of contemporary literature at Eastern Illinois University, writes poetry about the impact of his Polish parents' war traumas and migration on his own life and maintains a blog on the subject (http://lightning-and-ashes.blogspot.com/). His poem "Dumb Polacks" (2009) expresses some of the tensions experienced between languages and cultures and between children and parent, which signal a shift in identity awareness:

Dumb Polacks

Good children, we played outside
while our tired mother slept inside
resting from working the night shift,
and then a boy came along.

A bully, he was big and hard
and threw the ball at us
again and again, and called us DPs
and Dumb Polacks. Frightened
we called to our mother softly
in the English we didn't know
and had only practiced in whispers,

"Mother, Mother, Mother."
She had no English at all
and didn't come, and the boy
kicked us 'til we both were screaming,
"Mother, Mother, Mother."

Back in the house later,
with our tears and fearfulness,

we told her what happened
and she said, "Why didn't you call?"

We just stood there in silence.
What could we say to her?

LANGUAGE AND IDENTITY

Award-winning author Eva Hoffman (1989, 2004) was 13 years old in 1959 when she moved from her native Cracow, Poland, to Vancouver with her parents and sister. In *Lost in Translation* (1989), she describes her process of dealing with inherited grief and acculturation with intellectual and spiritual depth. Although she received a PhD in literature from Harvard University and worked as an editor and writer for the *New York Times,* she continued to feel caught between two cultures and languages. It took more time and lived experience in English before it became her predominant language, the one of interior dialogue in quiet moments, and she could feel a clearer sense of integration. However, she still found Polish phrases to "have roundness and a surprising certainty, as if they were announcing the simple truth" (Hoffman, 1989, p. 272).

Anna Wierzbicka, a linguist at the Australian National University, has written several books on how language is the key element in understanding a culture's worldview as well as a person's sense of self. In *Emotions Across Languages and Cultures: Diversity and Universals* (1999), we learn that emotions cannot be assumed to be recognized and dealt with in quite the same way across cultures. A culture that has experienced much war and oppression may view emotion as an external energy or force coming on it rather than an internal response to an external event. Language is so fundamental to self-concept and self-expression; when we lose our first language we lose a direct point of contact not only with our culture and family of origin but also with our own self. This presents a significant layer of complexity in the process of acculturation for both the immigrant and those of the host culture who hope to support them.

IDENTITY AND CHRONIC LOSS

Questions of identity are a lived, often chronic, dilemma for immigrants and their families. Anniversaries, ongoing political conditions, and new questions regarding the veracity of what happened may prolong the pain of personal losses resulting from migration. As time goes on, the aging process lends breadth and depth to the predicament (Mahalingam, 2006). Children may be expected to live and maintain the culture of their parents even as they strive to fit in with new peers, marry, and advance in careers; parents may be expected to work in ways they have not imagined even as they strive to come to terms with their migration losses; elders struggle to face the reality that they may die, be buried on "foreign" soil, and mourned in ways their culture would not have considered ideal. If culture touches us spiritually, how will these changes in cultural mores affect the soul and its journey following the body's death?

IDENTITY AND GRIEF

When our world collapses and our heart is broken, we search for the familiar things we feel are sure to help relieve distress. We yearn to express ourselves to someone who can understand, support, and counsel us. We look to our environment for assurance that the world can go on as it should. A favorite tree, a place by the river, and a familiar building in the city can all offer the solace of past association and the promise of continuity. Imagine, then, living through a significant loss without such supports. Imagine trying to express your grief in a second or third language in which you are not yet fluent. Imagine being unable to mourn as you feel you should, due to distance, political and social upheaval, natural disaster, or absence of a familiar community. When our loss is not expressed in a culturally meaningful manner, we may experience an interior dissonance that can deeply fracture our sense of self. The emotional impact of being untrue to our beliefs at a time of significant loss may affect our self-concept for many years and even cross generations.

The second generation to bear conflicts of identity and loss due to migration face additional complications in their process of self-development. They are geographically, politically, and temporally removed from the scenes of their parents' stories; they may not be able to visit the land of their ancestors or live immersed in the family's original culture. Elders' stories and life lessons may be difficult to take seriously at first because their points of reference do not exist in the real world of the second generation. As a child, how could I relate to our ancestral village, wiped off the map of a land so far away? How could I pretend to understand life in a Siberian gulag, or an African refugee camp? Yet the emotional link to what my parents experienced was felt to be as much a part of me as the inherited color of my eyes and hair (Agnew, 2005; Hoffman, 1989). The challenge, then, is how to relate oneself to a narrative that means so much to those whom you love most, when the mere question of how to do it already indicates you are not really a part of it.

My maternal grandmother has had an important influence on my sense of self even though she died when my mother was only 12 years old. The family was fleeing the Soviet Union in 1942 under an amnesty declared by the Allies. They had managed to board a train carrying Polish soldiers freed from the gulags, my mother's brothers among them. Just a day before reaching the border and freedom, my grandmother succumbed to the effects of starvation and forced labor. The family had to leave her body beside the railway tracks to continue on with the train before the border closed. This unresolved grief, complicated by traumatic factors, affected my mother deeply as she grew into womanhood, motherhood, and elderhood. As her firstborn, I felt the painful imprinting of this grief on my own sense of self through the way my mother interacted with me. A new wife and mother, she missed her own mother's guidance terribly as she struggled to cope in a country where she was unfamiliar with the language and customs. I have spent many hours during my lifetime trying to picture who my grandmother was in an effort to understand her influence on my own identity. The following excerpt from a poem I wrote about her illustrates my process:

There are no photos,
no mementoes of you, Babcia,
other than the love and wisdom
carried by your husband and children.
How often I have tried
to piece together an image of you,
studying your children's faces as they age,
noting the mannerisms
that might have begun with your example.
The longing for you
has led me through a complicated grief, Babcia.
Yet your influence
has reached beyond time and space
to offer healing
as I become the age you were,
when you died.
When I work with those who suffer loss and grief,
you send compassion;
when my sons connect with your daughter,
you send gratitude and grace;
where courage rises despite a fear,
there I see your face.

Wanda Sawicki, 2006

INTEGRATING REALITY, WALKING TOWARD THE FUTURE

Each modification in speech, behavior, and values signals a departure from primary cultural mores—from the way one first formed a sense of self and found one's place in the world. Feelings of grief and remorse for being the first in a long line of generations to break with tradition can lead to an ongoing sense of alienation in which one continually feels "the outsider"—even between parent and child. It can be most acute for those unable to visit their homeland in hope of some level of reconnection. Even though acculturation, much like any developmental process, often brings with it positive and generative outcomes, the inherent losses of connection with one's original culture remain salient. Each gain reflects a loss.

The reconstruction of self that takes place during acculturation forms around a core of loss and grief and happens in a new language. As agency in the new culture grows, even when a balance of biculturalism is attained, a sense of loss highlights the awareness that although the self has grown one will never feel truly at home in either culture (Hoffman, 1989; Sawicki, 2001).

A special type of grief ensues when one becomes aware of the loss of continued personal growth and maturation within one's original cultural context. One can no longer solidly and uniquely belong to that culture, and there can be no complete return. The process may be pictured as running along a sandy beach at water's edge: Distance is covered, progress is made, but on looking back we see that our footsteps have already begun to disappear. Our path cannot be walked in the same way twice, but the journey has made it possible for us to move on, to walk forward knowing from whence we came.

THE GIFTS OF MY GRANDMOTHER'S STORY

My grandmother's story, my family's history, is as much a part of me as the physical attributes I have received from her. Her legacy is an acute awareness that war is real and can happen to me and my family at any time; we should therefore appreciate the freedom in which we live, the food we have to eat, and all those who are close to us. I have learned that grief, though a burden, can also be a companion that shows us how to honor what we have lost and to value the precious beauty of what we have. My family's grief, my grief, has opened me to empathy for others and has given me the strength to witness their grief without fear that it will consume me. My grandmother, faced with tremendous hardship, did not falter when it came to sustaining her family. Stories of how she made soups and teas out of "nothing" in the Siberian gulag have taught me to look for grains of possibility in my counseling work with people who feel they have "nothing" in their lives after a loss. I have chosen to uncover the inspiration of my grandmother's legacy by honoring the grief her loss brought to my life. When I remember or tell her story, I stand not by her unknown grave but by the strength in the life she lived.

FINDING A BALANCE IN JUGGLING CULTURES

I am fortunate that my mother taught me to speak, read, and write in Polish before I learned English. Despite the initial culture shock this precipitated on the first day of school in Saskatoon, it is a gift that remains with me still and affords a bivalent view of the world along with a bilingual possibility of expressing myself within it. I feel an intimacy with Canadian soil, where I was born, but it does not match the special resonance in my body when I step onto Polish soil. The feeling leaves no question as to where my genes and blood have come from, but it does not affirm that I am home. While Canadians have called me Polish, the Poles consider me to be Canadian. I learned to accept the nebulous, uprooted status of otherness, much like my second-generation peers of many cultures, when I realized it freed me from the bounds of any one culture and afforded me an objective view of the world. The sense of unbelonging eventually became less painful as I gained fluency in other languages and cultural settings. I learned that my experiences as a second-generation survivor of migration loss were not unique to me but rather were experienced by many immigrants with similar histories (Dunlop, 2005; Sawicki, 1991). My losses, grief, and insights helped me to strive for better understanding of the human developmental process and promoted my spiritual growth. They provided me with the compassionate basis for my life's work as an art therapist with immigrants and refugees—particularly with elders who suffered traumatic losses when children, as my mother had (Sawicki & Zaczek, 2005), parents (Sawicki & Yepes-Millon, 1994), and with adolescents forming a sense of self while grieving migration losses (Sawicki, 1999).

CORE IDENTITY AND PERSONAL NARRATIVE

When our sense of identity wavers, the only direction left in which to search for definition may be inward. The first step toward recognizing our core identity is one taken through our personal, remembered life experience. Our personal narrative, though shaped by external factors such as migration, is not reliant on them in generating a resonant sense of self. Rather, such narrative flows from our wellspring of perceptions, feelings, values, and hopes. Telling our story can externalize our struggles so that we may begin to see them more objectively and to create a new narrative of understanding, coping, and moving forward with newfound wisdom (White, 2005). Hoffman (1989, 2004) describes the healing process of telling her story backward and then forward again from the beginning in her second language, English, during therapy. It is a process that allows a safer stance through space and time in which to name and grieve losses with a supportive witness and to celebrate the strengths and sense of purpose that can come from them.

SHARING A PERSONAL NARRATIVE OF LOSS

Individuals, families, and cultural groups experience the need, at one time or another, to choose whether to tell their life story or to preserve it in silence. For those whose migration was forced by political upheaval or natural disaster, the sense of responsibility to preserve and convey their cultural history can be especially significant. This is particularly true for immigrants, whose plight is not known to the world at large (Akhtar, 1999; Sawicki & Zaczek, 2005; Winslow, 2004). Survivors carry a truth that needs to be told; they are curators of a culture's history and wisdom that must be shared for the integrity of their people to endure (Sawicki & Zaczek, 2005; White, 2005). The communication of a cultural narrative honors not only the integrity of the teller (of the first or subsequent generations) but also of all those who have lived and died by that culture. It can also offer hope to other cultural groups undergoing similar struggles and to those professionals or individuals who would like to lend their support.

Art and narrative therapy (White & Epston, 1990) have been found to be helpful in conveying personal and cultural narratives of loss and reconstruction of self (Allen, 2005; Baker, 2006; Golub, 1989; Parry & Doan, 1994; Sawicki & Zaczek, 2005; Simington, 2006). When words do not seem adequate, personal artwork can bridge communication enough to build empathy between the artist and therapist. Creative work becomes a physical process of empowerment through the use of materials and the evolution of personal imagery in the presence of a supportive witness. When the finished work is shared by the client, it facilitates the articulation of personal narrative through the presence of tangible, visual reference points within the image. In creating a work of art, or a story, we challenge the darkness of our pain with the spark that comes from making something out of "nothing." Much like my grandmother, who created nourishment from the most meager of elements, when we make our mark on a blank sheet of paper, we create the first definition of "something" to promote healing. It is the beginning of our essential narrative that comes from within. It is a picture of who we really are in the moment and points to how we may reshape our sense of self to include a positive inventory of capacities along with the articulation of our losses.

THE TRAIN: A POSTSCRIPT

As I boarded a comfortable, warm train with my mother on a very cold day in December 2008, I knew we were both thinking of her first train ride as a 10-year-old girl. It took her, with her family, from their village in the eastern borderlands of Poland to forced labor in Siberia. It was February 1940. The train wagon they were forced onto was a cattle car with open slats and no conveniences on board. Our train ride in 2008, however, would lend some balance to that painful memory. We were on our way to the Polish Consulate in Toronto for a ceremony in which my mother, along with other survivors, would receive the Siberian Cross medal to honor their survivorship and preservation of Polish culture in exile. There was no sense of urgency to this train ride but rather an impression of healing. The history of the deportees to Siberia had not been officially recognized by any government due to political reasons (Brodniewicz-Stawicki, 1999), but on this day, after the fall of communism, my mother's loss would be publicly and officially noted by the nation from which she came and to which she had always been true in her heart. This story, placed on the front page or our local newspaper as an inspiring item preceding Christmas (Dubinski, 2008), was a turning point in my mother's healing process. It was also a moment of healing and pride for her children and grandchildren.

It had taken great courage for my mother to give the interview; used to years of feeling the outsider, she found it hard to believe that others would relate to her story, let alone find it useful. However, her sense of cultural responsibility and pride lent her the strength to proceed. She was rewarded with the pleasure of experiencing the story's generative impact on those who read it. Many said that it provided a model of strength in the face of adversity that inspired them to look at their own life stories with new and appreciative eyes. This feedback helped her to rewrite her personal narrative of hardship to include the aspect of survivorship and positive contribution to "the world."

As a result of bearing witness to a positive shift in my mother's story, and in the stories of others like her, I have been able to integrate a healing shift in my own narrative of identity. I am comfortable with my position between cultures. I appreciate the journey of self-development and no longer strive to be home in any one place or culture. Rather, I savor the movement that allows me to walk in balance with others on a therapeutic journey. I am a pilgrim; I honor the land I came from as much as the land I walk on. I move toward those moments in space and time made sacred by the sharing of narratives for the benefit of history, culture, and personal growth. We are not like other people; we are all unique in our wounding and in our healing. Yet there is much to gain when we walk together and hear one another's life stories. *Remember this.*

REFERENCES

Agnew, V. (2005). Introduction. In V. Agnew (Ed.), *Diaspora, memory and identity: A search for home* (pp. 3–17). Toronto: University of Toronto Press.

Akhtar, S. (1999). *Immigration and identity: Turmoil, treatment, and transformation.* Northvale, NJ: Jason Aronson Inc.

Allen, P.B. (2005). *Art is a spiritual path.* Boston: Shambhala.

Baker, B.A. (2006). Art speaks in healing survivors of war: The use of art therapy in treating trauma survivors. In *Trauma treatment techniques: Innovative trends,* Garrick, J. & M.B. Williams, Eds. (pp. 183–198). Binghamton, NY: Haworth Maltreatment & Trauma Press.

Bowden, A.R. (2001). *A psychotherapist sings in Aotearoa: Psychotherapy in New Zealand.* Plimmerton, New Zealand: Caroy Publications.

Brodniewicz-Stawicki, M. (1999). *For your freedom and ours: The Polish armed forces in the Second World War.* St. Catharines, Canada: Vanwell Publishing.

Corey, G. (2005). *Theory and practice of counseling and psychotherapy* (7th ed.). Belmont, CA: Brooks/Cole-Thomson Learning.

Dubinski, K. (2008). A medal for surviving: Katherine Sawicki of London was among Poles shipped to Siberia by the Soviets. *London Free Press,* December 18, 2008, London, Ontario, Canada.

Dunlop, R. (2005). Memoirs of a sirdar's daughter in Canada: Hybridity and writing home. In V. Agnew (Ed.), *Diaspora, memory and identity: A search for home* (pp. 115–150). Toronto: University of Toronto Press.

Golub, D. (1989). Cross-cultural dimensions of art psychotherapy: Cambodian survivors of war trauma. In H. Wadeson, J. Durkin, & Perach, D. (Eds.), *Advances in art therapy* (pp. 5–42). New York: John Wiley & Sons, Inc.

Guzlowski, J. (2007). *Lightning and ashes.* Internet blog. http://lightning-and-ashes.blogspot.com/

Guzlowski, J. (2009). Second language poems. *The Cosmopolitan Review,* August 8, 2009. Retrieved October 17, 2009 from http://cosmopolitanreview.com/articles/poetry/131-second-language-poems-by-guzlowski

Halasz, G. (2001). *Children of child survivors of the Holocaust: Can trauma be transmitted across the generations?* Paper presented at the Legacy of the Holocaust: Children of the Holocaust conference, Jagiellonian University, Cracow, Poland, May 24–27. Retrieved October 28, 2006 from http://www.psychematters.com/papers/halasz.htm

Hoffman, E. (1989). *Lost in Translation: A life in a new language.* New York: Dutton, Penguin Group.

Hoffman, E. (2004). *After such knowledge: Memory, history, and the legacy of the Holocaust.* New York: Public Affairs, Perseus Books Group.

Kisiel Dion, K. (2006). On the development of identity: Perspectives from immigrant families. In R. Mahalingam (Ed.), *Cultural psychology of immigrants* (pp. 299–314). Mahwah, NJ: Lawrence Erlbaum Associates, Inc.

Levine, E. (2003). *Tending the fire: Studies in art therapy and creativity* (2nd ed.). Toronto: EGS Press.

Mahalingam, R. (2006). Cultural psychology of immigrants: An introduction. In Mahalingam, R., (Ed.), *Cultural psychology of immigrants* (pp. 1–12). Mahwah, NJ: Lawrence Erlbaum Associates, Inc.

Parry, A., & Doan, R. (1994). *Story re-visions: Narrative therapy in the postmodern world.* New York: Guilford Press.

Sawicki, W. (1991). *Juggling Cultures.* Multimedia resource kit with manual. London, Ontario, Canada: London InterCommunity Health Centre.

Sawicki, W. (2001). *Never throw bread in the garbage: Adult children of sybiraki share thoughts on parental war trauma.* Manuscript submitted for publication.

Sawicki, W., & Yepes-Millon, M. (1994). *Cross-cultural parenting.* London, Ontario, Canada: London InterCommunity Health Centre.

Sawicki, W., & Zaczek, M. (2005). *From red ribbons to trials of ice and fire: The healing journey of Polish senior women through narrative and art therapy.* Paper presented at the Ontario Art Therapy Association Conference, May 14–15, King's University College, London, Ontario, Canada.

Simington, J. (2006). *Healing soul pain.* (DVD). Edmonton, Alberta, Canada: Taking Flight Books.

White, M. (2005). *Workshop notes.* 28 pages. Retrieved March 20, 2007 from http://www.dulwichcentre.com.au/Michael%20White%20Workshop%20Notes.pdf

White, M., & Epston, D. (1990). *Narrative means to therapeutic ends.* New York: W.W. Norton & Co.

Wierzbicka, A. (1999). *Emotions across languages and cultures: Diversity and universals.* Cambridge, UK: Cambridge University Press.

Winslow, M. (2004). Oral history and Polish émigrés in Britain. In Stachura, P. (Ed.), *The Poles in Britain 1940–2000: From betrayal to assimilation* (pp. 58–97). London: Frank Cass Publishers.

Wright, J., & Naszynska, A. (2001). *A forgotten odyssey.* Video recording. London, England: Lest We Forget Productions.

15

Loss of Employment

DARCY L. HARRIS AND JESSICA ISENOR

INTRODUCTION

While sitting at my desk several months ago, I (D.H.) answered a phone call from one of the supervisors of a government-funded unemployment help agency. She told me that her staff was completely overwhelmed with the volume of unemployed individuals seeking help through their services in the previous 6 months, and she asked if I would come to speak with members of her staff about the losses that they and their clientele were experiencing. She stated that she contacted me because of my specialization in bereavement-related issues, and she said simply, "These people are all grieving so many losses, and my staff feel overwhelmed by the amount of human suffering that they are encountering as they try to help these individuals try to find work in an environment where there are no jobs." At first, I hesitated in response to her request. My specialization in bereavement had been focused on helping bereaved individuals after they experienced the death of a loved one. However, when I started to ponder what it would be like if I found myself suddenly unemployed, myriad losses immediately came to my mind—the first thoughts were of the loss of my roles as teacher, counselor, and wage earner. I then considered what it would feel like to lose my hard-earned position and reputation in the local and international community that are a part of my job. I realized that I would experience a huge amount of anxiety over the loss of my financial security. And then I realized that I would also lose the community and colleagues that are part of my work. It finally occurred to me that I would feel a sense of losing myself as I know myself to be through my work. In addition, what about the pride I have taken in the work that I have done—would that still matter or be a part of me? I called the supervisor back and agreed to her request.

THE SOCIAL CONTEXT OF UNEMPLOYMENT

Obviously, the most salient loss that occurs when someone becomes involuntarily unemployed is the loss of income and the threat to one's financial security. However, many aspects of unemployment affect an individual at various levels. After my encounter with the unemployment supervisor, I began to notice how much of daily life and social interactions focus on work. For instance, in social gatherings, after meeting someone for the first time almost always the first question asked is, "What do you do?" We live in a society that is obsessed with doing, being busy, and maintaining productivity at all costs. We are essentially defined by the work that we do, and the definition of *success* is associated with a high income and a strong dedication to one's career.

Socialization around work and career in capitalistic, industrialized countries includes a strong focus on defining oneself through work and income, and the ingrained belief that one can be successful by trying hard enough and putting out the required sacrifice and effort along the way (Garrett-Peters, 2009). There is very little room for tolerance if you are not part of this working "elite" group. Once again, the emphasis is on the individual being responsible for this effort and success. However, the irony is that the most recent economic downturn has largely occurred due to decisions that have been made at corporate and political levels, yet the individuals who have been laid off or who have lost a significant portion of their investments experience the fallout very personally. The social messages around these losses still focus on being able to "pull yourself up by the bootstraps" during a time when there literally are no boots to be found.

The reality is that the recent dramatic economic downtown and resulting level of unemployment follows a trend over the past decade toward corporate streamlining and identification of workers as vendors of services rather than as long-term employees who are rewarded for years of service and dedication. The buzzword for the past several years in career counseling training has been the identification of *transferrable skills*, which essentially means that you will be taking whatever you do in one company, and when you complete the required work at that company you will be expected to apply these skills in another position at another company or job, with the expectation that an individual will likely pass through a series of time-limited positions at different companies in the course of a career rather than maintain a long-term position with a single company (Bridges, 1995). There is also a trend toward hiring workers on contract to fulfill the short-term needs of a company. When the contract period is over, the company may choose not to renew the contract or to offer the contract to another individual whose pay requirements may be less than the person who has held the contract for a period of time. Most of these contracts do not include benefits, which further increases the vulnerability of the person who works in this context. However, the benefit for employers is the ability to hire cheaper labor and to avoid paying high amounts in benefits over and above the wages of an individual. This new "world of work" is very different from the expectations of a generation ago, and the implication is that very few individuals will have the same continuous full-time position within one company for their working life and that there are also fewer individuals with job security and benefits attached to their work (Bridges).

Walsch (2009) discusses the three areas considered to be core aspects of a person's life: *relationships, money,* and *health.* When an individual loses employment, each one of these areas is profoundly affected, resulting in feelings of grief, disequilibrium, shame, and anxiety that are experienced in almost every area of the person's thinking, feeling, and functioning:

- *Relationships*—include the loss of regular contact and community with coworkers and the workplace environment, strained relationships within the family system due to stress and anxiety over the loss of employment, and disagreement regarding next steps and the uncertainty of family income; also include individuals' relationships with themselves and how they now view themselves without the context of work and career in which to identify.
- *Money*—relates not just to having regular income and the ability to pay bills and maintain a certain standard of living but also the reality that in industrialized societies money is equated with power and the ability to determine one's choices. When individuals' lives are threatened in this area, so is their relationship to the society in which they live, as money and consumerism are essential parts of belonging to and participating in this same social structure.
- *Health*—many individuals have health insurance coverage and benefits through their work, and job loss means the loss of this coverage. Of importance are the difficulties associated with obtaining future coverage with another employer for any condition that preexisted coverage that may be reinstated on reemployment. As a result, this loss may never be recovered, which may have very significant ramifications for individuals who lose employment. There is also a vicious cycle that has been suggested between ongoing and long-term stress (which certainly can result from unwanted unemployment) and poor quality of health mentally and physically, which can then lead to more difficulties for individuals in their search for reemployment (Cohen et al., 2007; Garrett-Peters, 2009; Linn, Sandifer, & Stein, 1985). In my own practice, I have seen individuals become deeply depressed because of long-term unemployment and unable to pay for medications that were prescribed to assist with depression that occurred secondarily to their unemployment because they did not have access to drug benefits. As a result, many of their depressive symptoms were untreated, making it much more difficult for these individuals to actively search for employment opportunities, avail themselves of job assistance programs, or to perform well in interviews in which they were applying for another position.

GRIEF AND UNEMPLOYMENT

The emotional factors associated to involuntary unemployment, and their impact on people's ability to cope with job loss and search for new employment, are of relevant concern to the counseling profession and to state/provincial and federal employment assistance programs. While job loss as it pertains to feelings of grief is a relatively new and largely unknown area of study, the negative effects of unemployment on both physiological and psychological well-being are well documented (Andersen, 2009; Burgard, Brand, & House, 2007; Comino, Harris, Silove, Manicavasagar, & Harris, 2000; Bockerman & Ilmakunnas, 2006; Moorhouse & Caltabiano, 2007; Price, Choi, & Vinokur, 2002).

Job loss has been specifically linked to depression (Comino et al., 2000; Moorhouse & Caltabiano, 2007) and a decline in overall physical health (Burgard et al., 2007; Price et al., 2002). Moorhouse & Caltabiano examined adult resilience in the context of the adversity of unemployment and feelings of depression; they stated that the National Survey of Mental Health and Wellbeing in Australia reports 22% of unemployed respondents had high levels of depressive symptoms, much higher than the national average for depression among the general population. It is important to note the finding that the longer individuals have been job searching the more likely they are to experience depression (McKee-Ryan et al., as cited in Moorhouse & Caltabiano). Price et al. found that in unemployed persons a loss of personal control combined with financial adversity were linked to increased chronic health problems as well as impaired role and emotional functioning. Burgard et al. were able to expand and confirm these findings while controlling for health selection and other possible confounding factors; their results showed that involuntary unemployment can lead to significantly poorer levels of self-rated health and increased depression symptoms, all of which is magnified if the person experiences involuntary job loss for health-related reasons.

Comino et al. (2000) also found that unemployed persons who were suffering from depressive symptoms or other psychological health concerns were more often treated by their family doctors with prescription medication and not referred to psychological counseling or treatment compared with employed patients with similar symptoms. This research suggests that people who are involuntarily unemployed not only are suffering but also may not get access to the same medical and psychological resources to which employed people are being referred, therefore possibly experiencing additional harm.

Andersen (2009) provided some preliminary evidence suggesting that job loss does not decrease feelings of overall well-being in people of all socioeconomic statuses but has an inverse U effect, showing a stronger impact on those who were middle class prior to unemployment.

Only a few studies have looked directly at the experience of grief in relation to job loss. They suggest that feelings of grief, similar to that of bereavement of a family member, can occur in persons who are unemployed (Archer & Rhodes, 1993, 1995; Brewington, Nassar-McMillan, Flowers, & Furr, 2004). Archer and Rhodes interviewed unemployed men in Cumbria, England, a city experiencing an unemployment rate higher than the national average in the mid-to-late 1980s, first with a cross-sectional study and then with a longitudinal study; they found that not only did 24–27% of these men meet the authors' criterion for a grief-like reaction but also these feelings lasted in some men regardless of the length of time for which they had been unemployed.

Brewington et al. (2004) performed a preliminary investigation comparing unemployed persons, mostly women, with standardized responses of a bereaved population from the Grief Experience Inventory—Loss Version (Sanders et al., 1985, as cited in Brewington et al., 2004; Archer, 1999) and found that the response levels were similar on all measures of grief except for feelings of depersonalization, which were lower in the unemployment group. Brewington et al. (2004) also found small, but statistically significant, relationships between specific measures of grief and certain life factors such as feelings of guilt having a positive relationship with income loss and the time since the job loss having a positive relationship with feelings of despair, anger and hostility, social isolation, loss of control, depersonalization, death and anxiety, and the overall grief score.

There is also some evidence that people who are in the process of losing their jobs go through stages of grief similar to what had been described by Kubler-Ross (Blau, 2008). Blau used questionnaires to assess employees whose production plant was in the process of being closed or sold over a 2-year period. His results suggested that over the 2-year period mean levels of denial, bargaining, and depression declined while exploration, an additional stage added to the Kubler-Ross framework (Bridges, 1991, as cited in Blau, 2008), increased. Blau also found that mean levels of anger and acceptance remained stable over time with anger at a consistent moderately low level and acceptance remaining at a high level.

Continued research into the experience of job loss grief is needed so that new employment assistance programs can be developed and counselors can be better educated to assist people experiencing job loss grief. Professionals and programs that ignore the existence of job loss grief may cause psychological harm to those they are trying to help.

LOSS OF THE ASSUMPTIVE WORLD IN UNEMPLOYMENT

As has been discussed in the introduction to this book, the grief associated with nondeath loss is often focused on aspects where individuals' assumptive world is shattered or lost as a result of their experience. Individuals who find themselves involuntarily unemployed may experience the following assaults to their assumptive world:

- The view of the world and of others is challenged. That the world is not a safe place and that others cannot necessarily be trusted as one may have thought in the past is a very difficult and painful realization. Often, there is a profound recognition of how money, social acceptance, and power are entwined when one is no longer able to participate in society as a consumer, a breadwinner, or a worker.
- Assumptions about justice and life are shattered. We are often taught that if you work hard you will be rewarded. However, an individual's unemployment may have very little or no relationship to the quality of that person's work or work ethic. In addition, decisions made by companies regarding the downsizing of employees may not be based on the quality

of one's work or performance, leaving a strong sense of injustice regarding who was let go versus who was retained within a company.

- Views of oneself as valuable and worthy are invalidated. It is almost impossible to maintain positive self-regard and self-esteem when you cannot earn a living or define yourself with your work in a society that defines success through financial means. It is also very difficult not to take decisions regarding unemployment personally, even if the decisions were made for economic reasons at the corporate level (Beattie, 2006).

CLINICAL RECOMMENDATIONS

Clinicians who work with unemployed individuals are often called on to "dance" between active interventions to assist these individuals in their search for work and supportive work focusing on the inner processing of the grief, anxiety, depression, and stress that are all associated with unwanted unemployment. Suggestions for helping unemployed individuals are as follows:

- *Contextualize the loss of employment* as a difficult situation, and do not let what is situational become impressed as a personal failing of the unemployed individual. While it can be true that personal factors may contribute to what has happened with an individual's employment history, it is imperative to be able to realistically assess the current job market and economic factors that have underscored individuals' work status to avoid attaching personal blame and further shame to those who are already in a place of great angst and anxiety.
- *Become familiar with job search and unemployment resources in your community.* Many communities have back-to-work programs, including individual counseling and retraining that may be of benefit to unemployed individuals. It is important to know what is available in the community, including what types of referrals are accepted, funding sources, and what the programs include. In my own community, one of the resources for unemployed individuals is a workshop that helps individuals identify their strengths and preferences, which has often been a very helpful adjunct to assist my clients to once again focus on what they have to offer rather than on what they have lost.
- *Make a realistic appraisal of strengths, skills, and abilities.* It may be helpful to try to help clients maintain connection with the assets and abilities that are innately theirs, even if they are not currently being expressed in a work-related venue. Many of my (D.H.) clients have found various temperament indicators, personality and preference sorters, and self-descriptor measures to be helpful in identifying strengths in themselves and others as well as tools for appreciating diversity within their contacts and relationships.
- *Recognize the toll of being in limbo.* Make a list with clients of all the areas of their lives affected by the loss of their employment to validate their grief and anxiety as normal rather than abnormal. After making this

list, look at the ways they have coped and demonstrated their strengths in the midst of great adversity. The key here is the recognition that there may be many losses, including a sense of losing one's self—but core aspects of a person's resilience and strength can still be found.

- *Focus on developing self-trust.* Clients may repeatedly struggle with issues of trust and anxiety after they have faced significant unemployment. In the process of counseling, gently remind clients that they can really trust only themselves. We often explore their perceptions of themselves as an avenue to open up the possibility of "befriending" themselves and developing self-trust regarding their decision making and intentions. This work helps clients to feel more of a sense of agency when participating in the job search and the interview process as well.

- *Take a realistic stance on control.* Most of us have been taught that we are responsible for our lives and success, and the implication is that we can control our own destiny. In reality, the only thing we can really control is our response to the life events that occur to us. It may be helpful to try to help clients reframe this emphasis on control to one that is more personal and realistic: If you learn to trust yourself and partner with yourself, you will rest in knowing that you will take care of yourself and respond in the best way possible to the things that you cannot trust and that you cannot control. This step often addresses the shame and humiliation that accompany unemployment, which can cause paralysis and more stress to individuals who are already struggling. There is no shame in refusing to take responsibility for what you cannot control. However, there is also an important step of realistically appraising what you can control so that you have an opportunity to actively participate in the recovery process.

REFERENCES

Andersen, S. H. (2009). Unemployment and subjective well-being: A question of class? *Work and Occupations, 36*(1), 3–25.

Archer, J. (1999). *The nature of grief: The evolution and psychology of reactions to loss.* New York: Routledge. Retrieved November 30, 2009 at http://books.google.ca/books?id=CEOBLjIw_1EC&pg=PA22&lpg=PA22&dq=GEI+sanders+question&source=bl&ots=_8wCtdaBbj&sig=hITSqLasfwcnlgXYDZqn_A-bqTs&hl=en&ei=H-oZS7b7OI-G9lAfX7-nxCQ&sa=X&oi=book_result&ct=result&resnum=3&ved=0CBgQ6AEwAg#v=onepage&q=GEI%20sanders%20question&f=false

Archer, J., & Rhodes, V. (1993). The grief process and job loss: A cross-sectional study. *British Journal of Psychology, 84,* 395–410.

Archer J., & Rhodes, V. (1995). A longitudinal study of job loss in relation to the grief process. *Journal of Community & Applied Social Psychology, 5,* 183–188.

Beattie, M. (2006). *The grief club: The secret to getting through all kinds of change.* Center City, MN: Hazelden.

Blau, G. (2008). Exploring antecedents of individual grieving stages during an anticipated worksite closure. *Journal of Occupational and Organizational Psychology, 81,* 529–550.

Böckerman, P., & Ilmakunnas, P. (2006). Elusive effects of unemployment on happiness. *Social Indicators Research, 79*, 159–169.

Brewington, J. O., Nassar-McMillan, S. C., Flowers, C. P., & Furr, S. R. (2004). A preliminary investigation of factors associated with job loss grief. *Career Development Quarterly, 53*(1), 78–83.

Bridges, W. (1991). *Managing transitions: Making the most of change.* Reading, MA: Addison Wesley.

Bridges, W. (1995). *JobShift.* Cambridge, MA: DeCapo Press.

Burgard, S. A., Brand, J. E., & House, J. S. (2007). Toward a better estimation of the effect of job loss on health. *Journal of Health and Social Behavior, 48*(4), 369–384.

Cohen, F., Kemeny, M. E., Zegans, L. S., Johnson, P., Kearney, K. A., & Stites, D. P. (2007). Immune function declines with unemployment and recovers after stressor termination. *Psychosomatic Medicine, 69*, 225–234.

Comino, E. J., Harris, E., Silove, D., Manicavasagar, V., & Harris, M. F. (2000). Prevalence, detection and management anxiety and depressive symptoms in unemployed patients attending general practitioners. *Australian and New Zealand Journal of Psychiatry, 34*, 107–113.

Garrett-Peters, R. (2009). "If I don't have to work anymore, who am I?": Job loss and collaborative self-concept repair. *Journal of Contemporary Ethnography, 38*(5), 547–583.

Linn, M. W., Sandifer, R., & Stein, S. (1985). Effects of unemployment on mental and physical health. *American Journal of Public Health, 75*(5), 502–506.

McKee-Ryan, F. M., Song, Z., Wanberg, C. R., & Kinicki, A. J. (2005). Psychological and physical well-being during unemployment: A meta-analytic study. *Journal of Applied Psychology, 90*(1), 53–76.

Moorhouse, A., & Caltabiano, M. L. (2007). Resilience and unemployment: Exploring risk and protective influences for the outcome variables of depression and assertive job searching. *Journal of Employment Counseling, 44*(3), 115–125.

Price, R. H., Choi, J. N., & Vinokur, A. D. (2002). Links in the chain of adversity following job loss: How financial strain and loss of personal control lead to depression, impaired functioning, and poor health. *Journal of Occupational Health Psychology, 7*(4), 302–312.

Sanders, C. M., Mauger, P. A., & Strong, P. N. (1985). Grief Experience Inventory, Loss Version. Colchester, VT: The Center for the Study of Separation and Loss.

Walsch, N. D. (2009). *When everything changes, change everything.* Charlottesville, VA: Hampton Roads.

16

Infertility and Reproductive Loss

DARCY L. HARRIS

INTRODUCTION

The inability to conceive or to successfully carry a pregnancy to term is a heartbreaking loss for many individuals. Several factors contribute to the impact of this particular loss, ranging from social expectations and the construction of motherhood as a defining role for women in the context of a pronatalist society to the personal struggle and pain that many women experience in their private lives in their longing to hold a child after enduring painful and often humiliating treatments for infertility. Even with the rise of women who are able to obtain high levels of professional accomplishment, the role of mother still holds the ideal of identification with being feminine and complete for most women; thus, the inability to conceive is often seen as a loss of identity for a woman. For couples that are unable to have biological children, the losses often include their friends and family members, who cannot comprehend the depth of their pain and struggle and who readily move on in their lives with the children they have conceived without difficulty. This chapter will focus on the unique aspects of the inability to conceive or to give birth to one's biological child, the social context of infertility, and the psychological effects of undergoing medical treatment for infertility.

Infertility is identified as the inability to conceive after 1 year of unprotected intercourse or the inability to carry a pregnancy to term. For women over 35, the definition of infertility changes to the inability to conceive after 6 months. The incidence of infertility in North America is approximately one in five couples. At present, infertility rates are increasing, and the cause of the increase is thought to be due to the changing roles of women and delayed child bearing, a higher incidence of sperm abnormalities, and the long-term effects of sexually transmitted diseases (STDs) on the reproductive system (Burns & Covington, 2006; McShane, 1997).

PSYCHOLOGICAL EFFECTS OF INFERTILITY TREATMENT

Most women who enter infertility treatment are unaware of the high levels of physical, financial, and psychological stress they will encounter while undergoing treatment. Many have heard media accounts of sensational or near-miraculous conception and birth through the use of medical technology and believe that it will be only a "matter of time" before they will become pregnant with their efforts (Bateman-Cass, 2000; Daniluk, 2001; Greil, 1991). There are myriad references to the life-altering impact of infertility and infertility treatment on women in the literature. Many of the women in these studies describe the "emotional roller-coaster" effect of treatment (Bateman-Cass; Daniluk, 1991). Several authors describe the diagnosis and treatment of infertility as a life crisis (Applegarth, 2006; Chester, 2003; Daniluk, 1997; Dupuis, 1997; Gerrity, 2001; Hart, 2002; Johansson & Berg, 2005; Lieblum & Greenfeld, 1997). Many women speak of their awareness of their infertility and going through the treatments as "devastating" and as "the worst experience of their lives" (Bateman-Cass; Domar, 1997). Burns (2005) refers to the entrance into infertility treatment as "paradise lost," as the woman loses the view of herself as healthy, procreative, and in control of her life. In their research, Domar, Zuttermeister, and Friedman (1993) described anxiety and depression scores in infertile women as similar to women who were suffering from cancer, hypertension, and cardiac rehabilitation.

Most of the studies that explore the psychological effects of infertility treatment on women report that anxiety and depression are frequent companions. In an analysis of 50 returned questionnaires from women after their first failed in vitro fertilization (IVF) attempt, Baram, Tourtelot, Muechler, and Huang (1988) reported that 60% of these women met the criteria for clinical depression. With more than two failed attempts, 94% of the women in their study reported severe symptoms of depression, including overwhelming sadness, helplessness, loss, guilt, reduced appetite, nightmares or disturbed sleep patterns, panic attacks, and anxiety. A total of 13% of these same women reported suicidal ideation. A similar finding was reported in a study by Garner, Arnold, and Gray (1984), who found that 64% of women in infertility treatment were clinically depressed, as assessed by the Beck Depression Inventory.

Many authors cite the experience of infertility and of undergoing infertility treatment as traumatic for many women (Deveraux & Hammerman, 1998; Diamond, Diamond, & Jaffe, 1999). Watson (2005) describes trauma in this context as an "experience of being emotionally and, at times, physically overwhelmed by an event that has grave negative consequences for the traumatized person" (p. 219). Although infertility is not comparable to a natural disaster or to abuse, it is unexpected and can have a profoundly negative effect on the woman (Zucker, 1999). Traumatic symptoms are also associated with feelings of powerlessness, helplessness, and loss of control, which "overwhelm the ordinary human adaptation to life" (Herman, 1992, p. 33). As already described, infertility and its treatment can, and often does, engender these very feelings. Women who may have previously felt a sense of confidence in their abilities and resourcefulness often find they are not prepared for the assault to their self-identity or loss of the sense of agency that can result from the realization of their infertile status and unsuccessful attempts to remedy their problem medically.

Compounding their infertile status, the invasiveness of the medical treatments and the ways they are sometimes implemented may further add to women's feelings of loss of control over their lives, their bodies, and their future. In her autobiographical article, Karen Eriksen (2001) gives a detailed personal account of her entry into medical treatment for infertility. In her description, she discusses how entrance into medical treatment required that she give the medical practitioners complete control over her body and her privacy. She describes having multiple procedures performed by doctors whom she had never met prior to them coming into the procedure room where she was already undressed and on the examination table.

> When I arrived for my first ultrasound, a doctor I had never met greeted me. How was I to spread my legs for someone who came in, introduced himself, and then just got down to business? He seemed nonplussed when I asked about it, saying "That's the way we do things around here." Different male doctors appeared for the next 3 days of ultrasounds as well. Why is it that the clinic would expect us to feel comfortable with this? Surely someone ought to know that having different men stick things in our "private parts" each morning is not a way to allay anxiety during an already anxiety-ridden time. (p. 58)

Women must consent to this type of treatment (and do) because of their desperation to try to become pregnant. Many women feel they have no choice but to be compliant and to submit to pelvic examinations and procedures by strangers to try to conceive the child they desire, even though having to do so causes them significant distress (Chester, 2003; Eriksen, 2001; Lauritzen, 1990; McLeod, 2002). In a study by Daniluk (2001) where couples were asked to retrospectively reflect on their experiences in infertility treatment, incidents of insensitivity by the medical care team were repeatedly cited as causing a significant amount of stress and anxiety. The psychological consequences for this way of treating infertile women, many of whom are already vulnerable due to the amount of powerlessness and helplessness that they feel, may indeed further traumatize them (Watson, 2005).

Infertile women frequently report feelings of increased stress when in the presence of pregnant women and babies. They are often unable to attend baby showers or holiday functions that are focused on children and family, and they avoid certain parts of stores that contain baby supplies or clothing because exposure to these stimuli increases their personal anxiety and distress (Dupuis, 1997; Verhaak & Burns, 2006). Some women report acute anxiety when entering the infertility clinic itself or even driving past the location where the clinic is located. Avoidance functions to protect these women from an escalation in their feelings of powerlessness and despair, much as avoidance of places and reminders that are associated with a traumatic event serves the purpose of protecting trauma survivors from experiencing acute anxiety related to their experiences (Dupuis; Eriksen, 2001; Hart, 2002; Watson, 2005). In addition to the self-imposed isolation and avoidance that may be used as a means of coping with stress and anxiety, many women feel marginalized in society as a result of their infertility, which adds to their isolation—they do not "fit in" with women who readily conceived or who have children, and they do not belong to the group of individuals who have chosen for themselves to live child free (Johansson & Berg, 2005). In a personal story written about her experience with infertility and how she felt in social contexts, Chester (2003) refers to herself as an "unmother."

THE EXPERIENCE OF LOSS IN INFERTILITY TREATMENT

The close monitoring, imagery, and medical procedures in infertility treatment allow a woman the opportunity to be highly involved and invested in a pregnancy at preconception levels, and all of her time and energy is devoted to continuing through the rigors of the treatment cycle (Sandelowski, Harris, & Holditch-Davis, 1990). Kluger-Bell (1998) noted that the high level of involvement by women during the treatment cycles and the technology that allows visualization of the entire process can contribute to attachment and emotional bonding to a *potential* pregnancy during the ultrasound monitoring of the woman's follicles.

Hurwitz (1989) describes a failed IVF cycle as more than the loss of a fantasized child, comparing it more closely to the loss of a real child due to the awareness of the woman that there was an embryo or embryos. In an earlier study, Greenfeld and Haseltine (1986) reported that women who felt they were pregnant at the time of the embryo transfer experienced grief reactions similar to women who have experienced a miscarriage. Garner et al. (1984) reported that many women viewed the embryo transfer in IVF to be the time of conception; when the pregnancy tests were performed 2 weeks later with negative results, these women grieved the loss of their children. For many, the losses are not only the chronic ongoing loss of fertility and the identification with or the dream of being a mother but also the loss of the children conceived in the Petri dish that "disappeared" after they were transferred into the woman's body. For some women, this loss includes the potential life in the follicles they saw on an ultrasound screen during treatment monitoring (Salzer, 1993; Seibel & Levin, 1987). It may therefore not be too much of a stretch to entertain the possibility that women who receive infertility treatments (as previously described) may form an attachment bond to another living being, even at times earlier than conception, and that their investment in the pregnancy (or potential pregnancy) is extremely high (Bateman-Cass, 2000; Glazer, 1997; Johansson & Berg, 2005). Many bereavement researchers identify the grief response as the result of a broken attachment bond (Bowlby, 1982; Parkes & Weiss, 1983). The grief of these women is real, even though there is no apparent "death."

For women, the loss experience in infertility and failed infertility treatment is a "layered" loss (Bateman-Cass, 2000). Women experience a loss of their dream of being a mother, while at the same time the intensity of the medical treatments strengthens their focus on and investment in this role. They also experience loss of control over their body and their life, the loss of their relationships with their partners as they once experienced them, and the ability to connect with friends and other family members who now have children and have moved on in the developmental milestones associated with parenthood.

UNRECOGNIZED LOSSES

Infertile women mourn losses that are often invisible and unrecognized by others (Bateman-Cass, 2000; Kirkman, 2003). In infertility, there is no baby to hold and no deceased person with whom experiences have been shared. The losses associated with infertility and infertility treatment are often misunderstood, invalidated, and dismissed. The grief associated with infertility is thus one that is *disenfranchised*, and there is often little social recognition and support available (Chester, 2003; Doka, 2002). Many individuals keep their infertility treatment private; thus, family and friends may not even know about their difficulties. However, even if family members and friends are informed of the infertility treatments, they often do not understand the complexities involved in these treatments or the intense and invasive nature of the procedures (Klock, 1997). Infertile women are still told by well-meaning others that they will conceive if they relax (which is unproven) or that they can always adopt a child, which is often not the case (Dupuis, 1997; Grant, 1994). Infertile women are often lectured about the advantages of not being encumbered by children's demands by others who think this information will somehow assuage the pain of their inability to conceive a much-desired baby. Many of these women become isolated in their grief due to the loss of their existing supports, as others are often unable to tolerate the intensity of the experiences and to understand grief from a loss that is unrecognized (Dupuis).

LIFETIME EFFECTS

Pavone (2005) conducted a qualitative study using in-depth interviews of eight working women as they underwent infertility treatment. In her study, she noted that many of the women who were working full time when they entered infertility treatment were either fired from their jobs or were forced to convert to part-time employment to accommodate the side effects of the medications or the intense scheduling requirements of the procedures. Many did not return back to full-time employment. Her conclusion was that the experience of infertility and infertility treatments changed the lives of these women as well as their view of the world and their view of themselves.

Many women in infertility treatment report months and sometimes years of facing not just the monthly awareness that conception has not occurred but also the loss of their identity and their hopes and dreams regarding the future. These women experience a form of chronic, ongoing loss that has no definitive ending, which can be appropriately described as *chronic sorrow*, and this topic is discussed at length in a preceding chapter of this book. In a narrative study of 31 infertile women, Kirkman (2003) references the construct of chronic sorrow in infertile women, describing the ongoing, chronic losses of these women as they mourn the loss of their hoped-for children and the mother role.

Johansson and Berg (2005) conducted a study of eight childless women using in-depth interviews 2 years after their last IVF treatment. In their study, the term *life grief* was used to describe the essence of these women's ongoing grief over being childless and unable to reproduce. It also included the loss of the mother role that these women experienced, which was accompanied by feelings of emptiness, pain, and despair. These authors further describe the life grief of their partici-pants as a form of suffering that is chronic in nature, with the women's monthly menstrual cycle serving as an ongoing reminder of their grief and pain. Daniluk (1991) describes infertility as being "like a death for which there are no rituals and little public acknowledgment" (p. 318). In addition to the loss of the hope and dream of having a child, women experience many other losses, such as loss of their health due to side effects from medication, loss of normalcy in their lives, loss of income from having to take time off work for treatments (or job loss as a result of inability to fulfill work commitments during treatments), loss of friends who have children or who cannot understand the intensity of the infertility experience, loss of self-identity and self-esteem, and the loss of equilibrium in their lives (Bateman-Cass, 2000; Burns, 2005; Daniluk, 1997; Domar, 1997; Harris & Daniluk, 2010; Johansson & Berg; Pavone, 2005).

CLINICAL IMPLICATIONS AND RECOMMENDATIONS

Being Present

In my private practice and also in the study that I completed with infertile women (Harris, 2009; Harris & Daniluk, 2010), one of the most helpful means of support identified by women in treatment was expressed as the presence of supportive individuals who would "just be there" and not try to make them feel better because they recognized that it was not possible to change what had already happened or to do anything different than what they were already doing. Many women stated that it was helpful to talk with someone who had been through similar experi-ences. Several described the importance of support from family, friends, and pro-fessionals who did not try to give advice or to "fix" things for them. Counselors must keep in mind that support needs to be founded on empathetic presence before attempting to focus on interventions aimed at cognitive reframing or solu-tions with a specific endpoint in mind.

Recognize, Name, and Validate All of the Losses

Counselors who work with individuals undergoing medical treatment for infertility must be prepared for the layers of loss that accompany this experience and must recognize that each aspect of loss needs to be named, validated, and grieved for what it represents to these individuals. As described in this chapter, these losses are both tangible and intangible, and each type of loss is significant and will mean something different to each person. Most individuals in infertility treatment typi-cally find that their experiences and the accompanying losses are minimized or dismissed by others. It is impossible to make things better by giving advice or attempting to smooth things over with placating comments. It is important to nor-malize the intensity of the treatment process, as the treatments and the focus on having a baby often rob the couple of their normal everyday routine and their relationship with each other as they have known it in the past. Validation of the many losses helps to name and give credence to the experiences and is cited by Doka (1989, 2002) as the first step in offering support to individuals who have experienced disenfranchised grief.

Consistency in Caregivers

Since the majority of infertility treatment occurs in the context of larger medical centers, which are often a part of a teaching program, women who seek medical treatment for infertility are frequently exposed to a variety of medical and ancillary health-care providers during the time that they are in treatment. Many women cannot even recall the names and roles of these providers because there are so many of them. It is very important that there be at least one or two primary care providers who are reliably present when the woman undergoes treatments or when treatment options are being considered. Due to the invasive nature of many of the procedures and the highly personal nature of the information in infertility treatment, it is important that women going through treatment feel that the health-care team is sensitive to their needs for privacy, that they are able to enter into dialogue with health-care team members regarding their decisions and feelings, and that they are not treated as objects on which a procedure can be performed without a relational context to the experience (i.e., meeting a physician before a pelvic examination, or knowing and consenting to who will be in a room where they will be undressed and having a procedure performed).

Informed Support

Individuals involved in infertility treatment need for their professional supports to understand the ins and outs of infertility treatment, including what is involved in specific types of treatment, typical medications and their side effects, what the various procedures involve, and a general understanding of the terminology that accompanies the treatment. Counselors who work with individuals in infertility treatment need to be informed about the specific medical and technical aspects of this experience to follow their clients' stories and to understand their experiences more deeply. A list of qualification guidelines for mental health professionals in reproductive medicine can be found in Covington and Burns (2006, Appendix 1). These guidelines specify that training in the medical aspects of infertility treatment is essential to provide informed support to individuals in infertility treatment.

Focus on Both the Process and the Goal

Clinicians in these contexts need to be aware of the valid need for control that these patients have and to actively seek to preserve the patients' autonomy in these settings. Because patients seek infertility treatment with a goal in mind, it can be very easy to repeatedly focus on the endpoint and outcome of treatment (i.e., pregnant or not). However, individuals in infertility treatment repeatedly state that the support by the clinical staff they received through the process of trying to conceive helped them immensely, even when the treatments were futile (for a discussion of the need to go through infertility treatment to psychologically move forward, see Daniluk, 2001; Harris, 2009). In these studies, support offered by clinical staff regarding the process and the impact of the treatments and how participants navigated their decision making along the way empowered the participants to make important treatment decisions that were congruent with their beliefs, values, and emotional resources.

Daniluk (1991) makes a point to emphasize that one of the tasks of counselors who work with infertile couples is to help them navigate through the places where they have control and where they need to be able to relinquish control. The need for control by these patients is often misinterpreted as a challenge to the authority of the care provider, and the participants in these studies emphasized the importance of being given control over the process and decision making as a key factor in their feeling supported by the health-care providers in the clinical setting.

Include Male Partners in Support

It is easy for clinicians to become very focused on the women's experiences because infertility treatments are usually concentrated on their bodies and women tend to be more verbal regarding their feelings. There is also a good deal of sympathy for women who are involuntarily childless because of the socialization to the role of mother for most women and the acceptance of pronatalism in Western society. However, literature exploring the experiences of couples in infertility treatment confirms that male partners are also profoundly affected by the inconvenience and intrusiveness of the treatments, the moods and despair of their partners and themselves, the financial hardships that may occur as a result of the treatments, and feeling helpless as they watch their female partners endure hardship for them to become parents (Daniluk, 1991, 1997; Diamond et al., 1999; Harris, 2009).

In studies that explored couples' responses to infertility, the male experience of infertility was often described to be more understated and focused on different aspects of the process than that of their female partners, but the men's experiences were certainly no less important than the women's experiences. It is important in clinical practice to make sure that male partners are included in offers of support and validated in their experiences of loss and powerlessness, although it may be interpreted and felt differently than the women's experiences. The experiences and needs of male partners in infertility are explored in literature by Daniluk (1991, 1997), Diamond et al. (1999), Epstein and Rosenberg (1997), and Newton (2006).

CONCLUSION

It is apparent that infertility is a life-altering experience for many who are unable to conceive or carry a biological child to term. Although infertility does not necessarily entail an acknowledged death, the impact of the losses associated with infertility and its treatment are profound for those who are involuntarily childless. The level of intensity and the ongoing nature of the losses demand a high degree of understanding and sensitivity to offer appropriate support to individuals who go through this experience. Sensational media accounts of births to older women add to unrealistic expectations about the success of medical treatment, and inaccurate information about the process and costs of adoption often lead to individuals making unhelpful and insensitive comments to individuals who are struggling with infertility. Women who are infertile are often faced with a profound loss of their identity as a "whole" person and as fully feminine according to social norms. Hopefully, more professionals will begin to understand the complexity of this issue and become well versed in the unique losses surrounding those who are infertile.

REFERENCES

Applegarth, L. D. (2006). Individual counseling and psychotherapy. In S. N. Covington & L. H. Burns (Eds.), *Infertility counseling: A comprehensive handbook for clinicians* (2nd ed., pp. 129–142). New York: Cambridge University Press.

Baram, D., Tourtelot, E., Muechler, E., & Huang, K. (1988). Psychosocial adjustment following unsuccessful in vitro fertilization. *Journal of Psychosomatic Obstetrics and Gynecology, 9,* 181–190.

Bateman-Cass, C. (2000). The loss within a loss: Understanding the psychological implications of assisted reproductive technologies for the treatment of infertility. *Dissertation Abstracts International, 61*(3), 1624B. (UMI No. 9965385)

Bowlby, J. (1982). *Attachment.* New York: Basic Books.

Burns, L. H. (2005). Psychological changes in infertility patients. In A. Rosen & J. Rosen (Eds.), *Frozen dreams: Psychodynamic dimensions of infertility and assisted reproduction* (pp. 3–29). Hillsdale, NJ: Analytic Press.

Burns, L. H., & Covington, S. N. (2006). Psychology of infertility. In S. N. Covington & L. H. Burns (Eds.), *Infertility counseling: A comprehensive handbook for clinicians* (2nd ed., pp. 1–19). New York: Cambridge University Press.

Chester, D. H. (2003). Mother. Unmother: A storied look at infertility, identity, and transformation. *Qualitative Inquiry, 9*(5), 774–784.

Covington, S. N., & Burns, L. H. (2006). *Infertility counseling: A comprehensive handbook for clinicians* (2nd ed.). New York: Cambridge University Press.

Daniluk, J. C. (1991). Strategies for counseling infertile couples. *Journal of Counseling & Development, 69,* 317–320.

Daniluk, J. C. (1997). Gender and infertility. In S. R. Lieblum (Ed.), *Infertility: Psychological issues and counseling strategies* (pp. 103–125). New York: Wiley.

Daniluk, J. C. (2001). "If we had it to do over again…": Couples' reflections of their experiences of infertility treatments. *Family Journal of Counseling and Therapy for Couples and Families, 9*(2), 122–133.

Deveraux, L. L., & Hammerman, A. J. (1998). *Infertility and identity.* San Francisco: Jossey-Bass.

Diamond, D. J., Diamond, M. O., & Jaffe, J. (1999). Infertility, pregnancy loss, and other reproductive traumas: A developmental perspective. *San Diego Psychologist, 8*(2), 1–3.

Doka, K. J. (1989). *Disenfranchised grief: Recognizing hidden sorrow.* Lexington, MA: Lexington Books.

Doka, K. J. (2002). *Disenfranchised grief: New directions, challenges, and strategies for practice.* Champaign, IL: Research Press.

Domar, A. D. (1997). Stress and infertility in women. In S. R. Lieblum (Ed.), *Infertility: Psychological issues and counseling strategies* (pp. 67–82). New York: Wiley.

Domar, A. D., Zuttermeister, P., & Friedman, R. (1993). The psychological impact of infertility: A comparison with patients with other medical conditions. *Journal of Psychosomatic Obstetrics and Gynecology, 14,* 45–52.

Dupuis, S. R. (1997). Understanding reproductive loss. *Dissertation Abstracts International, 58*(1), 414B. (UMI No. 9717693)

Epstein, Y. M., & Rosenberg, H. S. (1997). He does, she doesn't; she does, he doesn't: Couple conflicts about infertility. In S. R. Lieblum (Ed.), *Infertility: Psychological issues and counseling strategies* (pp. 129–148). New York: Wiley.

Eriksen, K. (2001). Infertility and the search for family. *Family Journal: Counseling and Therapy for Couples and Families, 9*(1), 55–61.

Garner, C. H., Arnold, E. W., & Gray, H. (1984). The psychological impact of in vitro fertilization. *Fertility and Sterility, 41*(2), 13.

Gerrity, D. (2001). Five medical treatment stages of infertility: Implications for counselors. *Family Journal: Counseling and Therapy for Couples and Families, 9*(2), 140–150.

Glazer, E. S. (1997). Miscarriage and its aftermath. In S. R. Lieblum (Ed.), *Infertility: Psychological issues and counseling strategies* (pp. 230–245). New York: Wiley.

Grant, K. R. (1994). The new reproductive technologies: Boon or bane? In B. S. Bolaria & H. D. Dickinson (Eds.), *Health, illness, and health care in Canada* (2nd ed., pp. 362–383). Toronto: Harcourt Brace.

Greenfeld, D. A., & Haseltine, F. (1986). Candidate selection and psychosocial considerations of in-vitro fertilization procedures. *Clinical Obstetrics and Gynecology, 29*(1), 119–126.

Greil, A. L. (1991). *Not yet pregnant: Infertile couples in contemporary America.* New Brunswick, NJ: Rutgers University Press.

Harris, D. L. (2009). *The experience of spontaneous pregnancy loss in infertile women who have conceived with the assistance of medical intervention.* Retrieved August 9, 2010 from ProQuest Digital Dissertations. (UMI no. 3351170).

Harris, D., & Daniluk, J. C. (2010). The experience of spontaneous pregnancy loss for infertile women who have conceived through assisted reproduction technology. *Human Reproduction, 25*(3), 714–720.

Hart, V. A. (2002). Infertility and the role of psychotherapy. *Issues in Mental Health Nursing, 23*(1), 31–41.

Herman, J. (1992). *Trauma and recovery.* New York: Basic Books.

Hurwitz, N. (1989). The psychological aspects of in vitro fertilization. *Pre- & Peri-Natal Psychology Journal, 4*(1), 43–50.

Johansson, M., & Berg, M. (2005). Women's experiences of childlessness 2 years after the end of in vitro fertilization treatment. *Scandanavian Journal of Caring Sciences, 19*(1), 58–63.

Kirkman, M. (2003). Infertile women and the narrative work of mourning: Barriers to the revision of autobiographical narratives of motherhood. *Narrative Inquiry, 13*(1), 243–262.

Klock, S. C. (1997). To tell or not to tell: The issue of privacy and disclosure in infertility treatment. In S. R. Lieblum (Ed.), *Infertility: Psychological issues and counseling strategies* (pp. 167–188). New York: John Wiley & Sons.

Kluger-Bell, K. (1998). *Unspeakable losses: Understanding the experience of pregnancy loss, miscarriage, and abortion.* New York: W. W. Norton.

Lauritzen, P. (1990). What price parenthood? *Hastings Center Report, 20*(2), 38–46.

Lieblum, S. R., & Greenfeld, D. A. (1997). The course of infertility: Immediate and long-term reactions. In S. R. Lieblum (Ed.), *Infertility: Psychological issues and counseling strategies* (pp. 83–102). New York: Wiley & Sons.

McLeod, C. (2002). *Self-trust and reproductive autonomy.* London: MIT Press.

McShane, P. M. (1997). Infertility diagnosis and reproductive options: A primer. In S. R. Lieblum (Ed.), *Infertility: Psychological issues and counseling strategies* (pp. 20–40). New York: Wiley & Sons.

Newton, C. (2006). Counseling the infertile couple. In S. N. Covington & L. H. Burns (Eds.), *Infertility counseling: A comprehensive handbook for clinicians* (2nd ed., pp. 143–155). New York: Cambridge University Press.

Parkes, C. M., & Weiss, R. S. (1983). *Recovery from bereavement*. New York: Basic Books.

Pavone, T. (2005). A phenomenological heuristic study of the emotional impact of infertility on the working woman. *Dissertation Abstracts International, 66*(6), 3453B. (UMI No. 3178455)

Salzer, L. (1993, August). The emotional experience of IVF. *RESOLVE: Emotional Aspects of Infertility*, 6–7.

Sandelowski, M., Harris, B. G., & Holditch-Davis, D. (1990). Pregnant moments: The process of conception in infertile couples. *Research in Nursing & Health, 13*, 273–282.

Seibel, M. M., & Levin, S. (1987). A new era in reproductive technologies: The emotional stages of in vitro fertilization. *Journal of In Vitro Fertilization and Embryo Transfer, 4*(3), 135–140.

Verhaak, C. M., & Burns, L. H. (2006). Behavioral medicine approaches to infertility counseling. In S. N. Convington & L. H. Burns (Eds.), *Infertility counseling: A comprehensive handbook for clinicians* (2nd ed., pp. 169–195). New York: Cambridge University Press.

Watson, R. I. (2005). When the patient has experienced severe trauma. In A. R. Rosen & J. Rosen (Eds.), *Frozen dreams: Psychodynamic dimensions of infertility and assisted reproduction* (pp. 219–235). Hillsdale, NJ: Analytic Press.

Zucker, A. N. (1999). The psychological impact of reproductive difficulties on women's lives. *Sex Roles, 40*(9–10), 767–786.

17

Coming Out
Intrapersonal Loss in the Acquisition of a Stigmatized Identity

DEREK SCOTT

*C*oming out of the closet is generally viewed by people within the queer communities and "liberal" others as a good thing. The ability to be authentic, engage with fellow members of a community, and form close, meaningful relationships with others of the same sex must surely be seen as goals anyone would desire—sort of like joining the Scouts or Guides. Why then are so many members of these communities plagued by mental health issues?

While I wholly agree with Moradi, Mohr, Worthington, and Fassinger (2009) that "defining a sexual minority population of focus carries with it challenging scientific (and political) tensions and consequences" (p. 6), the length and scope of this piece necessitates choices about population groups. I am choosing to simplify the discussion by focusing on gay or lesbian identified individuals and regret that space considerations do not permit a fuller discussion of bisexual, transgendered, and other queer identities.

According to Frost and Meyer (2009), "Theories of identity development among lesbians, gay men, and bisexuals (LGB) suggest that … overcoming internalized homophobia is essential to the development of a healthy self-concept" (p. 98). For Kashubeck-West, Szymanski, and Meyer (2008), "It is imperative that counseling psychologists adequately assess and address external and internalized heterosexism" (p. 616), because, as Hatzenbuehler (2009) comments after a comprehensive review of the research, "stigma-related stress ultimately influences the pathogenesis of mental health among sexual minorities" (p. 710).

The term *coming out* is considered herein to be the process whereby one's assumption, present throughout one's early years, that one has an exclusively heterosexual orientation is gradually replaced by the recognition of a homosexual orientation. Troiden (1989) reports on the "identity confusion stage, which usually occurs during adolescence, (followed by) … the identity assumption stage, the individual comes out as a homosexual" (as cited in Beatty, 1999, p. 597). Coming out, then, is an internal process that may or may not involve external declaration, and queers "have internalized an abundance of consistently negative and devaluing messages about homosexuality even before the subjective awareness of sexual attraction to members of the same sex. These values are usually ingrained well before the beginning process of labeling oneself as gay" (Burgoyne, 1994, cited in Cornelson, 1998, p. 265). And "since sexuality is a manifestation and expression of sexual orientation, the ability … to integrate … orientation into [the] overall personality is crucial to [the] achievement and maintenance of a healthy sexuality" (Cornelson, p. 263).

The queer identity then is one that is acquired—unlike some other stigmatized identities that may have been present from birth. Fundamental to the acquisition of this identity is the necessary loss of privileges attending the heterosexual identity, yet this profound loss is scarcely addressed within writings on homophobia. Jones (1985) and Walter (2003) are notable exceptions, as they observe that "these losses … might include rites of passage such as marriage and children in a climate of open support, or the right to speak openly about a partner" (cited in Green & Grant, 2008, p. 282).

What does it mean to lose the assumption that one is heterosexual? Janoff-Bulman (1992) identifies three major categories of assumptions: that the world is benevolent, meaningful, "a good, decent, moral person deserves positive outcomes" (p. 9), and the self is worthy and of value. When queers metaphorically step out of the world of the majority into the realm of the sexual minority (when the "them" becomes "me"), they become "victims" of heterosexism. What characterizes victim populations is that their members hold "basic assumptions about the benevolence of the world, the meaningfulness of the world and their own self-worth [that] are generally more negative than those of their non-victim counterparts" (Janoff-Bulman, p. 73).

It is a commonly held belief that queer-identified people "choose" their orientation (as evidenced by the still-prevalent use of the term *sexual preference*) and therefore deserve to suffer, in accordance with the "just world theory" postulated by Melvin Lerner (cited in Janoff-Bulman, 1992, p. 9). This etiologic myth, combined with the support heterosexism receives from its embedded ideological position within dominant culture, places mourning the loss of heterosexual privilege under the rubric of disenfranchised grief. The "disenfranchised griever is prone to experience an underlying sense of alienation and loneliness, shame and abandonment" (Kauffman, 2002, p. 68). A state of being that approximates that of the victim populations.

At this point I would like to invite you to participate in an exercise I have used repeatedly with individual clients and when providing workshops on diversity awareness, as it invites both empathy and compassion for anyone (including the self) engaged in the coming out process and may enrich the discussion. If you do not have time to do this right now by all means skip ahead, but please consider returning to it later:

1. Write "Gay/Lesbian" in the center of a piece of paper and circle it.
2. Generate as many derogatory terms as you can think of to describe gay men and lesbians, and write them down around the outside of the circle with arrows pointing toward the center. Clients may need to be encouraged to do this fully as some of the words are "rude." The list will generate responses such as *faggot* and *muff-diver.*
3. Now write down (if possible in a different color) the thoughts or feelings behind these words. Examples of thoughts might be, "They threaten the family," or "They should be locked up." Again, send arrows from these words to the center.
4. Consider what messages some of our institutions might add to this circle, and write them down. As an example, some religious institutions may proclaim that homosexuals are damned for eternity. Similarly, a medical establishment may not regard two men as both being a child's father.
5. Have a look at this circle. Notice the thoughts, feelings, and beliefs targeting the center. Now erase the words "gay/lesbian" and replace with the word "Me." Imagine suddenly finding yourself in the middle of this circle. Imagine that happening at 17 if you are a boy, 19 if a girl (the average age of coming out to self; McKay, 2006).
6. Now write down how you think you would feel about yourself. Consider to whom you would turn and with whom you might share this insight into yourself. Imagine for a moment what you have lost. Write down these losses.

This exercise is helpful in normalizing internalized homophobia and locating the source as heterosexism external to the individual. It also begins to normalize associated losses.

What grief theory has to offer queer reality is, I think, an acknowledgment that these losses are legitimate. For Kauffman (2002), the disenfranchised grieving self is turned inward, wishing repair but instead repeatedly attacking itself with its own worthlessness. Self delivers and receives on behalf of society a message such as, "Do not allow this grief to be real for you." Self enforces and abides by the order disallowing grief (Doka, 2002, p. 61). So the mourner is denied the possibility of moving through a process that facilitates integrative healing.

Ramirez (1991) and Steenbarger (1993) stress that multicultural therapists emphasize "it is the lack of fit between the minority client and the dominant culture—and not a deficit internal to the client—that is often the source of presenting problems" (as cited in Leahy & Dowd, 2002, p. 199). Yet merely reframing the experience for individuals and inviting them to consider their losses in light of this understanding are not sufficient interventions to mediate the negative mental health outcomes associated with the acquisition of a queer identity. We must instead look more closely at the process of internalizing negative beliefs and the function of shame in disenfranchised grief. We may then be better positioned to understand how individuals may, in the words of Frost and Meyer (2009), "negotiate this stigma and develop positive self-concepts in the face of it through counseling" (p. 107).

For Kauffman (2002), "Shame is the psychological regulator allowing and disallowing recognition of grief" (p. 63). It seems that without the belief that the mourner is entitled to grieve, grief will not occur. Corr (1998/1999) sees the disenfranchising of the grief process as an "active situation of disavowal, renunciation and rejection" (as cited in Green & Grant, 2008, p. 284). In self-disenfranchisement who may we regard as initiating this activity and who is the recipient?

Given that we are talking about mechanisms that occur within the psyche, an exploration of some of the assumptions about the psyche that inform personality theories may be helpful in pointing to ways self-disenfranchisement may be best approached. The traditional model of grieving is heavily influenced by psychoanalytic assumptions. Sigmund Freud understood grief as an "intrapsychic process of decathexis, the painful divestment of libidinal energy from memories of the lost object" (Whiting & James, 2006, para. 1). Most mainstream bereavement theories "have been psychologically orientated stage or phase theories, whilst others have been task focused" (Corr, 1998/1999; Greenstreet, 2004; Walter, 1999 in Green & Grant, p. 277). In recent years, however, these theories have been criticized for "on the one hand for being overly generalizing and prescriptive, and on the other hand for not acknowledging the socially constructed nature of categories that are highly regulatory and normative" (Corr, 1998/1999; Greenstreet, 2004; Walter, 1999 in Green & Grant, p. 277).

These and other critiques invite us to consider "a more growth-oriented paradigm of bereavement ... as counselors ... jettison explicit models of grieving altogether ... to work in a way that has greater fidelity to the lived experience of their clients" (Neimeyer, cited in Rothaupt & Becker, 2007, p. 13). In support of this shift "both Worden (2002) and Rando (1995) have argued for a fluid understanding of mourning," one in which these elements (formerly ascribed to a specific stage or task) can and do exist simultaneously" (cited in Servaty-Seib, 2004, para. 10).

Contemporary cognitive psychotherapy holds the view that "emotional and behavioral problems ... reflect the operation of a cognitive deficit or vulnerability... the primary therapeutic agenda is to change the client's beliefs in the direction of warranted standards of rational and/or objective thinking" (Lyddon & Weill cited in Leahy & Dowd, 2002, p. 198). In practice the goal here is to get clients to think like the therapist. Interpersonal and systems theorists maintain "an ongoing dialectical controversy regarding the relative degree of causation attributable to interpersonal and interactional as opposed to individual forces in determining behaviour" (Barone, Hersen, & Van Hasselt, 2004, p. 57).

All of these frameworks for counseling and therapy have embedded within them the assumption of the single subject, however, as Chandella (2008) points out: "Long before Freud, monistic definitions of self were being supplanted by hypotheses of dipsychism (dual selves) and polypsychism (multiple selves). There has been a discursive explosion in recent years around the concept of 'identity', within a variety of disciplinary areas, all of them, in one way or another critical of the notion of an integral and unified identity" (p. 61).

Bereavement counseling, as currently practiced, is rooted in the notion of a single fixed identity, which makes a discussion of intrapsychic loss problematic and confusing. I would like to introduce the concept of intrapersonal loss to more clearly define the mourning process that is occurring within the individual. The language forms we have supporting the monolithic model of the personality are not adequate for the task of describing this process and result in confusion. Kauffman's (2002) work exemplifies some of the difficulty: "Giving to oneself, self is, in the very difference between giving and receiving, not itself. That is, in the very act of giving, constituting itself, self is not itself" (pp. 67–68).

The notion of the self may be a relatively recent construct. Passmore (1985) explains that the "historic European idea of 'self' equated personal identity with the continuity of memory: 'identity' was linked to our ability to think of ourselves as being one and the same indivisible self at different times and different places" (cited in Dunning, 1993, para. 7). Revisiting this construct has led Dunning to declare, "The indivisible Cartesian self seems to be an anachronism at the close of the twentieth century" (para. 3). For Howell (2008), "The 'self' is plural, variegated, polyphonic and multi-voiced. We experience an illusion of unity as a result of the mind's capacity to fill in the blanks and to forge links" (p. 38).

Implicit in Freud's decathecting from the internalized loss object is the single "I," yet object relations theory, which may be regarded as the bedrock of grief counseling, offers the possibility of a polypsychic model. Leowald (1962) determined that "internalization may be understood as "certain processes of transformation by which relationships and interactions between the psychic apparatus and the environment are changed into inner relationships and interactions …. This is the process by which internal objects are constituted" (as cited by Kauffman, 2002, p. 73). So *object relations* may refer not simply to one subject engaging with multiple objects but also to multiple internal relationships with multiple internal subjects. Howell (2008) supports this view, stating that "an internalized object must include the assumption of an internalized object relationship (in which) … both the self component and the object component have subjectivity," which inevitably leads us to "conceptualizing a multiple self as internalizing relationships" (p. 42).

Clayton (2005) addresses the resistance the view of multiple selves encounters: "In the health professions there is widespread agreement that dissociative identity is dysfunctional and needs to be cured. This position is based on the assumption that the healthy self is unitary and therefore multiplicity must be disordered" (p. 9). Adopting a more open view of multiplicity then "depends on and informs a major shift in notions of the self, therapeutic research and practice, and social attitudes in general" (Clayton, p. 17). All of these shifts challenge us as counselors and as human beings.

Rowan (1990) regards the development of subpersonalities as "autonomous or semi-autonomous parts of the person" (p. 61), noting that it "seems to be a regular temptation of people working in this field, to try to classify the subpersonalities in some way" (p. 85). He refers to many theorists, including Freud on the superego, Carl Jung's complexes, Ferrucci's subpersonalities, Watkins and Johnson's ego-state theory, Berne's model of transactional analysis, Stewart Shapiro's concept of subselves, the voice dialogue work of Hal Stone and Sidra Winkelman, the "potentials" of Alvin Mahrer, Virginia Satir's work with parts, and the work of Genie Laborde in neurolinguistic programming.

Similarly, Schwartz (1995) observes that "self psychology speaks of grandiose selves versus idealizing selves; Jungians identify archetypes and complexes .... Gestalt therapy works with the top dog and the underdog; and cognitive-behavioural therapists describe a variety of schemata and possible selves ... [suggesting] that the mind is far from unitary" (p. 12). For Nerken (1993), "Alone among entities, the self reflects on itself—is at once subject and object" (cited in Rothaupt & Becker, 2007, p. 6), and this theme is echoed again in Rivera (1996): "The unmentioned or hidden 'multiplicity' in all of us comprises the many distinct and separate facets of a person's personality, the many ways of being which make up the 'whole' individual called 'I'" (cited in Clayton, 2005, p. 12).

Schwartz's (1995) Internal Family Systems (IFS) model appears to be the most effective for addressing intrapersonal loss when compared with other models that incorporate multiplicity. Pedigo (1996) notes, "it is apparent that IFS includes a fuller, more articulated concept of self" and that the "multiplicity of the mind is the most fundamental principle in the IFS model" (p. 269). Deacon and Davis (2001) agree that "IFS has moved family therapy into the new realm of the internal system" (p. 45). Rothaupt and Becker (2007) in their review of Western bereavement theories conclude that "new methodologies are providing in-depth exploration into the art and transformation of bereavement" (p. 13). IFS is one such methodology, and "to understand the IFS model is to ... appreciate a new paradigm in the fields of individual and family therapy" (Pedigo, p. 269). Within the IFS framework the mind is made up of many parts. A part is a "discrete and autonomous mental system that has an idiosyncratic range of emotion, style of expression, set of abilities, desires and view of the world" (Schwartz, p. 34).

The final concept central to the model is the self. The self has the capacity to view the whole system from an overall metaperspective and may be regarded as the "centerpiece of the IFS model" (Schwartz, 1995, p. 35). The self is characterized by the presence of the following qualities: calmness, clarity, curiousity, compassion, confidence, courage, creativity, and connectedness.

In his book *Internal Family Systems Therapy* (1995), Schwartz offers a critique of many of the embedded beliefs that inform the contemporary view of the self, including original sin; Darwinism and its influence on Freudian, behavioral, and evolutionary psychology; and developmental psychology and learning theory. He offers a move away from the pathogenic view of the human being. His understanding of self corresponds somewhat to the "willingness, openness and ... gentle, kindly, friendly awareness" present in mindfulness-based treatment approaches (Baer, 2005, p. 15), but what makes his approach truly salutogenic is his recognition that, unlike the view held by many mindfulness-based practitioners, "avoidance (of painful material) is not necessary and may be maladaptive" (Baer, p. 15). Schwartz maintains that all "parts" (including avoidant parts) are functioning in ways they regard as necessary for maintaining the health and integrity of the system. While some may be "destructive in their present state," these behaviors may be seen as a result of a "good part forced into a bad role" (Baer, p. 16). Bringing the quality of nonjudgmental curiosity to those parts reveals "the reasons that had forced them into those roles and their shame at what they had done" (Baer, p. 16).

However, for Schwartz (2001), the self is not merely the passive observer; it has "emergent compassion, lucidity, and wisdom to get to know and care for these inner personalities" (p. 36). He maintains that "most people have a poor self-concept because they believe that the many extreme thoughts and feelings they experience constitute who they are" (Schwarz, 1995, p. 17), so as Lester (2007) rightly concludes, "The possibility of attributing negatively valued aspects ... of oneself to one or more subselves may enable the individual to maintain high self-esteem" (p. 10). Within the IFS model we have a method for working concretely with the parts of the system associated with disenfranchised grief.

Returning to Kauffman's (2002) understanding of shame as the psychological regulator that disallows grief through internal attack, we can now inquire about how the shaming part may be of value to the system. When a part is bringing criticism into the system such as that described by Kauffman, the IFS model understands that part to be a protective "manager." These protectors are invested in controlling "your relationships and environment so that you're never ... humiliated, abandoned, rejected, attacked or anything else unexpected and hurtful" (Schwartz, 2001, p. 127). We generally do not like the parts with the critical voice, but if we can bring qualities of self to them—such as curiosity about their role— they will tell us more about their function and beliefs.

We can "interview" a part using direct access whereby the therapist or counselor speaks directly to the part, as in this example from Yalom (2002): "I also know there is some particularly reckless or careless part of you. I want to meet and to converse with that part" (p. 120). Or we can invite the client to focus internally and engage with the part. There may be parts of the client who do not wish to engage with the manager part—so those parts can be asked to step aside and allow the client's self to get to know the protector. When the manager part is asked about its protective role it will often reveal that it is preventing the system from becoming overwhelmed by other parts. In the case of a shaming manager, it might fear that if it did not do its job then parts grieving the loss of heterosexual identity and privilege would overwhelm the system—with what it perceives as disastrous results.

The parts that carry extreme feelings and extreme beliefs that the manager parts seek to protect us from are called "exiled" parts in this model. These are the parts that experience our vulnerability, and according to Schwartz (2001) there are good reasons to fear them: "They can pull us into black holes of emotion or memory, interfere with our functioning, draw us toward or keep us attached to hurtful people, and get us rejected or humiliated by people who disdain vulnerability" (p. 118).

In working with the shaming manager part we can be curious about and address its concerns. It may be worried that the exiles will overwhelm; we can assure it that they can regulate their affect. It may have anxiety that getting to know exiled parts will result in "external" changes in behavior; we can assure it that no change will occur without its permission. It may wish to negotiate a different role—more of a valve than a block—so that it will let some information through to the system from the exiled parts. When its concerns have been heard and addressed and its conditions satisfied, it may be willing to allow access to the exiled parts. When that happens we are in the familiar territory of affect-laden grieving parts. For people transitioning to a queer identity there will be a part or parts that need to vent their protest, others in shock and disbelief, some with intense sadness, shame, and regret, others still in depression, and even sometimes despairing and suicidal parts—all existing simultaneously and wanting our attention. Small wonder the manager part feels such a strong need to protect us.

When individuals are finally able to hear the parts of their system grieving the loss of heterosexual identity and privilege and when those parts are responded to with compassion, then grief is no longer disenfranchised, and the individuals are freed up to engage in the process that will lead to a healthy integration of the new identity.

I have focused this discussion narrowly on a specific area of disenfranchised grief but the process of working with intrapersonal losses can be of value for any acquired stigmatizing identity—for example, that of becoming disabled or a woman. This method can also be used for any loss in which shame may be a factor inhibiting access to the grieving parts. Additionally I consider the IFS method to be a valuable tool in working with past losses that may be activated by present circumstances.

If indeed as Atig (1996) asserts, "Bereavement therefore prompts us to 'relearn the self'" (cited in Neimeyer, Prigerson, & Davies, 2002, p. 239), then it behooves bereavement theorists to reexamine our understanding of our own self and consider how our unexamined beliefs may inform and limit our practice. If in so doing we notice a voice saying, "I don't need to do that," and another that is more open to the idea, perhaps we may get an inkling of our own interpersonal processes, opening the door to our increased receptivity to the experience of those we seek to serve.

REFERENCES

Baer, R. (2005). *Mindfulness-based treatment approaches: Clinician's guide to evidence base and applications*. San Diego: Academic Press.

Barone, D. F., Hersen, M., & Van Hasselt, V. B. (Eds.). (1998). *Advanced personality*. New York: Plenum.

Beaty, L. (1999). Identity development of homosexual youth and parental and familial influences on the coming out process. *Adolescence, 34*(135), 597–601.

Burgoyne, R. (1994). Counselling gay male couples living with HIV. *Canadian Journal of Human Sexuality, 3*, 114.

Chandella, N. (2008). I have that within which passeth show. *International Journal of the Humanities, 6*(2), 61–70.

Clayton, K. (2005). Critiquing the requirement of oneness over multiplicity: An examination of dissociative identity (disorder) in five clinical texts. *E-Journal of Applied Psychology, 1*(2), 9–19.

Cornelson, B. (1998). Addressing the sexual health needs of gay and bisexual men in health care settings. *Canadian Journal of Human Sexuality, 7*(3), 261–271.

Corr, C. A. (1998/1999). Enhancing the concept of disenfranchised grief. *Omega: The Journal of Death and Dying, 38*, 1, 1–20.

Deacon, S., & Davis, J. (2001). Internal family systems theory: A technical integration. *Journal of Systemic Therapies, 20*(1), 45–58.

Dunning, W. (1993). Post-modernism and the construct of the divisible self. *British Journal of Aesthetics, 33*(2), 132–141.

Frost, D., & Meyer, I. (2009). Internalized homophobia and relationship quality among lesbians, gay men, and bisexuals. *Journal of Counseling Psychology, 56*(1), 97–109.

Gold, S., & Bacigalupe, G. (2004). Interpersonal and systemic theories of the personality. In D. Barone, M. Hersen, & V. Van Hasselt (Eds.), *Advanced personality*. New York: Plenum Press.

Green, L., & Grant, V. (2008). "Gagged grief and beleaguered bereavements?" An analysis of multidisciplinary theory and research relating to same sex partnership bereavement. *Sexualities, 11*(3), 275–300.

Greenstreet, W. (2004). Why nurses need to understand the principles of bereavement theory. *British Journal of Nursing, 13*, 10, 590–593.

Hatzenbuehler, M. (2009). How does sexual minority stigma "get under the skin"? A psychological mediation framework. *Psychological Bulletin, 135*(5), 707–730.

Howell, E. (2008). *The dissociative mind*. New York: Routledge.

Janoff-Bulman, R. (1992). *Shattered assumptions: Towards a new psychology of trauma*. Toronto: Maxwell Macmillan.

Jones, L. (1985). The psychological experience of bereavement: Lesbian women's perceptions of the response of the social network to the death of a partner, Dissertation Abstracts International 46/09: 2566.

Kashubeck-West, S., Szymanski, D., & Meyer, J. (2008). Internalized heterosexism: Clinical implications and training considerations. *Counseling Psychologist, 36*(4), 615–630.

Kauffman, J. (2002) The psychology of disenfranchised grief: Liberation, shame, and self-disenfranchisement. In Doka, K. (Ed.), *Disenfranchised grief: New directions, challenges, and strategies for practice*. Champaign, IL: Research Press.

Leahy, R., & Dowd, T. (2002). *Clinical advances in cognitive psychotherapy: Theory and application*. New York: Springer Publishing Company.

Lester, D. (2007). A subself theory of personality. *Current Psychology, 26*, 1–15.

Lyddon, W. J., & Weill, R. (1997). Cognitive psychotherapy and postmodernism: Emerging themes and challenges. *Journal of Cognitive Psychotherapy, 11*, 2, 75–91.

McKay, A. (2006). Sex research update. (1), 47.

Moradi, B., Mohr, J., Worthington, R., & Fassinger, R. (2009). Counseling psychology research on sexual (orientation) minority issues: Conceptual and methodological challenges and opportunities. *Journal of Counseling Psychology, 56*(1), 5–22.

Neimeyer, R., Prigerson, H., & Davies, B. (2002). Mourning and meaning. *American Behavioral Scientist, 46*(2), 235–251.

Pedigo, T. B. (1996). Richard C. Schwartz: Internal family systems therapy. *Family Journal, 4*(3), 268–277.

Ramirez, M. III. (1991). *Psychotherapy and counseling with minorities: A cognitive approach to individual and cultural differences*. New York: Pergamon.

Rothaupt, J., & Becker, K. (2007). A literature review of Western bereavement theory: From decathecting to continuing bonds. *Family Journal, 15*(1), 6–15.

Rowan, J. (1990). *Subpersonalities: The people inside us*. London: Routledge.

Schwartz, R. (1995). *Internal family systems therapy*. New York: Guilford Press.

Schwartz, R. (2001). *Introduction to the internal family systems model*. Trailheads Publications.

Servaty-Seib, H. (2004). Connections between counseling theories and current theories of grief and mourning. *Journal of Mental Health Counseling, 26*(2), 125–145.

Steenbarger, B. N. (1993). A multicontextual model of counseling: Bridging brevity and diversity. *Journal of Counseling and Development, 72*, 8–15.

Troiden, R. R. (1989). The formation of homosexual identities. *Journal of Homosexuality, 17*(1/2), 43–73.

Walter, C. A. (2003). *The loss of life partner: Narratives of the bereaved*. New York: Columbia University Press.

Walter, T. (1999). *The revival of death*. London: Routledge.

Whiting, P., & James, E. (2006). *Bearing witness to the story: Narrative reconstruction in grief counseling.* VISTAS 2006 Online: American Counseling Association. Retrieved December 14, 2009 from http://counselingoutfitters.com/James.htm

Yalom, I. D. (2002). *The gift of therapy: An open letter to a new generation of therapists and their patients.* New York: HarperCollins Publishers.

Section *IIIB*

Loss of Functionality

18

Chronic Degenerative Conditions, Disability, and Loss

EUNICE GORMAN

Illness is the night side of life, a more onerous citizenship. Everyone who is born holds dual citizenship in the kingdom of the well and in the kingdom of the sick.

Susan Sontag

*I*t seems appropriate in a book dealing with change, transition, and loss that we pay attention to disability or chronic degenerative health conditions. Individuals experience very few life-altering events that cause as much upheaval, outside of the death of a loved one, than the diagnosis of a health-care problem that will stay with them throughout their life. For many, their chronic illness will take them through exacerbations, or flare-ups, and periods of relative quiet, or remissions. What will no doubt remain constant is the fear of further disability and the ongoing struggle to adapt, adjust, and cope as a condition continues or progresses and deteriorates. It is important to recognize the profound loss experiences that accompany a chronic illness, especially for young people in the prime of their lives, who may feel robbed of a future they had planned so meticulously. Older people also suffer numerous disruptions and grieve accordingly; however, they may feel less surprised by ill health, accepting it as part of the normal aging process. Either way the illness experience is fraught with changes, transitions, and losses that result in grief in individuals and their families.

Much has been written about the nature of disability over the last few decades (Davis, 2006; Kutscher, 2004; Murphy & Pardek, 2005). However even with this attention in the literature there remains some confusion about the meanings of various terms related to chronic illness.

To begin a discussion of chronic illness and degenerative health conditions it is important to define some key terms:

Disease: A change in the body, diagnosed, tested for, and treated. Everyone who has this condition has these signs and symptoms or objective findings; for instance, everyone with a diagnosis of multiple sclerosis, Alzheimer's disease, diabetes, or other conditions will have many of the same presenting problems (Campling & Sharpe, 2006).

Illness: The experience of being unwell—your illness, your reaction, your disabilities, your abilities, your personal subjective experience of disease (Campling & Sharpe, 2006).

Disability: A biological condition. Any restriction of mobility, vision, hearing, mental faculties, or developmental milestones resulting from an impairment of ability to perform an activity within the range of what might be considered normal.

Impairment: Any loss or abnormality of psychological, physiological, anatomical structure, or function.

Handicap: The function of the relationship between disabled persons and their environment. Handicap occurs when people encounter cultural, physical, or social barriers or obstacles that prevent them from fully participating in society. Handicap is the loss or limitation of opportunities to take part in the life of the community as fully as others who are not handicapped. For instance, transportation, housing, support services, and employment opportunities that are not accessible or appropriate can render a disabled person handicapped (WHO, 2001).

COMPLEXITY IN ILLNESS

Chronic illness is multifaceted, dynamic, and complex. By their very definitions chronic illnesses continue for life and do not have a cure, and often there is increasing disability and dysfunction that contributes to morbidity and mortality. Even more confounding is the fact that there is often no known cause or trigger associated with the onset of many chronic conditions. The why and how questions so central to our efforts to make meaning or gain understanding remain unanswerable. Chronic illnesses are often marked by degenerative conditions characterized by remissions and relapses. Patterns of onset, course, kind, and degree of disability vary from illness to illness. People with chronic illnesses are likely to experience more problems as they enter into the normal aging process or are diagnosed with concurrent illnesses. Care and management become key concepts when cure is not a possibility as is the case with chronic illnesses. Perhaps even more challenging are the misunderstandings associated with invisible or hidden disabilities. Furthermore, individuals who acquire disabilities over the course of their lives may experience different challenges from those who are born with chronic health problems or disabilities; the former group must adjust at each phase of development and life. Whether the onset is sudden or gradual or whether the condition runs in the family, chronic illness and the demands of illness are disruptive causing disequilibrium and thrusting the person and family into a medical system where compliance, adherence, medical regimes, adverse effects of treatments, and iatrogenic suffering (caused by the treatment or system) become key components of the illness experience.

BECOMING ILL

Chronic illness is a major unsettling experience, and the day to day is radically disturbed. This is true of any major change in a person's life. With the diagnosis of a chronic illness, what individuals take for granted and their explanatory systems are disrupted, causing a fundamental rethinking of biography and self-concept. They are thrown into a medical and health-care system and soon realize that they must mobilize resources and cope with uncertainty and that, often, medical knowledge is incomplete and treatment regimens are time-consuming, painful, or costly.

Corbin and Strauss (1988) proposed the following trajectory framework for chronic illness to explain the illness journey and the experience of becoming entwined with the medical system:

Pretrajectory: before illness begins, preventative phase, no signs and symptoms
Trajectory onset: signs and symptoms begin to be present, diagnostic phase
Crisis: life-threatening situation requiring emergency or critical care
Acute active illness: complications that require hospitalization
Stable illness course: symptoms are controlled by a regimen
Unstable illness course: symptoms are not controlled by regimens but do not require hospitalization
Downward: progressive deterioration in physical and mental status characterized by increasing disability and symptoms
Dying: immediate weeks, days, hours preceding death

Doka and Davidson (1997) outlined five phases, or stages, of the illness experience: (1) prediagnostic, (2) acute, (3) chronic, (4) recovery, and (5) terminal. People with chronic illnesses are stalled at stage 3 after a period of wondering if there might be something wrong with them because they do not feel right. Perhaps they are struggling with vague symptoms that can easily be explained away by fatigue, the seasonal flu, or stress. Eventually as time goes by and the vague feelings shift and change into more insidious problems that cause concern and require adjustments in day-to-day living, these persons will be compelled to visit a physician. Thus begins the diagnostic phase. Often after a long wait for appointments with specialists and after misdiagnoses, ambiguity, and misconceptions about their signs and symptoms, they will get a final answer and a name for what has been ailing them. Once the bad news is delivered, people react in a number of ways. For some chronic illness is viewed alternatively as a challenge, the enemy, or a sign of weakness. Some believe that chronic illness is a punishment; others see the diagnosis as a relief after what can sometimes be years of searching for a name and treatment plan for various symptoms that have been difficult for clinicians to pin down. For still others, it is a catalyst for spiritual growth. Chronic illness can result in a sense of belonging or of isolation and disconnection. For others, chronic illness can be a strategy to have more power and control over their lives and what they will do with their limited energies. Other individuals find that they come to see their chronic health problems as a gift.

Whether you come to view chronic degenerative conditions from a biomedical view (disease as a health problem), an economic model, a sociopolitical view (sick role, passing), feminist theory (gendered nature of human experience), or a cultural viewpoint, barriers exist for people who are living with chronic illness. Numerous misconceptions continue to plague those who are differently abled, and those with chronic illnesses are often neglected or misunderstood. If, as is often the case, physical illnesses are accompanied by other diagnoses or intellectual disabilities the person is rendered even more disadvantaged and thrust into the "sick role," which can begin to define them.

UNCERTAINTY

Perhaps one of the biggest hurdles to overcome for people who have been diagnosed with a chronic illness is the loss of a sense of certainty about the world and themselves in the world. Even though rationally we may understand that we have limited control in our lives, it still comes as a shock when the feared becomes actualized. Many people travel through life hoping, and even believing, that they will die quietly in their sleep at 94 after a long, healthy, and happy life. Most of us do not plan for chronic health concerns. Mishel (1988) outlines the challenges related to uncertainty including how hard it is for these individuals to structure meaning because of the ambiguity concerning the state of their illness. The complexity of treatments, negotiating a confusing and complex system of care, coping with a lack of information about the diagnosis or the potential seriousness of the illness, as well as an unpredictable illness course all combine to magnify the losses associated with disability. This uncertainty makes it challenging to make meaning of illness (Bruhn, 1990; Fife, 1994, 1995; Mishel, 1990) or to create meaning in illness—what Yalom (1982) referred to as terrestrial meaning or the meaning of my life.

According to Ellis (2005), uncertainty usually has four forms: (1) ambiguity concerning the state of illness or event, (2) complexity regarding treatment and system of care, (3) lack of information about the diagnosis or the seriousness of the illness or the event, and (4) unpredictability of the course of the disease and prognosis. At the same time that people are trying to cope with uncertainty they must manage grief (Bevan & Thompson, 2003), mourn the loss of the optimal self (Callahan, 1993), cope with the dread of pain and suffering and struggle with exclusion and stigma. Moreover, the accompanying sense of lack of control, or perceived lack of control, is sometimes the most difficult issue related to chronic illness for people to reconcile themselves to. We live in a society that stresses autonomy, self-control, and individuals' rights and freedoms, and to suddenly feel that control slipping away can be shocking. Helplessness, powerlessness, vulnerability, and role captivity are often new experiences for people newly diagnosed with a chronic illness and not welcome ones at that. The stress caused by unpredictability, flare-ups, setbacks, exacerbations, and recurrences further complicates the experience of loss of functionality in chronic illness.

TABLE 18.1   Potential Losses Associated With Chronic Illness

Health	Networks	Range of choices
Relationships	Sense of omnipotence	Socioeconomic status
Independence	Housing	Sense of worthiness
Freedom of movement	Options	Hobbies, recreational pursuits
Sense of certainty	Opportunities	Control
Capacity	Voice, say, input	Decision-making power
Idea of an endless future	Job lock	Rights (human, political, civil, social)
Personal power	Income	Taken-for-grantedness
Roles	Sexuality changes	Privacy
Place	Dating, intimacy	Confidentiality, disclosure
Status	Social capital	Access
Work	Identity	Experiencing discrimination
Livelihood	Intimacy	
Autonomy	Body image	

Some of the changes, transitions, and losses associated with chronic illness center around the issue of predictability, capacity, belonging, and the loss of a planned-for future (Frank, 1991, 1992, 1995, 1998). Losses can be categorized as behavioral losses (individual actions), cognitive losses (how you perceive or know things), emotional losses (consciousness or how you feel), physical losses (how your body feels and reacts), and spiritual losses (aspects of spirit) (Neeld, 2005).

The losses associated with the onset of a chronic degenerative illness are unique and varied to each individual. Each person may encounter only some of the potential losses listed in Table 18.1, whereas others may live through many of those losses listed.

The potential responses to the losses, changes, and transitions associated with chronic illness, listed in Table 18.2, are wide ranging, and the list in the table should in no way be seen as all inclusive.

As always, the onset of disability or chronic illness can be complicated by concurrent stressors and a history of abuse or power struggles. Other oppressions including gender, race, ethnicity, sexual orientation, or class may be magnified when coupled with chronic illness, leaving a person feeling disadvantaged on many fronts.

BECOMING A "PATIENT"

The experience of becoming a "patient," of being bombarded by helpful suggestions from others, or of begin ignored and talked over can be galling. Feeling the pressure to be optimistic and positive to make dealing with family, friends, even health care-workers easier can be exhausting. Trying to find ways to preserve relationships with family, friends, and coworkers, if individuals are able to continue working, can seem daunting. Coping with the insensitivity of strangers being asked to make complex decisions about medical care and alternative and complementary therapies can be confusing and intimidating. Managing relationships

TABLE 18.2   Potential Responses to the Onset of a Debilitating Chronic Condition

Fear (of a body out of control, dependence, death, disability, the future, care of children, abandonment, loss of love, more, and loss of approval)	Anxiety	Behavioral changes
	Denial	Feeling like a burden
	Shock	Physical changes
	Numbness	Economic changes
Loss of self-esteem	Depression, suicidal ideation	Social or psychological changes
Relationship stress	Relapses of previous substance abuse	Cognitive changes
Privacy issues	Lack of adequate information or education	Spiritual crisis
Hopeless		Family and friends overprotective or underprotective
Suffering	Shame	
Why me?	Feeling trapped	
Stress	Isolation	Passing as healthy
Adjustment issues	Worry	Guilt
Anger, rage	Reliance on caregivers	
Blaming	Discomfort	

with formal and informal caregivers and negotiating the system complicates the experience of loss of functionality even further. Other tasks related to illness include adjusting to pain and incapacitation and dealing with the hospital environment, procedures, and special treatments. Preserving reasonable emotional balance while fearing for what the future might bring is challenging. And through all of these adjustments there is, at least initially, grief: mourning what has been lost; capacity; the illusion of control; belonging; treasured activities in which these individuals are no longer able to take part, a sense of ease in their body and its movements; and a future that may be filled with even more disability if their condition worsens.

WHAT IS NORMAL?

The privileging and foregrounding of health in society is problematic for people diagnosed with a chronic illness. All illnesses have a neutral valence (Weiser, 1996) until their meanings are socially and culturally constructed (Freud, 1999; Wendell, 1996). These authors and others remind us of the moral ambivalence society has toward different kinds of illness; hence, we have created categories of "innocent victims" and "guilty agents." Chronically ill individuals are often viewed as "other." They are subject to blame-the-victim mentality as if somehow they might have avoided this health catastrophe or perhaps even may have brought it on themselves or somehow deserve it. Labeling, exclusion, silencing, and prejudice are all very much a part of the chronic illness experience. In a world where access and ableism, or discrimination, in belief or in practice, against those who are disabled exists it is not unusual for people with chronic illnesses to be seen as living outside the definition of "normality." This is especially true for those who struggle with addictions or mental health problems where such chronic conditions are often viewed as a sign of weakness, bad behavior, self-indulgence, or simply a lack of willpower. The fallout from the social disadvantage of illness and disability is problematic when we make the distinction between illness as "deviance" and health as conformity. Society has thrust the disabled into inferior bargaining positions. They face inequality, discrimination, and marginalization. We as a society continue to fear disability and the disabled—especially those with mental health concerns. Limited understanding contributes to fear and distancing. Stigma associated with disability does not just stop at the person but extends to their families and friends. Goffman (1963) referred to this experience as "courtesy stigma." Survival disparities, socioeconomic downward drift, insurance issues, red tape, competing priorities, and negotiation become norms for people who find themselves diagnosed with a chronic condition.

Many have written about the impact of chronic illness: multiple sclerosis, fibromyalgia, mental health problems, chronic fatigue syndrome, Crohn's disease, ostomies, Parkinson's disease, chronic pain and the impact of chronic illness on caregivers and spouses. Some have referred to chronic illness rather poetically as a dangerous opportunity (Frank, 1991), a biographical disruption (Bury, 1982), or the loss of the destination and map (Frank, 1995). No matter how we might conceptualize, or think about, loss of function we need to remember that there is a growing group of chronically critical individuals being created in a world of high-tech care where multiple needs can be met in people who would normally have died only 10 years ago.

THE LOSS NARRATIVE

It is important to note that the loss narrative is being rejected by many disabled people who do not agree with the traditional negative lexicon of disability. The loss narrative implies incompleteness, vulnerability, and need for rehabilitation that is not necessarily reflective of the joy and happiness often experienced within disability or the disabled (Watermeyer, 2009). Moreover, the loss narrative implies that all disabled people have aspirations to achieve so-called normality. Rather, by rejecting the loss template the disabled are highlighting the benefits of "ballpark normalcy" (Klein & Kemp, 2004). A strong disability identity, thriving disability rights, and independent living movements have emerged over the past few decades. These social and political movements seek to fight the negative stereotypes often attached to loss of functionality and chronic illness.

BENEFIT FINDING

Benefit finding in chronic illness within the self and in relationships has received much attention in the literature of late (Galvin, 2002, 2003, 2005; Pakenham, 2007; Tennen & Affleck, 2002). Researchers and people with disabilities and chronic illness point to positive meaning in illness, thus challenging the way we have looked at people who have chronic disabling conditions. The central and crucial difference is that we view the person first and the disability second. Nosek (1996) talks about wellness in disability across key life tasks: (1) spirituality, (2) friendships, (3) love, (4) work, and (5) self-regulation, and Daudet (2002) reminds us that suffering can be instructive. On a cautionary note, Tomich and Helgeson (2004) warn that benefit finding may interfere with self-care if it is not realistic or it causes individuals and family members to ignore elements of the disease experience that need attention or intervention.

The field of disability studies has taken hold at many universities and colleges, where social and cultural constructions of illness, disability, and health are being investigated. A similarly driven movement to clarify disability etiquette has emerged that cautions caring individuals to always be cognizant of the stress of asking for, and receiving, help (Cohen & Silver, 2006).

Rather than viewing chronic illness or disability as a tragedy, many are transformed. They go on to do well, they remain active, engaged, and connected within their families and communities, and they come to some level of acceptance of their "new normal." Some individuals living with chronic illnesses do not see themselves as diminished or living in devalued bodies but instead find a "survivor self" within (Wolin & Wolin, 1993). Wolin and Wolin characterize this newfound strength as encompassing insight, independence, relationship, initiative, creativity, humor, and morality. Drawing on past coping strategies, reactions, and responses to stress and developing new methods and mechanisms can assist with adaptation to the primary, secondary, and collateral losses associated with chronic illness.

Shifting from a discourse of deficits to one of possibilities (Madsen, 2007) can go a long way toward shifting from the medical model that stresses illness, diagnosis, deficit, deformity, and disability as defining elements of the chronic illness experience to a more social model of disability that stresses different ways social identities are devalued (Table 18.3).

TABLE 18.3 Potential Gains Associated With Chronic Illness

Giving back	Wisdom	Learning to work system
Mastery	Increased personal power	Self-discovery
Introspection	Awareness of mortality	Acceptance
Self-renewal	New priorities	Sense of purpose
Strength	Restoring personal agency	Educating others
Catalyst for change	Spirituality	Volunteering
Participating in research	Understanding	Acts of kindness and charity directed at
Caring for others	Sense of coherence	you (or performed by you)
Reflection	Sense of connection	Slowing down
Influence	Second chances	Redefining what is important
New identity in a new body	Inner directedness	Living more consciously
Insight	Turning point	Meaning making
Self-actualization	Hope	

Sources: Altemus, 2003; Frank, 1998; Groopman, 2004; Martz & Livneh, 2007; Papathanassoglou & Patiraki, 2003; Rioux & Daly, 2006; Seligman & Darling, 2007.

CLINICAL CONSIDERATIONS

Instrumental Support

The onset of a chronic and potentially disabling and degenerative illness requires that people and their families be given information, education, system navigation and negotiation tips, care, and in many cases either financial aid or information about accessing benefits and insurance. Assistance might include advocacy, information, and training opportunities so that individuals and their families can take on medical self-management with confidence. Our assessment of what needs to be done and what service we might be helpful needs to be thorough and timely and might include some or all of the pieces of information listed in Table 18.4.

Self-Efficacy

When the myth of control is shattered, people, their families, and friends are challenged to reorganize and to reconstruct their reality, their sense of self, their sense of the world, and their sense of themselves in the world. Personal agency, attitude toward chronic illness, and choice are stressed in the literature about chronic illnesses. Part of our work as professionals is to support people in their attempts to cope with chronic illness. Assisting individuals with problem solving, communication, resilience, and flexibility and identifying coping mechanisms and behavioral changes can lead to better adaptation over time.

TABLE 18.4   Assessment and Things to Consider

Culture	Attitude	Flexibility
Family	Faith	Children and care
Schooling and education	General health	Future fertility or infertility concerns
Past coping	Dependence	Range of coping strategies
Ethical issues and dilemmas	Location (urban, rural) remote	Workplace support
Family of origin	Perception of loss	Preexisting conditions or concerns
Self-esteem	History of loss	Legal issues
Mental health	Concurrent stressors	Culpability or possible prevention of
Housing	Personality style	loss or illness
Self-efficacy	Physical resources	Willing to attempt adaptation
Ego strengths	Self-care	Commitments
Fighting spirit	Gender	Time
Impact of normal aging	Prior successes	Birth order
Help seeking	Nature of illness and loss	Helper history
Help acceptance	Self-redefinition	Being helped history
Developmental stage	Uniqueness of what was lost	Insurance issues
Family life-cycle stage	Options available	Medical care
Illness knowledge	Social support	Relationship status
Religion	Finances	
Spirituality	Access	

Support

Maintaining personal integrity and dignity in light of treatments, procedures, tests, hospitalizations, and exacerbations requires both formal and informal social supports, information, and accessible and appropriate services. We cannot forget the family and friends in our efforts to support and care for people with disabilities. As with any loss there are direct (the person), indirect (family and friends of the person suffering a loss), and hidden (work mates, teachers, community members) groups who endure the impact of the loss experience and the subsequent grief and the efforts at adjustment. Each of these groups must be treated with compassion and respect.

Uncertainty and Lack of Control

Many people when faced with heath challenges become easily and quickly overwhelmed. They may freeze and be unable to make important decisions or be driven to extremes of pessimism or optimism about the future. Part of our role as professionals is to help people manage what is very much a hallmark of disabling conditions: uncertainty and lack of control. Finding ways to support control and to give control back to individuals is important.

Fostering Hope

Saleh & Brockopp (2001) outline six strategies to foster hope: (1) feeling connected with God, (2) affirming relationships, (3) staying positive, (4) anticipating survival, (5) living in the present, and (6) fostering ongoing accomplishment. Hope may shift, change, and evolve over time. What begins as a hope that the diagnosis that is feared or anticipated will not come to pass may end up as hope for a cure (Herth, 2000; Herth & Cutcliffe, 2002). Somewhere along the way, when cure is not an option, hope may become more realistic. Hope may then involve the sincere wish that efforts at coping and managing the illness will make a difference or that relationships will survive the ongoing barrage of medical problems or that a new treatment will manage chronic pain more efficiently and effectively.

Systemic Changes

These changes in the way we train and support health-care professionals are central to improved care and support of those diagnosed with a chronic degenerative illness. The growth of narrative medicine and recognition of the importance of the story may prove beneficial to those entering into long-term relationship with health-care professionals because of the ongoing nature of their condition (Charon, 2006, 2007; Raoul, Canam, Henderson, & Paterson, 2006).

Chronic illness causes multiple and often profound changes in people and their family's life. The transition from full and vigorous health to disability or ill health is a minefield of personal and social losses and gains. While supporting people's need to mourn what has been lost, we must also assist them, when appropriate, to examine what may have been found.

THINGS TO CONSIDER

1. Think about someone you know who has a chronic health problem. Has this person grieved the loss of preillness identity? Struggled with the insensitivity of others? Suffered because of stigma or illness reputation? Had to manage with reduced income, even poverty? Wrestled with the norms that accompany the label "patient"?
2. Consider invisible disabilities, or chronic illnesses, and the barriers and obstacles faced by people who have such conditions as deafness or hearing loss, partial blindness, chronic pain, severe allergies, fibromyalgia, depression, brittle diabetes, chronic daily headache, or other health issues that are not readily "seen."
3. How do families and communities assist with, or buffer, the impact of chronic degenerative health problems or loss of functionality?
4. Making meaning of chronic illness across symptoms, cultural significance, personal and social life world meanings, explanations, and emotions, according to Kleinman (1988), can be challenging. What do you imagine might be helpful to individuals trying to make meaning of their changed health status?

REFERENCES

Altemus, B. (2003). *The gift of pain: Transforming hurt into healing*. New York: The Berkley Publishing Group.

Asbring, P., & Narvanen, A.L. (2002). Women's experience of stigma in relation to chronic fatigue syndrome and fibromyalgia. *Qualitative Health Research, 12*(2), 148–160.

Bevan, D., & Thompson, N. (2003). The social basis of loss and grief: Age, disability and sexuality. *Journal of Social Work, 3*(2), 179–94.

Bruhn, J.G. (1990). The two sides of worry. *Southern Medical Journal, 83*, 5, 557–562.

Bruhn, J.G. (1994). *Managing boundaries in the health professions*. Springfield, IL: Charles C. Publishers.

Bury, M. (2001). Illness narratives: Fact or fiction? *Sociology of Health and Illness, 23*(3), 263–285.

Callahan, D. (1993). *The troubled dream of life: Living with mortality*. New York: Simon & Schuster.

Campling, F., & Sharpe, M. (2006). *Living with long term illness: The facts*. Oxford, UK: Oxford University Press.

Charon, R. (2006). *Narrative medicine: Honoring the stories of illness*. Oxford, UK: Oxford University Press.

Charon, R. (2007). What to do with stories: The sciences of narrative medicine. *Canadian Family Physician, 53*(8), 1265–1267.

Cohen, J., & Silver, Y. (2006). *Disability etiquette: Tips on interacting with people with disabilities*. Jackson Heights, NY: United Spinal Association.

Cohen, R.M. (2008). *Strong at the broken places: Voices of illness, a chorus of hope.* New York: Harper Collins.

Corbin, J.M., & Strauss, A. (1988). *Unending work and care: Managing chronic illness at home.* San Francisco: Jossey-Bass.

Daudet, A. (2002). *In the land of pain.* New York: Alfred A. Knopf.

Davis, L.J. (Ed.). (2006). *The disability studies reader* (2nd ed.). New York: Routledge.

Doka, K. (1993). *Living with life-threatening illness: A guide for patients, their families, and caregivers.* New York: Lexington Books.

Doka, K. & Davidson, J. (Eds.). (1997). *Living with grief when illness is prolonged.* Washington, D.C.: Hospice Foundation of America.

Drainoni, M.L., Lee-Hood, E., Tobias, C., Bachman, S.S., Andrew, J., & Maisels, L. (2006). Cross-disability experiences of barriers to health-care access. *Journal of Disability Policy Studies, 17*(2), 101–115.

Ellis, K. (2005). Disability rights in practice: The relationship between human rights and social rights in contemporary social care. *Disability and Society, 20*(7), 691–704.

Fife, B.L. (1994). The conceptualization of meaning in illness. *Social Science of Medicine, 38*(2), 309–316.

Fife, B.L. (1995). The measurement of meaning in illness. *Social Science of Medicine, 40*(8), 1021–1028.

Frank, A.W. (1991). At *the will of the body: Reflections on illness.* Boston: Houghton Mifflin.

Frank, A.W. (1992). What kind of phoenix? Illness and self-knowledge. *Second Opinion, 18*(2), 31–41.

Frank, A.W. (1995). *The wounded storyteller: Body, illness and ethics.* Chicago: University of Chicago Press.

Frank, A.W. (1998). Stories of illness as care of the self: Foucauldian dialogue. *Health, 2*(3, July), 329–348.

Frank, A.W. (2004). *The renewal of generosity: Illness, medicine, and how to live.* Chicago: University of Chicago Press.

Freud, S. (1999). The social construction of normality. *Families in Society, 80*(4), 333–339.

Galvin, R.D. (2002). Disturbing notions of chronic illness and individual responsibility: Towards a genealogy of morals. *Health, 6,* 2, 107–137.

Galvin, R.D. (2003). The paradox of disability culture: The need to combine versus the imperative to let go. *Disability & Society, 18,* 5, 675–690.

Galvin, R.D. (2005). Researching the disabled identity: Contextualising the identity transformations which accompany the onset of impairment. *Sociology of Health & Illness, 27,* 3, 393–413.

Galambos, C.M. (2004). Social work practice with people with disabilities: Are we doing enough? *Health & Social Work, 29*(3), 163–165.

Glenton, C. (2003). Chronic back pain sufferers—striving for the sick role. *Social Science and Medicine, 57*(11), 2243–2252.

Goffman, E. (1963). *Stigma: Notes on the management of spoiled identity.* Englewood Cliffs, NJ: Prentice-Hall Inc.

Groopman, J. (2004). *The anatomy of hope: How people prevail in the face of illness.* New York: Random House.

Herth, K.A. (2000). Enhancing hope in people with a first recurrence of cancer. *Journal of Advanced Nursing, 32*(6), 1431–1441.

Herth, K., & Cutcliffe, J.R. (2002). The concept of hope and nursing 3: Hope and palliative care nursing. *British Journal of Nursing, 11*(14), 977–983.

Klein, S.D., & Kemp, J.D. (Eds.). (2004). *Reflections from a different journey: What adults with disabilities wish all parents knew.* New York: McGraw-Hill.

Kleinman, A. (1988). *The illness narratives: Suffering, healing, and the human condition.* New York: Basic Books.

Kutscher, A.H. (2004). *Living under the sword: Psychosocial aspects of recurrent and progressive life-threatening illness.* Lanham, MD: Scarecrow.

Madsen, W.C. (2007). *Collaborative therapy with multi-stressed families* (2nd ed.). New York: Guilford.

Martz, E., & Livneh, H. (Eds.). (2007). *Coping with chronic illness and disability: Theoretical, empirical and clinical aspects.* New York: Springer.

Miller, J., & Timson, D. (2004). Exploring the experiences of partners who live with a chronic low back pain sufferer. *Health and Social Care in the Community, 12*(1), 34–42.

Mishel, M.H. (1988). Uncertainty in illness. *Image: Journal of Nursing Scholarship, 20,* 225–232.

Mishel, M.H. (1990). Reconceptualization of the uncertainty in illness theory. *Image: Journal of Nursing Scholarship, 22*(4), 256–263.

Murphy, J.W., & Pardeck, J.T. (2005). *Disability issues for social workers and human service professionals in the 21st century.* Binghamton, NY: Haworth Press.

Neeld, E.H. (2005). *Tough transitions: Navigating your way through difficult times.* New York: Warner.

Nosek, M.A. (1996). Wellness among women with physical disabilities. In D. Krotoski, M.A. Nosek, & M.A. Turk (Eds.). *Women with physical disabilities achieving and maintaining health and well-being* (pp. 17–33). Baltimore: Paul H. Brookes Publishing Co.

Ohman, M., & Soderberg, S. (2004). The experience of close relatives living with a person with serious chronic illness. *Qualitative Health Research, 14*(3), 396–410.

Pakenham, K.I. (2007). The nature of benefit finding in multiple sclerosis. *Psychology, Health and Medicine, 12*(2), 190–196.

Papathanassoglou, E.D., & Patiraki, E.I. (2003). Transformations of self: A phenomenological investigation into the lived experience of survivors of critical illness. *Nursing in Critical Care, 8*(1), 13–21.

Parish, S.L., & Huh, J. (2006). Health care for women with disabilities: Population-based evidence of disparities. *Health & Social Work, 31*(1), 7–15. (Reader)

Peolsson, M., Hyden, L.C., & Larsson, U.S. (2000). Living with chronic pain: A dynamic learning process. *Scandinavian Journal of Occupational Therapy, 7*(3), 114–125.

Raoul, V., Canam, C., Henderson, A.D., & Paterson, C.V. (Eds.). (2006). *Unfitting stories: Narrative approaches to disease, disability and trauma.* Waterloo/Kitchener, Ontario, Canada: Wilfrid Laurier University Press.

Raske, M. (2005). The disability discrimination model in social work practice. In G.E. May & M.B. Raske (Eds.), *Ending disability discrimination: Strategies for social workers* (pp. 99–112). Boston: Pearson Allyn & Bacon.

Richardson, J.C., Ong, B.N., & Sim, J. (2007). Experiencing chronic widespread pain in a family context: Giving and receiving practical and emotional support. *Sociology of Health and Illness, 29*(3), 347–365.

Rioux, M., & Daly, T. (2006). Constructing disability and illness. In D. Raphael, T. Bryant, & M. Rioux (Eds.), *Staying alive: Critical perspectives on health, illness, and health care* (pp. 305–324). Toronto: Canadian Scholars Press.

Saleh, U.S., & Brockopp, D.Y. (2001). Hope among patients with cancer hospitalized for bone marrow transplantation: A phenomenologic study. *Cancer Nursing, 24*(4), 308–314.

Seligman, M., & Darling, R.B. (2007). *Ordinary families, special children: A systems approach to childhood disability* (3rd ed.). New York: Guilford Press.

Snyder, C.R. (Ed.). (2000). *Handbook of hope: Theory, measures and applications.* San Diego: Academic Press.

Stewart, A.E., Robert, A., & Neimeyer, R.A. (2001). Emplotting the traumatic self: Narrative revision and the construction of coherence. *The Humanistic Psychologist, 29,* 8–39.

Stewart, D.E., Wong, F., Duff, S., Melancon, C.H., & Cheung, A.M. (2001). What doesn't kill you makes you stronger: An ovarian cancer survivor survey. *Gynaecologic Oncology, 83,* 3, 537–42.

Tennen, H., & Affleck, G. (2002). Benefit finding and benefit reminding. In C.R. Snyder and S.J. Lopez (Eds.), *Handbook of Positive Psychology* (pp. 584–597). London: Oxford University Press.

Tomich, P.L., & Helgeson, V.S. (2004). Is finding something good in the bad always good? Benefit finding among women with breast cancer. *Health Psychology, 23*(1), 16–23.

Trevillion, S. (2007). Health, disability and social work: New directions in social work research. *British Journal of Social Work, 37*(5), 937–946.

Watermeyer, B. (2009). Claiming loss in disability. *Disability and Society, 24*(1), 91–102.

Weiser, J. (1996). Psychosocial consequences of living with HIV/AIDS, or what I learned from my clients and friends. *Social Worker, 64*(4), 18–33.

Wendell, S. (1996). *The rejected body: Feminist philosophical reflections on disability.* New York: Routledge.

Wolin, S.J., & Wolin, S. (1993). *The resilient self: How survivors of troubled families rise above adversity.* New York: Villard Books.

World Health Organization. (WHO). World Health Assembly. Statement on Disability, International Classification of Functioning Disability and Health ICF. Geneva, Switzerland, May 22, 2001.

Wright, L.M. (2005). *Spirituality, suffering, and illness: Ideas for healing.* Philadelphia: F.A. Davis Co.

Yalom, I. (1982). The "terrestrial" meanings of life. *International Forum for Logotherapy, 1*(5), 92–102.

19

Loss of Functionality
Traumatic Brain Injury

PHYLLIS S. KOSMINSKY

INTRODUCTION

The theme of loss and how it affects identity is one touched on by many of the authors included in this volume. What we think of as the *self* is a composite of internal states and interactions with the world we inhabit. Our physical and emotional health, our beliefs, our relationships, and our affiliations—all these and more make up our sense of self. The loss or significant alteration of any one of these components can alter our feelings about who we are and can undermine our confidence in ourselves. But while any loss has the potential to leave us feeling somehow "less than" we were, some losses manifestly reduce our ability to function, deprive us of a significant portion of our mental, physical, and emotional capacities, and transform our lives in ways that cannot easily be accommodated. In addressing the loss of capacity that can result from a traumatic brain injury, we are looking at what may be the deepest insult to a person's sense of self, and surely one of the most all-encompassing, as it affects every aspect of functioning and impacts every role and every relationship. In short, suffering a brain injury is like falling into a hole and losing contact with much of the world above.

Every year in the United States, approximately 1.9 million people experience an acquired traumatic brain injury (TBI), with some 80,000 people experiencing continuing and significant disability (Thurman, Alverson, Dunn, Guerro, & Sniezek, 1999). Complications related to brain injury vary, as does the extent of recovery. Some complications respond well to treatment, whereas others may never improve. Loss of memory, diminished ability to process information, difficulties in communicating, and personality changes are a few of the losses someone with a brain injury is likely to suffer. Depending on the nature and severity of the injury, people with brain injuries face a future that is at best uncertain and at worst promises only a continuing series of disappointments and painful reminders of what they have lost.

THE EXPERIENCE OF BRAIN INJURY: FIRST-PERSON ACCOUNTS

Thanks to a number of intrepid authors, we now have a picture of what acquired brain injury feels like from the inside out. Although these accounts are by no means a comprehensive view of the impact of brain injury, they do highlight the kinds of problems commonly experienced by people with brain injuries and their families. Much of what has been described relates to the consequences of damage to the frontal lobes, the so-called center of executive functioning. Functions affected include planning and initiation as well as inhibitory processes, which negate impulsive expression (Cicerone, 2005). These functional impairments significantly impact the expression of emotion and the ability to moderate emotional response.

While difficulties with planning, remembering, and so forth make it difficult for those with a brain injury to return to work or school, it is the impairment of their ability to moderate emotional response and control emotional expression that is most damaging with respect to their relationships with others. Friends and family members are likely to experience frustration and even disbelief when confronted with the changes in personality, behavior, and function that are present. More marginal relationships are likely to wither as people find themselves unable or unwilling to deal with those who have become argumentative, socially inappropriate, self-involved, and generally difficult to recognize as the persons they once knew.

In *I'll Carry the Fork* (2003), Kara Swanson, who survived an automobile accident but was left with effects that others could not see and therefore could not understand, writes that the hardest part of her life with TBI was the loneliness. Many old friends disappeared, while others gradually fell away after encountering the changes in Kara: "I got angry at nothing. I interrupted people. They could tell me they just found the cure for cancer and I would cut them off and talk about how pretty the car next to us was" (p. 33). Like many people faced with loss of function, Kara found it difficult to ask for help but became furious when she could not accomplish a task.

Besides the wound to her pride involved in asking for help, Kara had to deal with the problems attendant to simply communicating with words that no longer were at her command. "The inability to organize my thoughts confounded me. I had some idea of what I wanted to say, but I couldn't keep other ideas from popping in here and there, and my first attempts were a tangled mess.... It was like trying to get gum out of my hair with mittens" (Swanson, 2003, p. 98).

For anyone, the loss of something they previously took for granted as a strength is difficult. The more independent someone was, the harder it is for them to ask for or accept help. The more someone took pride in their ability to express themselves with words, the harder it is for them to live with the loss of fluency. The impact on their self-esteem, their interest in being with others, and their desire to struggle to regain some foothold in the non-brain-injured world is tremendous. Even the strongest, most determined survivor of TBI will face months and even years of work and will need the support of committed caregivers.

Of all the losses attendant to acquired brain injury, perhaps the most devastating is the loss of hope. With so much less to build on, the future seems a fragile possibility at best. If the injury occurs in adolescence or early adulthood (as many accident-related injuries do), whatever roads a person planned to travel now seem closed. Life goals—to pursue a career, to fall in love, to have a family—now seem impossibly out of reach. The despair that accompanies such a demolition of self can scarcely be put into words, but Claudia Osborn (1998), a physician who suffered a brain injury after being struck by a car, wants us to understand how it feels:

> I sat for hours, a boneless, jellylike blob with a swollen pain, relieved intermittently by stupor, only to return again and again to consciousness and unbearable grief. I could not live like this. Without my intellect, I did not want to live. I was a remnant of who I was. I was unlovable. I wanted to end my pain. (p. 118)

Rather than offering consolation or respite, Osborn's (1998) periodic experience of an escape from the prison of her injury served only to deepen her depression. Referring to "adynamia," which is the loss of animation and enthusiasm often accompanying brain injury, Osborn writes:

> To be adynamic is to be an eagle with clipped wings. It might be more tolerable if I had never flown, or was still so unaware of my situation that I didn't know I could no longer fly. (p. 98)

ADAPTATION AND COPING

How can our understanding of bereavement and how people recover from loss shed light on how people cope with the loss of functionality, of which acquired brain injury is a prime example? Whatever differences exist with respect to individuals' loss and their healing from that loss, recovery generally begins with the *recognition* that a loss has occurred (Rando, 1993). Quite reasonably, it is assumed that a person cannot begin to recover from a loss until the fact of the loss is acknowledged. In the absence of such recognition, individuals will try to continue to live as if the loss had not occurred—for example, as if the loved one is still present. This kind of delayed acceptance of painful reality and its impact on mourning are part of the daily experience of therapists who work with the bereaved (Kosminsky, 2007). The denial that circumstances have changed inhibits any move toward adaptation to those changed circumstances. Over time, the effort of suppressing recognition becomes too much, and the mourner begins the painful but unavoidable work of rebuilding, of imagining and then constructing a new identity, a new life.

The same process of delayed recognition followed by gradual acceptance is evident in people who have survived a brain injury. Recalling visits from family in the early days of her recovery, Osborn (1998) observes, "We were all busy weaving a net of delusion" (p. 27). Everyone was pretending that she would eventually be able to return to work as a doctor. It was following a group session at the rehabilitation clinic that she experienced what she describes as "the collapse of my dreams":

> One word, hiding in my unconscious, lying in wait on the periphery of my knowledge, had stripped me of hope and shattered my dreams. *Permanent.* Sobbing in near hysteria, I lay down on the sofa, using the armrest for a pillow.... I felt numb about my self-knowledge. I could never, at least not for very long, slip back into my former innocence when I believed my losses were all correctable, but I still had a long way to go before reaching emotional acceptance of my head-injured persona. (p. 113)

What is the role of the clinician in moving individuals with brain injury toward recognition of their changed state? Langer (1999) explains the particular issues that arise in treating someone who is in denial regarding the nature of their injury or is even unaware of cognitive and physical changes that have resulted. Langer emphasizes that we need to "balance the risk of despair, versus the need to maintain hope; the risk of shame, versus the need to maintain self-esteem and self-respect...and the nature and level of distress and the patient's ability to tolerate it" (p. 92). As with bereavement following the death of a loved one, denial here serves a therapeutic purpose to the extent that it allows the individuals to gradually absorb a reality that is otherwise too painful to tolerate. It may be frustrating, and it may take time, but this is a process that cannot be unduly accelerated without the risk of further harm to someone at a painfully vulnerable time.

Yet reality must eventually be confronted and must become the basis on which these individuals' lives, going forward, are constructed. Here, too, bereavement theory provides insight regarding what it means to accept "reality" within the context of irreparable loss.

CONTINUING BONDS

Much has been made in recent years of the idea that relationships do not end or, more to the point, need not end with the death of one of the participants. We speak of "continuing bonds" with loved ones who have died, acknowledging that although we have been parted from the person's physical presence we remain connected to them, through memory, through love, through shared experience. Even when all is lost, all is not lost. We can apply this idea as well to the preservation of one's relationship to oneself after the loss that accompanies brain injury. While accommodation is a feature of any healthy adjustment to loss, the belief that not all has been lost, that the old self can still be recognized and the relationship to the old self maintained, can be a source of hope at a hopeless time. Osborn (1998) fought against the full realization of her loss of functionality and was plunged into hopelessness when she could no longer pretend that she would be able to return to her work as a doctor. However, she did not stop there; rather than continuing to mourn the person she had lost, she began to identify the elements of her identity that remained available to her and to imagine the ways in which what remained of herself was enough to make life worth living:

> Though there are aspects to the quality of my thinking that still elude me, I have regained the sustaining element in my enjoyment of life—my passion for art, music, nature, love, poetry and life. To paraphrase Irving Berlin, I am ready to "face the music and dance." (p. 133)

WHAT DOES "RECOVERY" MEAN?

If we have learned anything about how people heal from loss it is that the potential for healing is affected by a multitude of factors; characteristics of the person, the relationship, and the loss all play a part. We would not venture to say that recovery ought to be the goal of therapy with people who have sustained a brain injury, if by recovery we mean severing the relationship with the old self and genially embracing one's new, injured self. However, we have seen that recovery of the desire to be engaged with the world, to participate fully with everything we have, is possible after even the most devastating personal losses, whether those losses are the loss of a loved one or the loss of beloved parts of the self. Helping people maintain a relationship is part of our work with many clients devastated by the loss of a loved one, and as we have said is relevant here. So too is our experience with structuring therapeutic interventions to facilitate the discovery of latent capacities that may have been untapped in clients' preloss lives. In short, loss alters personal reality and restricts but does not deprive us of future possibility, as Osborn (1998) tells us:

> Longing for what one had has a way of popping up at unexpected times. But over time, the intensity eases. If I were asked, I would counsel someone with a devastating injury not to focus on their loss and what might have been, but to fully live the life they have now and to carve out new and achievable dreams to fit it…. I was a happy woman before my injury, and I am a happy one today. (p. 232)

Of course, this level of adaptation and reentry to the premorbid level of functioning is by no means universal. No one knows this better than TBI survivors, their family and friends, and the professionals charged with doing something, anything, to bring back someone who is not dead but not quite alive either.

> J. is 34 years old. At 19, he suffered a traumatic brain injury when a car being driven by his friend went off the road and hit a tree. His friend died instantly, "but I lived-ish." By all accounts a formerly gifted student and promising writer, J. suffered severe cognitive impairment and physical problems as the result of his accident. He exhibits all the emotional and interpersonal problems associated with damage to the frontal lobe—he is prone to outbursts of anger, depression comes over him in waves, he has difficulty focusing on what anyone else is saying, and he returns again and again to a few, mostly delusional, "memories" of his past life. Despite years of intensive inpatient and outpatient treatment, J. has not been able to resume any kind of regular

employment or study. He despairs of ever having a relationship with a woman or of having a family of his own (Kosminsky, personal files, 2008).

Given this kind of devastating loss of self, it is not surprising that J. has often wished that he had not survived the accident that killed his friend. His days are filled with frustration and constant reminders of everything that he has lost: his professional hopes; his dreams of a family of his own. Finding meaning in the hours that stretch endlessly from when he wakes up to when he falls into restless sleep is a continuing struggle for J. and a source of ongoing sadness for his family. Significant loss, whether of a loved one or a cherished part of the self, challenges the individual and those who care for and about him or her to make sense of the world as it is while holding onto the hope that a return to some kind of normalcy is possible.

REFERENCES

Cicerone, K. D. (2005). Rehabilitation of executive function impairments. In W. M. High, A. Sander, M. Struchen, & K. Hart (Eds.), *Rehabilitation for traumatic brain injury* (pp. 71–87). New York: Oxford.

Kosminsky, P. (2007). *Getting back to life when grief won't heal.* New York: McGraw Hill.

Langer, K. G. (1999). Awareness and denial in psychotherapy. In K. G. Langer, L. Lewis, & L. Laatsch (Eds.), *Psychotherapeutic interventions for adults with brain injury or stroke* (pp. 75–96). Madison, CT: International Universities Press.

Osborn, C. (1998). *Over my head: A doctor's own story of head injury from the inside looking out.* Kansas City, MO: Andrews McNeel.

Rando, T. (1993). *Treatment of complicated mourning.* Champaign, IL: Research Press.

Swanson, K. (2003). *I'll carry the fork: Recovering a life after brain injury.* Scotts Valley, CA: Rising Star.

Thurman, D. J., Alverson, C., Dunn, K. A., Guerro, J., & Sniezek, J. E. (1999). Traumatic brain injury in the United States: A public health perspective. *Journal of Head Trauma Rehabilitation, 14*(6), 602–615.

20

"Who Did You *Used* To Be?" Loss for Older Adults

NIELI LANGER

INTRODUCTION

O ld age is a challenging period in people's lives that often includes sudden and multiple losses and unforeseen assaults to their person. For many people the period following retirement occupies an increasing segment of the life cycle, as medical advances extend life. Older people's needs change during this time of their lives, but many are ill prepared or completely unprepared for the biological, psychological, and social adjustments that may often include loss of independence.

First and foremost, loss is a deprivation. People are deprived of something that was a part of their lives. For older adults these deprivations often translate into fewer opportunities, shrinking of individuals' feelings of competence and self-esteem, physical frailty, and loss of independence. Independence is a precious commodity; older adults do not lose their desire for independence. If older persons perceive that the changes in their lives rob them of their identity and, therefore, their independence, they often begin to feel valueless or useless. This, in turn, affects their ability to interact with other people and to take an active role in everyday decisions. When losses make older adults feel frightened and uncertain of future direction or threaten their independence, they feel more vulnerable and less in control of their lives. The extent to which they accept and adapt to these losses directly affects the quality of life they can achieve and maintain.

WILL I RESIST DEPENDENCY?

In today's society, dependency in old age is viewed as a negative process, whereas independence is seen as the ideal way of life. Cott and Gignac (2000) conducted in-depth interviews with a physically compromised older cohort of men and women. The study demonstrated that elderly people placed great importance on being independent. The respondents were learning to cope with their problems instead of becoming dependent on someone else. "Being independent was an identity goal that they were actively struggling to maintain" (Cott & Gignac, p. 7).

In another study, the terms *independence* and *dependence* were examined and defined (Secker, Hill, Villeneau, & Parkman, 2003). The authors concluded that for older people independence is not solely the absence of relying on someone else but also entailed "self-esteem, self-determination, purpose in life, personal growth and the continuity of self" (Secker et al., p. 375). Similar to Cott and Gignac's (2000) results, being able to look after oneself and not by someone else, and freedom to choose what to do and when to do it, were the recurring themes. It should be noted that in the United States and Europe, every effort is made to avoid becoming dependent on someone else, even if older persons' health or lifestyle is worse off than it would be if someone was looking after them. In contrast, in cultures such as the Chinese, it is an honor for adult children to care for parents, and they, in turn, are proud to be taken care of by their children.

Concurring with the results of the previously mentioned studies, Mack, Salmoni, Viverais-Dressler, Porter, and Gary (1997) demonstrated that the respondents in their research perceived dependence on someone else as being negative and an unwanted part of life. The majority of the participants held that the main reason it was important to remain living in the community was because it maximized their independence (83%) and enhanced their sense of identity (53%). In all the studies cited, the majority of respondents were trying to escape the dependency process of aging.

CLINICAL RECOMMENDATIONS

The Search for Meaning in Clients' Lives

If our concern as care providers is to enable older persons to remain "independent" or "in the community" for as long as possible, we need to tap into the personal values and lifelong commitments that guide the way these persons use their time, solve problems, and ultimately live out their remaining years. An important aspect of adjustment to aging and loss is the ability to derive meaning from experiences and the realization that life has a purpose and is meaningful. When people are capable of transforming negative events into opportunities, the result is personal growth and life satisfaction (Langer, 2004).

In his book *Man's Search for Meaning* (1963), Victor Frankl contends that people always have the freedom to find meaning through meaningful attitudes even in apparently meaningless situations. For Frankl, ultimate meaning exists and is unique to each person and each situation. The ability of individuals to choose their attitude in any given set of circumstances is what gives meaning and purpose to life.

Personal meaning is a collection of themes of life's domains that have been, and will continue to be, essential to a person's existence. Together, these themes give purpose to individuals' lives and provide them with an identity (Prager, 1997). The meaning and purpose derived from life themes define spirituality. Spirituality also provides a "personal compass" by which individuals can assess and navigate their current needs. Human beings are able to contemplate questions about the meaning of existence and often reach backward and forward in time to weigh their relationships with others as well as unique events and values. Each theme of individuals' lives can be a source of spiritual nourishment. If they are conscious of their own life themes, spirituality is played out through the ordinary and the everyday events of life, and their existence is charged with meaning. A consensus reached among several researchers is that interpersonal relations, individual growth, success, service, hedonism, creativity, religion, and legacy are acknowledged life themes that are sources of meaning and purpose for most people (Fiske & Chiriboga, 1991; Hedlund & Birren, 1984; Thurnher, 1975). It is suggested that an individual's perception of personal meaning remains generally stable over the lifespan (Zika & Chamberlain, 1992). Therefore, individuals' identity or life themes do not appreciably change throughout the life course and provide stability and consistency.

Many older adults, facing a major loss or crisis, have the capacity to reorder their life themes so that they can "re-conceive their identity" or make meaning (Courtenay & Truluck, 1997, p. 190). This conceptualization implies that meaning in life is developmental and dynamic. What is critical in this approach is the unique way people translate an experience and assign meaning to it based on their personality traits, capacities, and levels of expectation. They may concurrently have to discard some old assumptions and adapt new ones that provide the anchors for a revised life stage. Older adults may experience many losses such as poor health, reduced financial circumstances, and a shrinking social network yet retain a general sense of well-being and the conviction that life has meaning. Baltes and Baltes (1990) note that even with pronounced signs of frailty aging adults are capable of making necessary modifications in goals and aspirations. When individuals continue to develop through their life experiences and find sources of meaning therein, then they are more empowered to cope with life's stresses and survive.

Understanding Clients' Sense of Control

Another resource that older people use to address adversity and potential loss of independence is *mastery.* Mastery, which is a sense of control, can help buffer the stresses of aging and loss of independence. Evidence of mastery can be drawn from past experience or from manageable areas in an individual's current life. To be resilient in old age, people need to embrace flexibility and to accept change. In some aspects, competence is comparable to resilience as the ability to maintain competence despite adversity (Masten, 1994). With a client's ability for self-direction, counselors can enhance the client's sense of achievement by seeking mutual solutions, can point out strengths, and can encourage access of available resources. As Pearlin and Skaff (1995) note, "The process of adapting to late life may involve staking one's mastery on domains over which one can exert control and yielding it where control is now more difficult" (p. 115).

Social service and health-care providers have witnessed and participated in the care of individuals whom they believed to possess the quality of inner strength when faced with adversity or loss. Assessing a client's spirituality and resiliency in its various expressions, identifying its use, and including it in individual counseling interventions may assist older clients to recognize their capacity to readjust during periods of disruption and loss. Clients are empowered to use the strengths they already possess (Langer, 2000). The strengths perspective focuses on capabilities, assets, and positive attributes rather than problems and pathologies. Saleebey (1992) captures the rationale of the strengths perspective with the following challenge:

> At the very least, the strengths perspective obligates counselors to understand that, however downtrodden or sick, individuals have survived (and in some cases even thrived). They have taken steps, summoned up resources and coped. We need to know what they have done, how they have done it, what they have learned from doing it, what resources (inner and outer) were available in their struggle to surmount their troubles. People are always working on their situations, even if just deciding to be resigned to them; as helpers we must tap into that work, elucidate it, find and build on its possibilities. (pp. 171–172)

While many older persons lead fulfilling lives, others feel a loss of meaning and purpose. Whereas some older adults find ways to adapt to the vicissitudes of getting old, many may require the assistance of counselors to help reclaim or reaffirm their identity (or spirituality). The professional helps clients to view how they may use their spirituality as an effective coping strategy for life's losses and stressors, as a source for reframing crises, and as a source of strength for facing the future. In the absence of a meaning perspective, clients and care providers risk working at cross-purposes. Care providers need to be open to clients' views and to be supportive of them. When professional caregivers are seen to value clients' spirituality, the clients are empowered to use the coping mechanisms they already have available. Professionals who recognize and acknowledge their own spirituality and the clients' values (life themes) can probably anticipate more positive and forthcoming responses. With appropriate opportunity to articulate their life themes and issues, these troubled older adults may be counseled into resolving some of their difficulties.

Understanding and Accessing Clients' Kin Support

Central to the relationships within the family are issues of independence and dependence. With adequate financial and housing resources, older adults choose to live independently of their adult children, although often in relative proximity. Parent–child interaction patterns do not generally emerge for the first time in later life. Lifelong patterns are present, and they become more evident over time. Thus, it appears especially important among the aged to know the history of a relationship of support exchanges (reciprocity) to be able to understand the current nature of the support relationship (Antonucci, 1990). This information will enable the service provider to more accurately assess the actual or potential strengths and weaknesses of older persons' social networks and to determine if the services of the formal social or health-care organizations need to be accessed.

People react to a loss of independence in different ways. This can be a difficult area for both older persons and their care providers (e.g., spouse, adult children, professional care provider). If being dependent is stigmatized in Western society, then older people will attempt to define their situation as independent. Autonomy is the freedom we have to make choices in our lives. While related to independence, it is not the same. Persons may be dependent on receiving care in a day-to-day routine but autonomous in making decisions about their health care. Since most people act out their daily lives involved in social networks in which they exchange, for example, money, goods, services, and emotional support with kin, friends, and neighbors, what evolves from an analysis of older persons living independently in the community is the concept of *interdependence*. When asked to define and describe their independence, participants in a study by White and Groves (2008) described how they were not dependent and not powerless. The key concepts in the maintenance of their independent lifestyle were control, mediation, and reciprocity of assistance. In the development of programs for the elderly, interdependence with an emphasis on reciprocity may be the key for aging adults to maintain autonomy and continue to reciprocate at whatever level they may be able to sustain.

Sometimes, in a care-giving situation, individuals' freedom to make decisions may be affected. Whenever possible, including all parties in the decision-making process (about health, financial, or other planning matters) helps to mitigate some of the losses and fosters positive adjustment. While faced with their own challenges, caregivers still need to recognize the care receiver's needs for some independence, autonomy, and dignity.

Group Services

Group services represent another referral source for community practitioners. To achieve reconnection after cumulative losses including independence and to adapt personal identity and evolving roles to accommodate the changes, the elderly need to share their thoughts, feelings, and past and present experiences with a cohort who understands and can validate their existence. Participation in a meaningful group provides older persons with vital emotional support and commonality of experiences.

Perhaps even more important is that group participation enables older persons to develop a reciprocal relationship with peers; it enables them to be givers as well as recipients of both emotional and tangible support. The opportunity to contribute empowers the elderly, building badly needed self-esteem and a continued sense of self-worth. The loss of significant others in one's life is often marked less by the sense of what one no longer is able to receive than from the fact that one can no longer contribute to the missing kin or friends and, subsequently, to receive validation from them. Being able to contribute something to others is ego supportive and, therefore, a highly effective antidote to depression. "Group associations can provide many opportunities to replace old friends with new ones, to substitute family ties with peer ties and to give new status and hence new relevance to one's existence" (Lowy, 1983, p. 25).

CONCLUSION

To meet the predicted service needs of a large and diverse older adult population, counselors will need to reexamine their own attitudes and the nature of agency programs. Preventive programs designed to support older adults' strengths have the potential to reduce the number of elders who may later need extensive mental health services. Older adults can build on their own inherent strengths, can find their own solutions, and can provide agencies with much needed information about their service needs (Greene, 2000).

REFERENCES

Antonucci, T. (1990). Social supports and social relationships. In *Handbook of aging and the social sciences* (3rd ed., pp. 205–226). San Diego: Academic Press.

Baltes, P., & Baltes, M. (1990). Psychological perspectives on successful aging: The model of selective optimization with compensation. In P.B. Baltes & M.M. Baltes (Eds.), *Successful aging: Perspectives from the behavioral sciences* (pp. 1–34). New York: Cambridge University Press.

Cott, C., & Gignac, M. (2000). Independence and dependence for older adults with osteoarthritis or osteoporosis. *Canadian Journal on Aging, 18*, 1–25.

Courtenay, B., & Truluck, J. (1997). The meaning of life and older learners: Addressing the fundamental issue through critical thinking and teaching. *Educational Gerontology, 23*, 175–195.

Fiske, M., & Chiriboga, D. (1991). *Change and continuity in adult life*. San Francisco: Jossey-Bass.

Frankl, V. (1963). *Man's search for meaning*. New York: Washington Square Press.

Greene, R. (2000). *Social work with the aged and their families*. New York: Aldine de Gruyter.

Hedlund, B., & Birren, J. (1984). *Distribution of types of meaning in life across women.* Paper presented at the Annual Meeting of the Gerontological Society of America, San Antonio, TX.

Langer, N. (2000). The importance of spirituality in later life. *Gerontology & Geriatrics Education, 20*(3), 41–50.

Langer, N. (2004). Resiliency and spirituality: Foundations of strengths perspective counseling with the elderly. *Educational Gerontology, 30*, 611–617.

Lowy, L. (1983). Social group work with vulnerable older persons: A theoretical perspective. *Social Work with Groups, 5*(2), 21–32.

Mack, R., Salmoni, A., Viverais-Dressler, G., Porter, E., & Gary, R. (1997). Perceived risks to independent living. *Gerontologist, 37*, 729–736.

Masten, A. (1994). Resilience in individual development: Successful adaptation despite risk and adversity. In M.C. Wang & E.W. Gordon (Eds.), *Educational resilience in inner-city America* (pp. 3–25). Hillsdale, NJ: Lawrence Erlbaum.

Pearlin, L., & Skaff, M. (1995). Stressors and adaptation in late life. In M. Gatz (Ed.), *Emerging issues in mental health and aging* (pp. 97–123). Washington, DC: APA.

Prager, E. (1997). Meaning in later life: An organizing theme for gerontological curriculum design. *Educational Gerontology, 23*, 1–13.

Saleebey, D. (Ed.). (1992). *The strengths perspective in social work practice.* New York: Longman.

Secker, J., Hill, R., Villeneau, L., & Parkman, S. (2003). Promoting independence: But promising what and how? *Ageing and Society, 23,* 375–391.

Thurnher, M. (1975). Continuities and discontinuities in value orientation. In M.F. Lowenthal, M. Thurnher, & D. Chiriboga (Eds.), *Four stages of life: A comparative study of women and men facing transitions* (pp. 176–200). San Francisco: Jossey-Bass.

White, A., & Groves, M. (2008). Interdependence and the aged stereotype. *Australasian Journal on Ageing, 16*(2), 83–89.

Zika, S., & Chamberlain, K. (1992). On the relation between meaning in life and psychological well-being. *British Journal of Psychology, 83,* 133–145.

Section *IV*

Coping With Losses in Life

21

Adaptation, Resilience, and Growth After Loss

EUNICE GORMAN

The world breaks everyone, and afterward, some grow strong at the broken places.

Ernest Hemingway, 1929

*I*t would be misleading in a book about change, transition, and loss to have the reader believe that grief is the only defining element of loss across the lifespan. In fact, readers who have lived through some of the losses described in other chapters know that often people emerge on the other side of challenging events and crises stronger and wiser. Much has been written about this phenomenon of "doing well," or posttraumatic growth (PTG) and resilience over the last several decades (Borawski, 2007; Cyrulnik, 2005; Y. Dolan, 1998; P. Dolan, 2008; Flach, 1997, 1988; Katz, 1997; Lesser, 2004; Miller, 2005; Rutter, 2007; Scaer, 2005; Sirois, 2006). The literature also refers to struggling well (O'Connell-Higgins, 1994), inner optimism (O'Gorman, 1994), learned resourcefulness (Bonanno, 2004), enduring transcendence (Weenolsen, 1988), tragic optimism (Frankl, 1984), toughness, and hardiness. Other terms used to refer to the ability to thrive after a traumatic event include *rebounding, self-righting,* and *ordinary magic* (Masten, 2007). Each of these terms refers to the ability seen in many people not only to survive but also to thrive after extremely adverse events or challenges. Not only do these individuals "bear up," but their suffering also becomes a gateway to wholeness and serves to unveil hidden strengths and talents. Wainrib (2006) refers to this as the *phoenix phenomenon* in reference to the fabled beautiful bird that rises from the ashes.

A crisis can act as a catalytic agent, a defining moment, or a seismic occurrence that has the ability to expand human potential and cause individuals to regenerate, renegotiate, and find redeeming value within stressful situations

(Folkman, 2008). In short, a crisis is seen as a wake-up call or an opportunity for an awakening experience. It is not viewed simply as a terrible event that puts people on a path of chronic sorrow or grief. For example, one young man talked about learning that his HIV test had come back positive. He stated, "I felt like I had just received a cosmic kick in the butt," although his reference to his derriere was made in more colorful language. As a result of this news about his health, he made numerous changes in his life. He felt lucky and glad to be alive and diagnosed in a time when there are more options for the treatment of AIDS should he develop more symptoms later on.

That is not to say that mourning and grief do not occur initially on learning bad news, because certainly these emotions are part of responding to sad, painful events in our lives. Rather, it is to point out that crises need not break individuals' spirits or ruin their ability to enjoy life or live life to the fullest. The concept of posttraumatic growth is meant to provide hope and reassurance, not to dismiss the very real sadness that people feel with a difficult change, transition, or loss. The types of traumatic events or losses that precede posttraumatic growth might include a house fire, theft, rape, a critical illness or health crisis, divorce, betrayal, or a tragic accident. The loss might fall into the following categories:

Primary or secondary
Minor or major
Actual or threatened
Internal or external
Direct or indirect
Imposed or chosen
Sudden or anticipated

As is always the case, it is people's own perception of the loss and how it is experienced that are the most important factors in describing and understanding the loss as lived. What might for one person be a long-threatened and anticipated loss may for another seem like a bolt out of the blue. For another individual what appears to be an imposed loss might actually be one that is chosen, such as unemployment or the dissolution of a relationship. For still others, the primary loss is not their own, but they are caught up in the secondary losses resulting from the initial change. For instance, the parents of a child who is ill have not lost their own good health but as the main support people and caregivers of their child will encounter numerous secondary losses associated with their child's health crisis. A loss might be felt internally with no tangible external link that another person looking on might be able to discern, such as is the case with the loss of faith or long-held and cherished beliefs. What seems on the surface to be a minor loss is, in fact, a major loss to another person faced with the same event. Loss is always a highly individualized experience. Posttraumatic growth and resilience are not easily predicted but rather are as unique to each person as responding to a changed worldview and grieving.

POSTTRAUMATIC GROWTH

Tedeschi and Calhoun (2004) explored posttraumatic growth in depth, as have many others (Calhoun and Tedeschi, 1990, 1998, 2006; Konrad, 2006; Linley & Joseph, 2004; Salick & Auerbach, 2006). These authors point to the ability to construe benefits and reframe negative experiences to make the crisis manageable and comprehensible. Individuals exhibiting posttraumatic growth are able to see the positives in the struggle, to reach a sense of coherence, to renew themselves, and even to flourish. Stress, crisis, and loss (Henry, 2007) can lead to positive outcomes including increased confidence, coherence, trust, or improved self-esteem. Other qualities associated with PTG include self-transcendence, connectedness, competence, and enhanced self-awareness. Posttraumatic growth can also lead to meaning reconstruction (Neimeyer, 2006), wisdom, spiritual development, strength, self-reliance, and emotional expressiveness. People often respond to a traumatic event by shifting their priorities, and, as a result, they enjoy an enhanced appreciation for life. Many people after a traumatic event find a renewed commitment to life and a deep desire to set new goals and live in new ways that better reflect who they are and who they have become because of facing hardship. Individuals report an improved sense of self-efficacy after weathering difficult and life-changing events. Tedeschi and Calhoun (2007) refer to these as "strange blessings" from grief/loss:

- Change in self: empathetic, stronger, fellow feeling
- Change in relationships: closer, connected, not taken for granted
- Change in philosophy of life: spiritual awareness, seeing life as precious; priorities shift

Positive psychological changes are hallmarks of posttraumatic growth (Hefferon, Grealy, & Mutrie, 2009). In a meta-analysis of the PTG literature, Prati and Pietrantoni (2009) found that optimism, social support, spirituality, acceptance coping, reappraisal coping, religious coping, and seeking-support coping were all associated with posttraumatic growth. People emerged from a crisis not seeing themselves as "victims" but rather as "survivors." Still others, who reject the survivor label, saw themselves as "living with" their diagnosis, disability, or the ongoing pain of what has been lost.

BENEFIT FINDING

Positive benefit finding can also be linked to posttraumatic growth (Pakenham, 2007). Benefit finding in trauma can lead to new possibilities being unveiled. Opportunities for personal and spiritual growth can emerge when people look for the silver lining in misfortune. Coming through a traumatic event can, and does, lead to improved understanding of what is important in life (Samios, Pakenham, & Sofronoff, 2009; Sears, Stanton, & Danhoff Burg, 2003). For instance, the person who has struggled with a devastating cancer diagnosis might reflect that "in a strange way it was the best thing that ever happened to me. I know what is important to me now and it is not getting ahead in the rat race. It is family and friends, and you sure find out who your friends are after something like this." Benefit reminding can also carry a person through rough patches when old hurts or memories intrude. Reminding oneself of what has been experienced, what has been gained, and the strength that has been shown can all be powerful coping mechanisms to draw upon (Tennen & Affleck, 2002).

RESILIENCE

Why is it that some people are able to weather the storms of life and others are not? This age-old question has been explored by social scientists for a number of years. Why do some people rise above their suffering while others are shattered by a similar set of circumstances and are never the same again? One area of research looks at the importance of resilience in coping with adversity. Resilience is the ability to transform challenges, to adapt and move forward, even while struggling with stress. Resilience and posttraumatic growth are linked in the sense that it is often people who are resilient who are able to find benefit, or grow, following a tumultuous period or critical event in their lives. Resilience is a product of the number of protective factors within the individual, the family, and community. Protective factors that help manage change, transition, and loss can be unique to individuals, qualities of family life and upbringing, or supports found within the community. Individual factors that support resilience include good health, self-esteem, problem-solving skills, communication skills, a sense of control, and an ability to have patience and know that hard times will not last forever. If things do not go exactly as planned, resilient people are able to change their priorities and remain flexible. They often have a sense of humor, possess empathy, and are able to put things in perspective (Flach, 1997, 1988). Sources within individuals might include good grounding with primary attachment figures, a history of receiving consistent love and respect, strong relationships with family, and a freely given space to grow, learn, and occasionally make mistakes. The ability to rebuild, reinvest, and integrate experience are foundational elements in resilience. Family factors include strong ties with one or both parents, nurturing extended family, and a warm, supportive, and caring environment where food, shelter, and support needs are met. Furthermore, boundaries, limits, and expectations that are consistent help to build resilience (Flach, 1997, 1988; Morris, 2004). Family resilience, according to Walsh (1998, 2007), comes from belief systems and the ability of the family to act as a shock absorber, to make meaning out of adversity, to provide a positive outlook, and to support flexibility. The family can nurture spirituality, can provide social and economic resources, can support affiliation, and can encourage hope. A family where open communication and collaborative problem solving are found will assist its members in managing stressful life events. Community factors that encourage resilience include positive school experiences, group opportunities such as Girl Guides and Girl Scouts, sports teams, youth groups, child care that is kind and consistent, and religious affiliations that are positive. The community provides protective factors through programming, resources, and finding ways of shielding and supporting the individual and family in challenging times. In fact, it has been found that in cases where individual or family resilience building was lacking a community role model or mentor made all the difference in the world (Flach, 1988). It can be a teacher, a social worker, or another adult who took an interest, saw something special in the young person, and nurtured a relationship that proved a lifeline for a troubled child heading down a self-destructive path.

Goldman (2005) asserts that resilience is closely aligned with acceptance and comfort, self-control, motivation, humor, insight, and courage. Factors such as self-discipline, self-confidence, empathy, creativity, perseverance, and appreciation of self add to children's ability to manage difficulties. Flach (1998) adds insight, the ability to tolerate pain, possessing an independent spirit, self-respect, and lifelong learning to the repertoire of characteristics necessary to foster resilience. The ability to make friends and depend on others, to be patient, to restore self-esteem, and to give, take, and ask for help add to the likelihood that one will be resilient. Resourcefulness, open-mindedness, a range of interests, and the ability to tolerate uncertainty are integral elements of resilience. Hurley (2009) reminds us that resilience is not something that is carved in stone, or static; rather, it is dynamic. Just because individuals showed remarkable resilience in one situation does not necessarily mean that they can summon the same ability to bounce back from difficulties in a new set of circumstances. Hurley refers to hidden resilience, lapses in resilience, situational resilience, sustained resilience, pockets of resilience, and shared resilience. In his work in the child protection field, Ungar (2002, 2004, 2006) reminds us that resilience is often hidden and not necessarily easily recognized until people are called on to be resilient or to show ways in which they might become more resilient.

POSTTRAUMAIC DEPRECIATION

While many people feel a sense of freedom, opportunity, or enhanced sense of personal strength and power following a crisis (Colville & Cream, 2009), not everyone responds to dramatic loss so positively. Not all individuals view finding themselves on the other side of a trauma as a second chance. Some may not see new possibilities and instead may experience alienation, self-hatred, shattered meaning, or *posttraumatic depreciation* (negative growth) or may become dispirited and demoralized (Tedeschi & Calhoun, 2007). Others may perceive personal suffering as punishment, a test, bad luck, or God's will and may respond with anger, resignation, fatalism, passivity, denial, gloom, and despair. These people may be predisposed to *posttraumatic stress disorder (PTSD)*. PTSD is a severe anxiety disorder that can develop after exposure to any event that results in psychological trauma overwhelming individuals' psychological defenses. Other names for PTSD include "shell shock" or "battle fatigue." The three defining characteristics of PTSD are (1) reexperiencing original traumas through flashbacks or nightmares; (2) avoidance of stimuli associated with the trauma; and (3) increased arousal, such as difficulty falling or staying asleep, anger, and hypervigilance. PTSD is a serious disorder that has a deleterious impact across all facets of the lives of those affected, including work, relationships, and the ability to manage self-care and day-to-day routines. Boscarino (2008) lists low self-esteem, previous negative life events, and lack of support as risk factors for PTSD after a traumatic event. Herman (2008) adds a history of child abuse and those who are helpless, overwhelmed, and younger as risk factors for developing posttraumatic stress disorder. Having said that, it is critical to state that even those who have lived through a cruel past can, and do, show resilience. Not everyone who is exposed to trauma will develop PTSD, just as not everyone will experience posttraumatic growth.

Adaptation therefore needs to be viewed as dynamic (Collishaw et al., 2007; Gilligan, 2000; Lathar, Cicchetti, & Becker, 2000). Those who have suffered a loss, to a point, have choices, or control, over whether they accept the affectional significance of the loss and attempt to move forward. Clearly, those who have more protective factors in their personal, family, and community background will be more likely to exercise choice and attempt coping and adjustment over the short and long term. At the same time, it is critical to recognize that it is likely that some people may experience both posttraumatic growth and posttraumatic depreciation at the same time and in response to the same highly stressful event (Baker, Kelly, Calhoun, Cann, & Tedeschi, 2009).

CLINICAL CONSIDERATIONS

Disaster strikes and forces people to reorder values and priorities, to come to terms with altered lives, to mourn the past and lose the future they had planned for, to make modifications, to accept trade-offs, and to learn new ways of being in the world. Some find inner strength and profound life lessons in loss and illness experiences. Some emerge with profound gratitude cherishing what is left. Still others emerge with a deeper appreciation for the simpler things in life. Understanding one's vulnerability can lead to epiphanies that promote healing, spiritual growth, strengthened relational and intergenerational bonds, authenticity, and shifts in self-perception. Some go as far as to say that they are better people after loss or bereavement (Dutton & Zisook, 2005).

Supporting Hope

Hope is an important concept and resource linked to posttraumatic growth and resilience. Critical elements of hope include mutuality, affiliation, a sense of the possible, and avoidance of seeing things in black and white only. Ways to instill or nurture "found hope" include establishing and achieving goals, promoting psychological health and well-being, seeking purpose and meaning in life, and mental and physical activation (Cohen, 2008). Hanging on to anticipation, optimism, and the belief that things will get better over time may be all one can manage in the early days of adjusting to difficult life events.

Interventions

Flach (1988) suggested ways to become more resilient including therapy, the reparative kindness of strangers, recruited relationships, altruistic peer relationships, and restorative animal love. Finding safe harbors that promote autonomy and competence is important. Engaging in activities that promote flexibility and balance can be useful. These active coping strategies suggest that even if you were not raised with much exposure to the protective factors already mentioned you can build resilience as an adult. Our ability to bounce back after adversity may improve as we face difficulties head on and test out coping mechanisms.

Relationship

No matter what intervention we might use it is critical that we approach all people with acceptance, sensitivity, compassion, and warmth. Asking for assistance, being able to receive care, and then being willing to explore loss are challenging activities. The power, and gift, of presence alone cannot be underestimated. Often a kind, patient, dependable person who is skilled in deep listening is one of the most effective means to find and promote resilience and to support posttraumatic growth. Moreover, normalizing the anger, fear, or guilt that people feel can provide an enormous amount of comfort and support. Giving people permission to feel whatever they are feeling, without trying to reshape their responses, allows individuals to feel heard and understood.

Telling the Story

The power of the story and in the retelling of a loss narrative is well documented (Beattie, 2006; Pennebaker, 2000). It is through talking about the loss experience that people are able to clarify what happened, to come to terms, to examine next steps, and to begin the healing process. Acknowledging the effects and the reality of loss allows people to appreciate the uniqueness of their experience while at the same time recognizing their membership in the human community. Trials are often painful, but they can also be instructive. Traveling through a crucial time in a person's life with all the accompanying losses can also be an important time of reclaiming the sense of self and getting accustomed to the "new normal."

Strengths Perspective

Part of this adaptation is an honest appraisal and reappraisal of strengths, capacities, competencies, possibilities, choices, and finding sources of power and potential. Focusing on values, beliefs, and affect regulation skills can assist with mobilizing internal and external resources. Examining past triumphs and coping mechanisms that served the person well can assist in transforming hurt into healing (Altemus, 2003). Resilience is a choice, according to Crawford (1998); dealing with beliefs, motivation, attitude, and self-image are challenging to be sure. Using the ASK method of self-talk while attempting to cope (Accurate, Supportive, Kind) is strongly encouraged by Crawford. Neeld (2005) talks about the importance of negotiating one's way through difficult times by responding, reviewing, rebuilding, and reorganizing to create meaning and to strengthen relationships. Part of what is needed to undertake such active (approach) coping over more passive (avoidance) coping is a realistic self-concept and the willingness to trust that getting through the crisis of loss will never completely dull the pain but may lead to a sense of competence, satisfaction, and what Simmons (2002) refers to as the blessings of an imperfect life. Bearing witness to suffering may ultimately lead to deeper spirituality, increased fellow feeling, enhanced quality of life, and even joy and thankfulness.

Sense of Control

Richardson (2002) reminds us that life consists of cycles of disruption and reintegration that we will go through many times. Through these periods of disruption and reintegration we can develop self-love and a sense of safety and nurturing. Hartling (2002) outlines six ways to strengthen resilience in yourself and others: (1) relationships that are mutually empathic and responsive, (2) listening to others compassionately and resourcefully, (3) finding effective resources and responses to adversity, (4) finding a mentor or being a mentor, (5) expanding relational competence by helping others and contributing to the community, and (6) using services that provide support and treatment, such as mutual support groups. Y. Dolan (1998) suggests that moving beyond being a survivor includes knowing yourself, enjoying the present, and nurturing yourself with a sense of home, good food, and daily rituals. Having hopes and dreams, working on relationships, and having supports and people who are willing to advocate on your behalf are central to developing resilience. Furthermore, Dolan suggests that it is important to have a plan for when the past rears its head. It is important to have responsive people around us but at the same time to understand that their patience to relive and rework the trauma or loss experiences may diminish over time. Sometimes their support needs to be supplemented by more formal caregivers such as doctors, therapists, local self-help groups, or spiritual leaders.

Mindfulness and Self-Care Strategies

Part of what can contribute to posttraumatic growth and resilience are such things as becoming mindful, making sense of what has happened or is continuing to happen, renegotiating public identities including the "hero" and the "victim," letting go, and shifting social roles and identities. It is important to be aware of one's own truths, and this is especially helpful when recognizing that you are feeling stuck. Struggling back to a sense of wholeness and belonging is important. Hurley and Martin (2009) outline the importance of the professional caregiver's roles in resilience as well as the agency's role in supporting and promoting resilience, not only in professional caregivers but also in the clients they serve (McMurray, Connolly, Preston-Shoot, & Wigley, 2008). Clearly, it is part of our role as professionals to assist movement in people toward posttraumatic growth. This may include education and information about self-care and encouragement to use a number of self-soothing or comforting strategies.

Rituals

Ellis (2006) reminds us of the importance of rituals in posttraumatic growth and resilience. Rituals help us to relate to one another and to our deeper selves;

TABLE 21.1   Interventions and Creative Activities Promoting PTG and Resilience

Memory books	Support groups	Hypnosis
Family meetings	Storytelling	Biofeedback
Poems	Guided imagery	Going on retreat
Songs	Aromatherapy	Cognitive behavioral therapy
Meditation	Making books with children	Drumming
Individual counseling	Religious services	Life review
Family counseling	Art therapy	Reminiscence
Couples counseling	Music therapy	Dream work
Journaling	Letter writing	Reunions
Life story writing	Healing circles	Bibliotherapy
Memorials	Talking circles	Cinema therapy
Rituals	Feeling circles	Forgiveness, reconciliation
Centering prayer	Excerise	Rituals
Reiki	Mapping formal and informal supports	Tai chi
Naming ceremonies		Qigong
Therapeutic touch	Yoga	Employee assistance programs (EAPs)
Healing touch	AA, NA, RA, OA	
Labyrinth walking	Relaxation kit	Bodywork
Deep breathing	Time away	Balance
Breath work	Time alone	Simplicity
Spiritual support and practices	Self-care activities	Burden basket—Native American tradition
Sand tray	Relaxation therapy	
Critical incident stress debriefing (CISD)	Stress management training	Scrapbooking
	Psycho-educational groups	Autobiography or biography
Creative visualization	Internet support groups	Famous role models of resilience
Gardening and horticultural therapy	Self-help groups	Relaxation kit
Candle lighting		Worry box

they shape our day-to-day lives. They assist in expressing connection and emotion and figure heavily in the maintenance of relationships. Rituals can involve daily activities like eating and sleeping or family traditions such as holiday celebrations and life cycle or developmental milestone rituals. Making, and marking, our own rituals can assist with healing, communication, relationships, and our sense of self. Rituals can provide grounding after particularly difficult life transitions, trauma, crises, or loss. They can help to reestablish order and to reaffirm meaning. Rituals need not be public or large gestures; they can be minimal and meaningful only to the person who has established them (Table 21.1).

Posttraumatic growth, resilience, benefit finding, and benefit reminding are key concepts in our understanding of change, transition, and loss across the lifespan. We can support coping and adjustment to stressful life events by having a fuller awareness of interventions and the power of the human spirit to overcome adversity and to grow, develop, and flourish following a tragedy. By knowing what is possible, we better prepare ourselves to be fully present to our clients and to provide exemplary psychosocial care. Believing that grief will stay deeply present and that no one could ever possibly go on after a difficult event in their lives is to short-change people and their family and friends. By the same token, this does not mean that we become false cheerleaders, pushing our patients to rally long before they are ready or able to do so. Care, kindness, and compassion must be at the center of all our efforts and interventions on behalf of those we assist.

THINGS TO CONSIDER

1. Have you ever had your sense of mastery or control shattered? Can you recall how you felt?
2. Some authors talk about reconstruction, renewal, renegotiation, revising, facing limitations, and finding joy; do these concepts ring true for you when you think about difficult events or periods of time in your life?
3. Have you ever heard a friend or family member say, "In a weird way, it was the best thing that could have happened to me/us"? What do you think about a statement like this?
4. Can you think of losses that have promoted your current resilience and ability to cope with what life throws at you?

REFERENCES

Altemus, B. (2003). *The gift of pain: Transforming hurt into healing*. New York: The Berkley Publishing Group.

Baker, J.M., Kelly, C., Calhoun, L.G., Cann, A., & Tedeschi, R.G. (2009). An examination of posttraumatic growth and post traumatic depreciation: Two exploratory studies. *Journal of Loss and Trauma, 13*(5), 450–465.

Beattie, M. (2006). *The grief club: The secret to getting through all kinds of change*. Center City, MN: Hazelden.

Bonanno, G.A. (2004). Loss, trauma, and human resilience: Have we underestimated the human capacity to thrive after extremely aversive events? *American Psychologist, 59*(1), 20–28.

Borawski, B.M. (2007). Reflecting on adversarial growth and trauma through autoethnography. *Journal of Loss and Trauma, 12*, 101–110.

Boscarino, J.A. (2008). Psychobiologic predictors of disease mortality after psychological trauma: Implications for research and clinical surveillance. *Journal of Nervous and Mental Disease, 196*(2), 100–107.

Calhoun, L.G., & Tedeschi, R.G. (1990). Positive aspects of critical life problems: Recollections of grief. *Omega, 20*(4), 265–272.

Calhoun, L.G., & Tedeschi, R.G. (1998). Posttraumatic growth—future directions. In R.G. Tedeschi, C.L. Park, & L.G. Calhoun (Eds.), *Posttraumatic growth: Positive changes in the aftermath of crisis*, Mahwah, NJ: Lawrence Erlbaum Associates, pp. 215–238.

Calhoun, L.G., & Tedeschi, R.G. (Eds.). (2006). *Handbook of posttraumatic growth: Research and practice*. New York: Guilford Press.

Cohen, R.M. (2008). *Strong at the broken places: Voices of illness, a chorus of hope*. New York: Harper Collins.

Collishaw, S., Pickles, A., Messer, J., Rutter, M., Shearer, C., & Maughan, B. (2007). Resilience to adult psychopathology following childhood maltreatment: Evidence from a community sample. *Child Abuse and Neglect, 31*, 211–229.

Colville, G., & Cream, P. (2009). Post-traumatic growth in parents after a child's admission to intensive care: Maybe Nietzsche was right? *Intensive Care Medicine, 35*, 919–923.

Crawford, R. (1998). *How high can you bounce? Turn setbacks into comebacks*. New York: Bantam Books.

Cyrulnik, B. (2005). *The whispering of ghosts: Trauma and resilience* (Susan Fairfield, Trans.). New York: Other Press.

Davis, C.G., Wohl, M.J.A., & Verberg, N. (2007). Profiles of posttraumatic growth following an unjust loss. *Death Studies, 31*(8), 693–712.

Davis Prend, A. (1994). *Transcending loss: Understanding the lifelong impact of grief and how to make it meaningful*. New York: Berkley Books.

Dolan, P. (2008). Prospective possibilities for building resilience in children, their families and communities. *Child Care in Practice, 14*(1), 83–91.

Dolan, Y. (1998). *One small step: Moving beyond trauma and therapy to a life of joy*. Watsonville, CA: Papier-Mache Press.

Dutton, Y.C., & Zisook, S. (2005) Adaptation to bereavement. *Death Studies, 29*, 877–903.

Ellis, R. (2006). *Are associate degree nursing graduates adequately prepared to meet the cultural needs of their patients at the end of life?* Master of Nursing degree thesis, Washington State University Intercollegiate College of Nursing, May.

Ellis, T.M. (2006). *This thing called grief: A new understanding of loss*. Minneapolis: Syren Book Company.

Flach, F. (1988). *Resilience: Discovering a new strength at times of stress*. New York: Fawcett Columbine.

Flach, F. (1997). *Resilience: How to bounce back when the going gets tough*. New York: Hatherleigh Press.

Folkman, S. (2008). The case for positive emotions in the stress process. *Anxiety Stress and Coping, 21*(1), 3–14.

Frankl, V.E. (1984). *Man's search for meaning*. New York: Simon & Schuster.

Gilligan, R. (2000). Adversity, resilience and young people: The protective value of positive school and spare time experience. *Children and Society, 14*, 37–47.

Goldman, L. (2005). *Raising our children to be resilient: A guide to helping children cope with trauma in today's world*. New York: Brunner-Routledge .

Hartling, L. (2002). Strengthening our resilience in a risky world: It is about relationships. *WCW Research and Action Report*, Fall–Winter, pp. 4–7.

Hefferon, K., Grealy, M., & Mutrie, N. (2009). Post-traumatic growth and life threatening physical illness: A systematic review of the qualitative literature. *British Journal of Health Psychology, 14*, 343–378.

Henry, J. (2007). Positive psychology and the development of well-being. In J. Hawoth & G. J. Hart (Eds.), *Well-Being: Individual, Community and Social Perspectives* (pp. 25–40). New York: Palgrave Macmillan.

Herman, J.L. (2008). Craft and science in the treatment of traumatized people. *Journal of Trauma and Dissociation, 9*(3), 293–300.

Hurley, D. (2008). *Resilience*. Paper presented at King's University College, March 7, University of Western Ontario, London, Ontario, Canada.

Hurley, D. (2009). *From the zone of risk to the zone of resilience*. Social Work Research day, November 6, King's University College at the University of Western Ontario, London, Ontario, Canada.

Hurley, D., & Martin, L. (2009). From the zone of risk to the zone of resilience. Social Work Research Day presentation. King's University College at the University of Western Ontario, London, Canada. November 6.

Katz, M. (1997). *On playing a poor hand well: Insights from the lives of those who have overcome childhood risks and adversities.* New York: W.W. Norton and Company.

Konrad, S.C. (2006). Posttraumatic growth in mothers of children with acquired disabilities. *Journal of Loss and Trauma, 11,* 101–113.

Lesser, E. (2004). *Broken open: How difficult times can help us grow.* New York: Villard.

Linley, A., & Joseph, S. (2004). Positive change following trauma and adversity: A review. *Journal of Traumatic Stress, 17,* 11–21.

Luthar, S.S., Cicchetti, D., & Becker, B. (2000). The construct of resilience: A critical evaluation and guidelines for future work. *Child Development, 71*(3), 543–562.

Madsen, W.C. (2007). *Collaborative therapy with multi-stressed families* (2nd ed.). New York: Guilford.

Masten, A.S. (2007). Resilience in developing systems: Progress and promise as the fourth wave rises. *Development and Psychopathology, 19,* 3, 921–930.

McMurray, I., Connolly, H., Preston-Shoot, M., & Wigley, V. (2008). Constructing resilience: Social workers' understandings and practice. *Health and Social Care in the Community, 16*(3), 299–309.

Miller, B. (2005). *The women's book of resilience: 12 qualities to cultivate.* York Beach, ME: Conari Press.

Morris T. (2004). *Stoic art of living: Inner resilience and outer results.* Chicago: Open Court Publishers.

Neeld, E.H. (2005). *Tough transitions: Navigating your way through difficult times.* New York: Warner.

Neimeyer R. (Ed.). (2004). *Meaning reconstruction and the experience of loss.* Compassion Books.

Neimeyer, R.A. (Ed.). (2003). Meaning reconstruction and the experience of loss. *Psycho-Oncology, 12*(3), 301.

Neimeyer, R.A. (2006). Narrating the dialogical self: Toward an expanded toolbox for the counselling psychologist. *Counselling Psychology Quarterly, 19*(1), 105–120.

O'Connell-Higgins, G. (1994). *Resilient adults: Overcoming a cruel past.* San Francisco: Jossey-Bass.

O'Gorman, P. (1994). *Dancing backwards in high heels: How women master the art of resilience.* Center City, MN: Hazelden.

Pakenham, K.I. (2007). The nature of benefit finding in multiple sclerosis. *Psychology, Health and Medicine, 12*(2), 190–196.

Pennebaker, J.W. (2000). Telling stories: The health benefits of narrative. *Literature and Medicine, 19*(1), 3–18.

Prati, G., & Pietrantoni, L. (2009). Optimism, social support and coping strategies as factors contributing to posttraumatic growth: A meta-analysis. *Journal of Loss and Trauma, 14*(5), 364–388.

Richardson, G.E. (2002). The metatheory of resilience and resiliency. *Journal of Clinical Psychology, 58*(3), 307–321.

Rutter, M. (2007). Resilience, competence and coping. *Child Abuse and Neglect, 31*(3), 205–209.

Salick, E., & Auerbach, C. (2006). From devastation to integration: Adjusting to and growing from medical trauma. *Qualitative Health Research, 16*(8), 1021–1037.

Samios, C., Pakenham, K.I., & Sofronoff, K. (2009). The nature of benefit finding in parents of a child with Asperger's syndrome. *Research in Autism Spectrum Disorders, 3,* 358–374.

Scaer, R.C. (2005). *The trauma spectrum: Hidden wounds and human resiliency*. New York: WW Norton and Co.

Sears, S.R., Stanton, A.L., & Danoff-Burg, D. (2003). The yellow brick road and the Emerald City: Benefit finding, positive reappraisal coping and posttraumatic growth in women with early stage breast cancer. *Health Psychology, 22*(5), 487–497.

Simmons, P. (2002). *Learning to fall: The blessings of an imperfect life.* New York: Bantam.

Sirois, M. (2006). *Every day counts: Lessons in love, faith, and resilience from children facing illness.* New York: Walker and Company.

Tedeschi, R.G., & Calhoun, L.G. (2004). Posttraumatic growth: Conceptual foundations and empirical evidence. *Psychological Inquiry, 15*(1), 1–18.

Tedeschi, R.G., & Calhoun, L.G. (2007). *PTG: Strange blessings*. ADEC keynote presentation, Indianapolis.

Tennen, H., & Affleck, G. (2002). Benefit finding and benefit reminding. In C.R. Snyder & S.J. Lopez (Eds.), *Handbook of positive psychology* (pp. 584–597). New York: Oxford University Press.

Ungar, M. (2002). *Playing at being bad: The hidden resilience of troubled teens*. Lawrencetown Beach, NS, Canada: Pottersfield Press.

Ungar, M. (2004). A constructivist discourse on resilience. *Youth and Society, 35*(3), 341–365.

Ungar, M. (2006). Nurturing hidden resilience in at-risk youth in different cultures. *Journal of Canadian Academy of Child and Adolescent Psychiatry, 15*(2), 53–58.

Wainrib, B.R. (2006). *Healing crisis and trauma with mind body and spirit*. New York: Springer.

Walsh, F. (1998). *Strengthening family resilience*. New York: Guilford Press.

Walsh, F. (2007). Traumatic loss and major disasters: Strengthening family and community resilience. *Family Process, 46*(2), 207–227.

Weenolsen, P. (1988). *Transcendence of loss over the life span.* New York: Hemisphere.

Wilkes, G. (2002). Abused child to nonabusive parent: Resilience and conceptual change. *Journal of Clinical Psychology, 58*(3), 261–276.

Wolin, S.J., & Wolin, S. (1993). *The resilient self: How survivors of troubled families rise above adversity.* New York: Villard Books.

22

Meaning Making and the Assumptive World in Nondeath Loss

DARCY L. HARRIS

INTRODUCTION

S o far, we have explored the concepts of nondeath and nonfinite loss, identified various "living losses," and described how coping, resilience, and posttraumatic growth may occur after such losses. A related exploration is the identification of the ways that individuals search for and find meaning after their assumptive worlds have been challenged by significant loss experiences. The idea of meaning making in bereavement has been well described (see Neimeyer, 2000 for a review). We now look at how meaning making may occur in losses that are ongoing in nature.

For those not familiar with the application of the concept of meaning making in the bereavement literature, a brief description may be helpful. Over the past 25 years, attempts to frame the grieving process in stages, tasks, and outcomes have not been necessarily supported by empirical research with bereaved individuals. There has also been a great deal of difficulty finding language that is accurate and descriptive of a process widely variable between individuals and very multidimensional in its expression. For instance, does one accommodate, integrate, or "work through" a significant loss experience, or does one "recover" from grief? In a comprehensive review of published studies of grief counseling, Neimeyer (2000) states that one of the more commonly described aspects of the experience of bereaved individuals was an attempt to attach meanings to loss experiences. Originally founded in constructivist psychology, the concept of making meaning extends from the idea that human beings construct life narratives, and part of this construction is also the assignment of meaning, or attaching significance to an event. I would also suggest that meaning making is one of the primary processes in which individuals engage when there is dissonance between their life experiences and their existing assumptive world.

MEANING MAKING AND ASSUMPTIONS

Most people typically move through life without consciously thinking about the foundational assumptions they have formed about how the world should work and how they belong in this same world. We can usually use our schemas and beliefs to make sense of the world and to venture into new areas of exploration with relative confidence. Because our core assumptions are usually positive, we remain contented—we feel safe, secure, and protected. Our tendency toward cognitive conservatism (as discussed in the introduction) suggests that our beliefs and assumptions about benevolence, meaning, and self-worth are deep-seated and as a result allow us to maintain an "illusion of invulnerability" (Janoff-Bulman, 1992, p. 51). We tend to interpret all of our experiences in light of cognitive conservatism, and our fundamental assumptions basically remain untouched. Challenges to one's assumptive world are usually met through the previously mentioned processes of *assimilation* (where events are interpreted through the lens of the assumptive world satisfactorily) or *accommodation* (where assumptions are gradually revised somewhat to explain a new set of experiences).

However, at times something may happen that defies belief or one's ability to integrate the experience with any known way of how the world should work. The phrase *loss of the assumptive world* is used when a negative life event has challenged one's basic assumptions about the world in a way that these assumptions no longer make sense and when there is no acceptable alternate way of seeing the world that will reconcile previously held beliefs with a new reality that does not fit these assumptions. For example, individuals' view of themselves as worthy and valuable may be assaulted when the person they love abandons the relationship for whatever reason. Another example might be when a person who was a spiritual mentor and authority figure abuses this position in some form, causing deep-seated doubts about the religious beliefs or sense of safety in the world to someone in the care of such an individual.

Preexisting assumptions that are no longer viable in describing the world and one's inner working models or schemata must somehow be reworked for the person to feel safe in the world again, and this process can be very difficult. As discussed in the introduction, Janoff-Bulman (1992) uses the term *shattered assumptions* to describe an experience that overwhelms individuals' core assumptions so completely that reconciliation of reality with their existing assumptive world is not possible. Tedeschi and Calhoun (2004) speak of "seismic life events" that "violate" individuals' schemas about how the world should work (p. 5). It is important to note in this discussion that the individual's subjective appraisal process is very important. How one interprets and perceives an event determines the significance of its impact upon the assumptive world. Many experiences—and in this context losses—can be very significant to individuals but may not necessarily be appreciated by others or by society, as has been well documented by Doka's (1989) exploration of disenfranchised grief in many contexts, including many of the losses we have discussed in this book.

Experiences that can shatter one's assumptive world are often labeled as traumatic events, and Janoff-Bulman (1992) describes the characteristics of these experiences as (1) outside of the normal range or expectation of a person, (2) markedly distressing to almost anyone, and (3) unexpected, with little chance of being able to psychologically prepare for them. The previously held assumption that "this couldn't happen to me" is now challenged by the reality that this negative event has indeed happened to this individual. What results is that the world that was once believed to be benevolent and meaningful is now seen as unsafe, negative, and threatening. The internal world of the survivor is thrown into a state of upheaval and disintegration, because the very assumptions that offered a sense of stability and coherence are now seen as totally inadequate and inaccurate in describing the world of the survivor. The reality is that our expectations (and therefore our assumptions) are that we will go through life and be healthy, will be fulfilled in our work and relationships, and will have many choices regarding our lifestyle and future. Rando (2002) discusses the problems associated with a lack of adversity in early life, as absence of struggle does not help individuals develop their coping strategies and adopt more realistic expectations.

Attempts to cope after such events are seen as attempts to rebuild one's assumptive world to recover the sense of security and safety once felt prior to the event or situation that threw a wrench into the well-oiled machine of day-to-day life. In a further interesting point, Janoff-Bulman (1992) states that victims of trauma can be seen as threatening to nonvictims because they raise the real possibility of a malevolent universe rather than a benevolent one. Individuals who collapse under the weight of seismic life events are threatening, not because they pose a direct physical threat but because their situation poses a threat to the most fundamental assumptions and core beliefs that enable others to feel safe, secure, and confident. This perception would offer an explanation as to why victims are often blamed for what has happened to them: Blaming a victim or holding a victim responsible for a negative event that has occurred protects others' beliefs and assumptions about benevolence, meaning, and self-worth (i.e., this event happened to that person because of something they did that was wrong, and I would not do that, so it will not happen to me). This explanation may also apply to why bereaved individuals are often isolated in their grief, as their presence challenges the death-denying and avoidance attitudes held in Western society. Their experiences demonstrate the reality that death can (and does) happen to people that we know and love.

Janoff-Bulman (1992) describes an oscillation between numbness (often described as avoidance of the event) with confrontation and retraumatization due to inability to integrate what has happened with a belief system that hinges on benevolence and meaning. This description by Janoff-Bulman is very similar to the dual process model of coping with grief as described by Stroebe and Schut (1999), which suggests the normalcy of the need to oscillate between avoidance of the reality of the loss by focusing on everyday functioning alternated with dwelling on the loss and its effects at other times.

Rebuilding a new assumptive world occurs as individuals compare their experience with others, interpret their role in what happened (which may sometimes involve self-blame as a means of assigning control), and attempt to reevaluate the event or experience in terms of benefits and potential purpose. Attig (1996) introduced the phrase *relearning the world,* which is described as a process of learning "how to be and act in the world differently" (p. 107) after a significant loss. In contrast to the cognitive focus of Janoff-Bulman's (1992) model, Attig's representation of relearning the world describes a multidimensional model of adjustment, involving both tasks and a search for meaning at a deeper level. Certainly, in my work with bereaved clients, this process is much more experiential in nature, with much trial and error involved in the attempts to return to some semblance of equilibrium.

Meaning making is the focus of many authors who explore responses to trauma, loss, and negative life events. Davis and Nolen-Hoeksema (2001) state that making sense of an event involves a process of attempts to reconcile the occurrence of the event with one's working models of the assumptive world. Viktor Frankl (1963), a concentration camp survivor and the developer of logotherapy, asserted that one can survive all forms of harm and harshness by finding meaning and purpose through what one has experienced. By choosing to reflect on the possibility of something positive occurring after the negative life event, individuals may be able to assign meaning to their experience, which helps to build the foundation for their assumptive world in a positive way again. Janoff-Bulman (2004) describes the existential issues that must also be addressed and assigned meaning after experiencing a critical event. Survivors are not interested just in why an event happened but also why an event happened to them in particular. She cites Sartre (1966) in her discussion of existential issues, stating that individuals must create their own meanings through deliberate choice in the face of meaninglessness. She concludes that we may not be able to prevent misfortune, but we have the ability to create lives of value in the wake of misfortune.

Searching for meaning after significant loss appears to be an almost universal phenomenon and an important part of the grieving process (Davis, 2001; Miles & Crandall, 1983; Parkes & Weiss, 1983; Wheeler, 2001). The trauma, shock, and anguish of significant losses challenge an individual's fundamental assumptions about the world. Meaning making can result from reinterpretation of negative events as opportunities to learn new lessons about oneself or life in general, as a means of helping others, or contributing to society in some way that is related to the experience that occurred (e.g., the formation of an advocacy group or efforts to help others in similar situations).

Neimeyer (2001; Neimeyer et al., 2002) discusses the social constructivist view of meaning making through the use of narrative reframing in individuals who have experienced significant losses. Neimeyer's (2001) description of the "master narrative," which is an "understanding of one's life and experiences, along with meanings attached to these" (p. 263), is very similar to earlier descriptions of the assumptive world by other writers. He states that significant losses disrupt taken-for-granted narratives and strain the assumptions that once sustained them. Individuals must find ways to make meaning of the life events that have been disruptive by a "reweaving" process that incorporates the new experiences into the existing narrative of their lives so that it is once again coherent and sustaining.

Searching for meaning in what seems to be a meaningless event is how human beings attempt to reestablish a sense of order and security in the world and to minimize the high degree of vulnerability that occurs after basic assumptions are shattered. Davis, Nolen-Hoeksema, and Larson (1998) focused on two aspects of meaning in their research. These two aspects consisted of meaning as the ability to find a benefit in what had happened or meaning as a way of making sense of the loss. Of interest is my own research with infertile women who adamantly stated that their experiences made no sense to them but that they were still able to find meaning in what they had endured (Harris, 2009). Attig (2001) further delineates the various conceptualizations of the search for meaning by distinguishing between meaning making and meaning finding. *Meaning making* refers to the conscious and active process of reinterpreting and bringing new meaning to one's experiences, actions, and suffering, and *meaning finding* refers to becoming aware of and accepting meaning that arises spontaneously out of grief and suffering. These two processes mix together as one rebuilds the assumptive world after a significant loss. Research published by Tedeschi and Calhoun (2004) suggests that there is potential for more than adjustment after exposure to "seismic" life events (described Chapter 21 in the section related to posttraumatic growth). These authors cite numerous instances in their research where individuals encountered tragic bereavement, catastrophic illness, violence, or political oppression, and their exposure to such events led to significant personal accounts of positive growth and development. Growth in this sense is not a direct result of exposure to these types of events but rather results from the struggle in which individuals engage with the new reality in the aftermath of these events.

CLINICAL REFLECTIONS

In exploring the material for this chapter, I was often struck by the juxtaposition of the written materials with the stories and experiences that my clients have shared with me as well as the descriptions of loss experiences included in the sections of this book by our contributors. It is common for clients who have experienced a major loss to state that the experience has changed their lives. Many of my clients have shared with me that they know that they will never be the same again or that their loss experience has affected every area of their lives—their relationships with others, their view of themselves, their goals in life, their sense of agency in the world, and their view of God or some higher life form. Many have shared with me that they felt completely "broken," not just because they were saddened or stressed but because of a feeling that something deep inside has been shattered. When I first encountered Janoff-Bulman's (1992, 2004) writings about the assumptive world, I found that much of what she wrote resonated with these accounts.

In the time I spend with clients, there is almost always the underlying question of "why" present in our sessions. Why has my body betrayed me? Why did my partner leave? Why can't I make this happen? Why don't others understand? Why would God allow this to happen to me? I am also mindful of Doka's (1989) discussion of disenfranchised grief, recognizing that many of the losses that we are discussing here as "living losses" are often unrecognized or minimized or carry some form of social stigma, making the rebuilding process one that often occurs in isolation for these individuals.

CONCLUSION

It is apparent that our assumptive world allows us to function in our lives with the feeling that there is continuity and meaning to life. We feel safe and secure when our assumptive world is stable and when we can usually integrate most life experiences into our assumptive world without great difficulty. However, certain negative life events can assault us at our most basic level of understanding the world. When our assumptive worlds are shattered by situations that defy our existing assumptions, the process is not one of integration but of ongoing, painful rebuilding that occurs at a foundational place in our mind, spirit, and awareness.

Janoff-Bulman (1992) assumes that we develop basically positive views of the world from our earliest experiences of attachment. She does not, however, discuss what effect insecure attachment might have on the development of the assumptive world or how traumatic experiences in infants and young children may affect the assumptions about the world that later develop. She uses a model of avoidance alternated with confrontation to describe how negative life events are eventually incorporated into one's assumptive world, similar to the dual process model proposed by Stroebe and Schut (1999). These bereavement researchers have incorporated varying attachment styles into their model. I would assume that this same extrapolation might be possible with Janoff-Bulman's model of accommodation and assimilation after exposure to a seismic life event.

After reviewing many of the readings for this chapter and the contributed chapters in this book, I became curious about what might happen to individuals who have experienced many repeated assaults to their assumptive world. I wondered if repeated assaults over time could foster a sense of competence in an individual so that previous experiences might have a positive influence in handling later challenges. Perhaps this is an area for future study, as many factors could influence both the process and outcome—for example, if the events happened with some time in between or all at once (allowing a sense of time to accommodate versus being completely overwhelmed), what previous coping had been like, and the supports and resources available. The chronic nature of nonfinite losses adds many layers of complexity to this exploration. In my clinical practice, I have often found that clients with exposure to many negative life events do still experience much pain and despair, but many do seem to have more confidence that they will come out on the "other side" of their pain. One of my clients once shared with me, "I know I'm eventually going to be OK, but I don't have a clue what 'OK' is going to look like."

I hope this exploration has provided a good foundation to reflect on how beliefs about how things that "should be" can be challenged at a very deep place when a significant loss occurs. Placing the template of the assumptive world and meaning making into the context of nonfinite losses allows us to embrace the complexity of losses that are ongoing in nature, with many layers of pain and adjustment. Perhaps in our deeper awareness, we can more readily accompany those who face these loss experiences, ensuring that their journey is not in isolation.

REFERENCES

Attig, T. A. (1996). *How we grieve: Relearning the world*. New York: Oxford University Press.
Attig, T. A. (2001). Relearning the world: Making and finding meanings. In R. A. Neimeyer (Ed.), *Meaning reconstruction and the experience of loss* (pp. 33–53). Washington, DC: APA.
Davis, C. G. (2001). The tormented and the transformed: Understanding responses to loss and trauma. In R. A. Neimeyer (Ed.), *Meaning reconstruction and the experience of loss* (pp. 137–155). Washington, DC: APA.
Davis, C. G., & Nolen-Hoeksema, S. (2001). Loss and meaning—how do people make sense of loss? *American Behavioral Scientist, 44*, 726–741.
Davis, C. G., Nolen-Hoeksema, S., & Larson, J. (1998). Making sense of loss and benefiting from the experience: Two construals of meaning. *Journal of Personality and Social Psychology, 75*(2), 561–574.
Doka, K. J. (1989). *Disenfranchised grief: Recognizing hidden sorrow*. Lexington, MA: Lexington Books.
Frankl, V. E. (1963). *Man's search for meaning: An introduction to logotherapy*. New York: Washington Square Press.
Harris, D. L. (2009). The experience of spontaneous pregnancy loss in infertile women who have conceived with the assistance of medical intervention. *Dissertation Abstracts International, 70*(03)A./ ProQuest Digital Dissertations (AAT 3351170).
Janoff-Bulman, R. (1992). *Shattered assumptions: Towards a new psychology of trauma*. New York: Free Press.
Janoff-Bulman, R. (2004). Posttraumatic growth: Three explanatory models. *Psychological Inquiry, 15*, 30–34.
Miles, M. S., & Crandall, E. K. B. (1983). The search for meaning and its potential for affecting growth in bereaved parents. *Health Values: Achieving High Level Wellness, 7*(1), 19–23.
Neimeyer, R. A. (2000). Searching for the meaning of meaning: Grief therapy and the process of reconstruction. *Death Studies, 24*, 541–558.
Neimeyer, R. A. (2001). The language of loss: Grief therapy as a process of meaning reconstruction. In R. A. Neimeyer (Ed.), *Meaning reconstruction & the experience of loss* (pp. 261–292). Washington, DC: APA.
Neimeyer, R. A., Botella, L., Herrero, O., Pecheco, M., Figueras, S., & Werner-Wilder, L. A. (2002). The meaning of your absence. In J. Kauffman (Ed.), *Loss of the assumptive world: A theory of traumatic loss* (pp. 31–47). New York: Brunner-Routledge.
Parkes, C. M., & Weiss, R. S. (1983). *Recovery from bereavement*. New York: Basic Books.
Rando, T. A. (2002). The "curse" of too good a childhood. In J. A. Kauffman (Ed.), *Loss of the assumptive world: A theory of traumatic loss* (pp. 171–192). New York: Routledge.
Sartre, J. P. (1966). *Being and nothingness: A phenomenological study of ontology*. New York: Washington Square Press.
Stroebe, M., & Schut, H. (1999). The dual process model of coping with bereavement: Rationale and description. *Death Studies, 23*(3), 197–224.

Tedeschi, R. G., & Calhoun, L. G. (2004). Posttraumatic growth: Conceptual foundations and empirical evidence. *Psychological Inquiry, 15,* 1–18.

Wheeler, I. (2001). Parental bereavement: The crisis of meaning. *Death Studies, 25,* 51–66.

23

Concluding Thoughts

DARCY L. HARRIS

When thinking about the experiences that would be represented in this book as examples of nondeath and nonfinite losses, it was apparent that this could, indeed, become a very large project. In fact, when I described the subject matter of this book, I encountered many individuals who asked if they could share their loss experiences with me. In reading through these chapters, it is apparent that loss is a frequent companion to life, and letting go is something that we must learn, even as we attempt to hold on tighter to what we know, value, and love. We lose those that we love through normal milestones, transitions, relational change and dissolution, distance, and death. We can lose objects that we value and bestow with meaning. We can lose a sense of connection to our community, our country, and our beliefs. We can even lose ourselves. The language of loss, expressed in the stories, associated feelings, and outgrowth of these experiences, makes up a large part of our human experience, albeit often unacknowledged as such.

Each of the chapters of this book offers insight into loss experiences that do not result from a death per se and that may be ongoing in nature. These events often result in profound grief, which is the adaptive process whereby individuals begin to rebuild their assumptive world after such experiences. This rebuilding process may involve adaptation, accommodation, or integration into a new way of living and being. It is important to recognize the significance of these experiences and to keep in mind the adaptive aspects of grief rather than pathologizing this response due to the influence of result of rigid social norms that focus on narrowly defined rules.

As a clinician, I often identify aspects of my clients' nondeath loss experiences within the context of various theories of bereavement that are widely known and accepted. I have framed my clients' experiences in different ways, depending on the aspects of the process that they share with me. For example, the dual process model of grief, which was posited by Stroebe and Schut (1999), describes the grieving process as one in which bereaved individuals oscillate between focusing on the loss and then changing the focus to the restorative activities of daily life and then back to the loss again. This theory is readily applicable to nondeath losses. An example of the application in a nondeath context would be with individuals who are struggling with the loss of an intimate relationship, in which there are times when they feel deep grief and pain at the loss of this relationship and what happened to cause it to end and at other times may focus on learning new skills and interests, seeking new relationships, and redefining themselves as single again.

Further to the dual process model, it is possible to identify where attachment theory comes into play in experiences that involve change, loss, and significant transition. As indicated in the introduction to this book, attachment is often identified as a key element in grief, and the attachment model provides an ethological element to the grieving process. In his research, Bowlby (1988) found similar behaviors in young children when they were separated from their mothers that were present in primate studies involving separation. Parkes (1996) expanded Bowlby's work into the area of adult bereavement, suggesting that the attachment system, and the resulting grief when that system is threatened by separation, is an extension of a process that has evolved over time to optimize feelings of safety and to enhance the chances for survival of the individual.

If grief and attachment are thus interrelated, then to what are we attached when we grieve a nondeath loss, such as loss of a sense of safety, or loss of our homeland, or loss of employment? It could be that these defining, overarching losses involve either the loss of an aspect of ourselves to which we are attached or to our place in the world, which makes us feel safe and secure. For example, it would be common for immigrants to a new country to yearn for their family and friends who are still present in their homeland, to search for what is familiar in their new environment, and to look for commonalities with their known culture in the new country of their arrival. The well-known term *comfort food* implies that identification with foods that are associated with our family and cultural roots provides a sense of comfort when we are stressed or in unfamiliar territory. In another example, individuals who have lost their jobs may pine for their old lives or self to return to them, reminiscing about what they used to do or who they used to be. The disequilibrium that results from these types of losses can activate the attachment system, motivating us to draw us closer to what is familiar and safe, and the grieving process enables us to adapt to some part of ourselves or our lives that is markedly different from what it was before. As discussed in the introduction, Janoff-Bulman (1992) draws a connection between one's assumptive world and one's attachment system, stating that how one relates to and views the world, others, and oneself is an extension of the attachment system that is formed at a very young age. Thus, it would make sense that threats to the assumptive world resonate back to the attachment system on which that world was built.

Stroebe (2002) describes how various attachment styles may shape the grieving process in ways that are congruent with individuals' previous ways of relating to the world and other individuals. Yalom (2009) alludes to the therapeutic encounter as a microcosm of clients' ways of interacting with individuals in their world. In my clinical practice, I frequently see glimpses of clients' attachment styles from their interactions with me and descriptions of their interactions with others. How these individuals process their loss experience is often consistent with how they form their close relationships and how they interact with others, which is an extension of their attachment style. I can identify many different normative responses to loss, as there are many different patterns of attachment and ways of being in the world as a result. Being informed by such insight and research in this area may help clinicians to normalize the diverse responses and processes of clients who are facing nondeath and nonfinite losses, even though this theorizing was initially based on grief after the death of a loved one.

Doka's (1989, 2002) concept of disenfranchised grief is highly applicable to the exploration of nondeath losses, as the lack of recognition of the losses leads to a tendency to deny their potential significance or to not recognize the degree to which these losses can affect an individual. In most of the experiences included in this book, there is often a social message of *so what?* that accompanies the experience or a sense of *just get over it and get on with your life* that many individuals feel when these losses are encountered. It is hoped that, in offering these descriptive chapters, there will be a greater awareness of the significance of these experiences and a heightened sensitivity to individuals facing these types of losses.

There are obvious differences between death-related and nondeath losses, which are readily highlighted by Boss's (1999) descriptions of ambiguous loss and Roos's (2002) elaboration of the concept of chronic sorrow. In situations of ambiguous loss or nonfinite loss, typically there are no socially accepted rituals that would give acknowledgment or credence to the experience of an individual in the way a funeral might provide for a bereaved individual. The absence of a body does not mean the absence of grief; however, in the absence of an overt or outward manifestation of the loss, the level of social recognition and support is often minimal or absent. The example given in the discussion of ambiguous loss relates the grief of a wife whose husband is physically present in the home but who is emotionally absent through his continued distraction and unavailability to her when he is there. Should her husband die in a car accident, much support and concern would be extended to this same woman, yet in both situations she is grieving the loss of her husband's presence.

As previously described, most of the current bereavement literature focuses on death-related losses, and many of the measures used in bereavement research are rooted in the identification of "separation distress" from another individual as the primary feature that distinguishes grief from other responses and states, such as posttraumatic stress, depression, and anxiety (Prigerson et al., 1999). Separation distress is characterized by yearning, longing, preoccupation, and searching for the deceased individual (Jacobs, Mazure, & Prigerson, 2000). However, the emphasis of grief being seen primarily as a response to the death of a person does not allow for the possibility of recognizing grief as the same adaptive process that allows individuals to integrate significant losses that are perhaps not as tangible. In reflecting on this aspect of bereavement theory and research, I believe we need to consider the possibility that the separation distress resulting from the death of a loved one is only one manifestation of the broader picture of loss and grief, which encompasses the distress that occurs when individuals' existing assumptive world is lost due to a significant life-changing event, or what Tedeschi and Calhoun (2004) refer to as a "seismic" life event. Indeed, Bowlby's (1977; 1988) descriptions of yearning, pining, longing, and searching (which are all considered hallmarks of separation distress over the loss of a significant attachment figure) could be recognized in the responses to many of the nondeath loss experiences described in this book.

As stated in the introduction and the chapter on meaning making and the assumptive world, these life-changing events can cause us to feel deeply vulnerable and unsafe, as the world we once knew, the people we relied on, and the images and perceptions of ourselves are no longer relevant in light of what we have now experienced. As a process that helps us to rebuild our assumptive world after it has been shattered, grief is both adaptive and necessary. It would certainly follow that the process of making meaning, which is now seen as very much a part of the grief response, is applicable to both death-related and non-death-related losses. I hope to see research in the future that addresses the process of grief after the experience of nondeath and nonfinite losses, as there are presently very few studies that explore grief after such events and very few measures that would be appropriate to nondeath loss events.

Finally, this book has been an exploration of the innate resilience that can be found in the human spirit. Each of the descriptive chapters explores a loss experience that can be felt as initially overwhelming, and even devastating, but that still has great potential for increasing awareness, growth, and depth in those who integrate these experiences into the fabric of their lives. May we, and those we accompany on their life's journey, be continually reminded that in the midst of our grief and painful life experiences there is often much to be discovered that we could not have possibly imagined in our previous way of being.

REFERENCES

Boss, P. (1999). *Ambiguous loss.* Cambridge, MA: Harvard University Press.

Bowlby, J. (1977). The making and breaking of affectional bonds. *British Journal of Psychotherapy, 130,* 421–431.

Bowlby, J. (1988). *A secure base: Parent-child attachment and healthy human development.* New York: Basic Books.

Doka, K. J. (1989). *Disenfranchised grief: Recognizing hidden sorrow.* Lexington, MA: Lexington Books.

Doka, K. J. (2002). *Disenfranchised grief: New directions, challenges, and strategies for practice.* Champaign, IL: Research Press.

Jacobs, S., Mazure, C., & Prigerson, H. (2000). Diagnostic criteria for traumatic grief. *Death Studies, 24,* 185–199.

Janoff-Bulman, R. (1992). *Shattered assumptions: Towards a new psychology of trauma.* New York: Free Press.

Parkes, C.M. (1996). *Bereavement: Studies of grief in adult life.* London: Routledge.

Prigerson, H. G., Shear, M. K., Jacobs, S.C., Reynolds, C.F., Maciejewski, P.K., Davidson, J.R., et al. (1999). Consensus criteria for traumatic grief: A preliminary empirical test. *British Journal of Psychiatry, 174,* 67–73.

Roos, S. (2002). *Chronic sorrow: A living loss.* New York: Brunner-Routledge.

Stroebe, M. (2002). Paving the way: From early attachment theory to contemporary bereavement research. *Mortality, 7*(2), 127–138.

Stroebe, M., & Schut, H. (1999). The dual process model of coping with bereavement: Rationale and description. *Death Studies, 23*(3), 197–224.

Tedeschl, R.G., & Calhoun, L.G. (2004). Posttraumatic growth: Conceptual foundations and empirical evidence. *Psychological Inquiry, 15*, 1–18.

Yalom, I. (2009). *The gift of therapy*. New York: Harper Collins.

Index